BF
311
R86

Rundle, Bede

Perception, sen-
sation and veri-
fication

PERCEPTION, SENSATION
AND VERIFICATION

PERCEPTION
SENSATION
AND
VERIFICATION

BEDE RUNDLE

FELLOW OF TRINITY COLLEGE, OXFORD

CLARENDON PRESS · OXFORD

1972

Oxford University Press, Ely House, London W.1

GLASGOW NEW YORK TORONTO MELBOURNE WELLINGTON
APE TOWN IBADAN NAIROBI DAR ES SALAAM LUSAKA ADDIS ABABA
DELHI BOMBAY CALCUTTA MADRAS KARACHI LAHORE DACCA
KUALA LUMPUR SINGAPORE HONG KONG TOKYO

PRINTED IN GREAT BRITAIN
BY BUTLER AND TANNER LTD
FROME AND LONDON

To Ros

PREFACE

THIS work is an investigation into the common part of two broad philosophical topics: the analysis of mental phenomena and the acceptability of an account of meaning and truth which restricts the range of what can be true to what can in principle be known to be true. Among the issues relating to the former a central place is given to perception and sensation, and to topics which these directly involve: light and sound, consciousness, purpose, and the relation of the mental to behaviour and the physical. These are to some extent discussed for their own sake, or with the aim of making the accounts of perception and sensation reasonably comprehensive, but the more general questions of meaning and truth which constitute the second principal theme are usually not far in the background.

The linking together of these two themes should require no explanation, and yet it is rare to find significant attention paid to the wider considerations relating to verification which actually make for one of the main problems associated with the analysis of mental phenomena, namely, the problem of our knowledge of other minds, even though the confusion and inconsistency which this neglect encourages is often evident enough. For instance, it is not uncommon to approach the problem from premises which, it would appear, can be satisfied only if some form of behaviourism can be vindicated. A programme along these lines is accordingly followed up, but, naturally enough, most philosophers shrink from a thoroughgoing behaviourism, however grudgingly they allow a place for the irreducibly mental at some point. By this stage, however, they tend to have forgotten the initial assumptions, verificationist in nature, which led them to push behaviourism as far as they could, even though it is difficult to see what principles could be enlisted to reconcile the eclectic positions which they finally adopt.

The particular direction given to the argument of this book is due in part to exasperation with this state of affairs, in part to an independent interest in each of the major themes. Unfortunately, a preoccupation with two such large issues leads to neither being developed in the detail which it deserves; despite their relevance, topics such as memory, the self, and phenomenalism are forced out of the discussion, and as far as the questions of truth and verification are concerned the argument is little more than an interlude within the general debate. However, I do try to bring as much thoroughness and clarity as I can to the chosen problem, and I hope that a reasonably well supported position finally emerges from the arguments assembled, despite their varying degrees of cogency and completeness.

BEDE RUNDLE

Trinity College, Oxford
July 1972

CONTENTS

INTRODUCTION

IN current philosophical jargon it is common to find the epithet 'mental' applied to pains and other sensations. We do, it is true, have some use for a notion of *mental pain*, as in the case of anguish at a bereavement, but it is an odd usage that describes the pain in my toe in that way, especially odd when confronted with the natural description of such a pain as a 'bodily' sensation. I suspect that we have here a reflection of a false conception of sensations and not simply an innocent liberty with language, but I shall fall in with this philosophical usage to the extent of interpreting the main question which will concern us—'how can we know what is going on in the mind of another?'—as embracing such particular questions as 'how can we tell that a man is in pain?' and 'how can we know that someone is feeling a tickle?' I shall also, but less misleadingly, use the term 'state' in a conveniently general way, speaking of 'mental states' when I do not mean to be restricted to states properly so called, but have in mind episodes, acts, and events, in short anything that might merit the title 'mental' in one sense or another.

The question, how can we know what is going on in the mind of another?—understood in this general fashion—defines the problem of other minds, and in this introduction I shall draw attention to certain features of the problem which will be the focus of our interest. We may note first that in asking how we can ascertain that another is thinking, feeling, perceiving, and so forth, we are not merely presenting a point of controversy between sceptic and non-sceptic, so understood that, should the possibility of knowledge of another's mental states eventually be ruled out, we could consider the issue settled—as though we just had to face that this was a region in which knowledge was not to be had; a matter for regret, no doubt, but a matter that ended there. A sceptical conclusion would be important, not simply because it would reveal a lacuna in our knowledge, but because it would cast doubt on our understanding of what we have to say, at a very elementary level, about other people. If, for instance, your being in pain is a state of affairs which I can never recognize as obtaining when it does obtain, but is something quite outside any knowledge which I can possibly have, then my claim even to understand what it is for you to be in pain would seem to be threatened. A sceptical conclusion to the initial question does not merely force us to concede that there are some things we can know, others we cannot, with, so it turns out, propositions relating to other minds falling in the latter category; it is the consequences of this conclusion which present us with the major problem, a problem concerning the meaning of the words we use in attempting to describe a reality of which we can have no knowledge.

Formulated in these terms, the problem naturally develops into a particular instance of a general dispute between proponents of two sharply opposed accounts of meaning. On the one side we have the view that the meaning of a statement, a form of words which can be true or false, must be specifiable in terms not simply of conditions which determine when the statement is true and when it is false, but conditions which we can recognize as obtaining when they do obtain. On the other side is the position which sees no necessity for insisting upon any such connection with know-ledge: we specify the meaning of a statement by specifying its truth-conditions, but we must allow the possibility that these truth-conditions should be conceived of independently of what we know or what we can come to know; to know the meaning of P is to know what it is for P to be the case, but whether P is in fact true or not is a matter which might well transcend any human knowledge.

Following Michael Dummett, I shall describe as 'anti-realist' the positon which requires that the truth-conditions of a factual statement fall within the range of what we can come to know (in a finite time); the view which is prepared to relax this qualification, claiming no more than that there must be something in the world in virtue of which a true statement is true, is correspondingly to be described as 'realist'. Dummett has made the largest contribu-tion towards identifying and clarifying the variety of disputes involving these contrasting viewpoints, and has argued in detail for positions which pay due regard to anti-realist considerations; for details see his articles 'Truth' and 'The Reality of the Past' in the *Proceedings of the Aristotelian Society* for 1958–9 and 1968–9 respectively. As presented by Dummett, anti-realism is a generali-zation of the Intuitionist conception of meaning and truth as applied to mathematical propositions, while realism corrseponds to the position implicit in classical mathematics. The latter allows an unrestricted use of the Law of Excluded Middle, 'every proposition is either true or false', whereas Intuitionism restricts its application to effectively decidable propositions, and, as is well known, a different logic and a different content to mathematics result from imposing this restriction.

One way or another, the debate between realist and anti-realist defines the central problem in a wide range of philosophical controversies, not merely the major problem in the philosophy of mathematics, and a decisive victory for either side would represent the most significant advance in any area in which the dispute arose. The general controversy is too large and unwieldy to be discussed here in any depth, but after indicating in greater detail the differences which separate the two positions on the questions which are our main concern, I shall offer a few remarks in clarification of the anti-realist's theory of meaning more broadly construed; not enough to enable us to adjudicate between the rival views, but enough, I should like to think, to forestall an overhasty dismissal of the theory and to help us recognize when a position is and when it is not in accord with the anti-realist's reasoning.

As well as examining our knowledge of other men's minds, we might also ask whether animals other than men feel pain, or whether this particular animal is feeling pain on this occasion. It is unusual to approach the question of other minds via this route, yet in some ways animals—and infants—pose far more difficult and intriguing questions than our fellow men; there is never any real doubt whether normal adult human beings can think, see, know, and suffer; putting the philosophical question in the form 'given that his behaviour is so-and-so, can we doubt that his mental state is such-and-such?' is generally just a way of dressing up a logical point in psychological terms; real doubt is not ordinarily being expressed, but it is a matter of the logical connection between statements of two apparently different classes, and the question becomes one of *how* we know certain things rather than *whether* we know them at all. By contrast, with an animal or insect we may genuinely wonder: how does the world look to this creature? can it really smell things? does it feel pain the way we do? This is not to say that the genuineness of our perplexity is of overriding importance; in both cases it is the logical question, the question of the relation between evidence and conclusion, that is central. But the reality of the doubt does make for an added interest: with animals we are not so likely to be trying to find reasons in support of something which we know in advance, or think we know in advance to be so. Thus, since it is hardly a real possibility that in the end our ostensible understanding of statements about other men's minds should have to be recognized as defective, the issue resolves into a choice between the verifiability of such statements and the rejection of anti-realism. With animals, on the other hand, it is not so obvious that the possibilities can be similarly reduced, but one outcome might just be that we are not talking sense when we use the language of sensation with reference to animals. Certainly, any theory which hopes to get to grips with mental phenomena can hardly afford to remain silent on this subject. It is instructive, though discouraging, to ask of any treatment of the other minds problem how much real help it offers, if only implicitly, in dispelling the very real perplexity occasioned by a consideration of animals and lesser forms of life, and in keeping this extended version of the problem to the fore I hope to stand a better chance of avoiding the one-sidedness which is a wellnigh universal feature of these discussions.

In order, then, to illustrate the kind of problem on which realist and anti-realist are more than likely to disagree, let us ask how we can tell whether an animal is in pain. We observe the animal, a dog, let us say, yelping and recoiling from contact with a very hot object, and closer inspection reveals that its body tissue has been damaged at this point. Can we conclude from such observations that the creature really did experience a painful sensation? The realist's natural response is twofold. On the one hand, whether or not this is the sort of question which can be answered with any certainty, it makes perfectly good sense, he believes, to suppose that the animal did feel pain; it either did or it didn't, whether or not we can tell which. Furthermore, even if we cannot establish conclusively that it did feel pain, we do have or can have considerable evidence pointing in that direction, namely the evidence of the animal's reactions, both behavioural and physiological, to the hot object. Admittedly, there is room here for error; the animal could react as it did yet not feel pain, since the pain is not, after all, to be identified with anything we can directly observe. Still, we know that when our behaviour is of this kind in such circumstances, it is almost inevitably because we feel pain, and such an analogy with our own case can give us all we need to make it reasonable to ascribe pain and other sensations to lower forms of life. Or, he might say, the supposition that the creature feels pain provides us with an explanatory hypothesis, a hypothesis which can be invoked to account for the behaviour which we observe. Perhaps it must for ever have the status of a hypothesis, but to ask for anything more is to attach an unreasonable importance to certainty. In practice human affairs can get along with a lot less, and in philosophy scepticism is not to be opposed by making the doubtful logically watertight.

The anti-realist will be dissatisfied with this reply at every point. If, he argues, the supposition that an animal is in pain is to be a genuine supposition, it must specify a situation which it is possible for us to recognize when it obtains. We do not get around this requirement by advancing the animal's behaviour as *evidence* for the supposition, but the requirement is presupposed by such a characterization of the behaviour or other data, in that we have no right to speak of A as evidence for B until we have found circumstances of the same types as these associated together; and this of course implies that a conclusion comparable with the present one should have been established at some time without the help of evidence. Footprints in the snow can furnish evidence of a human presence because we have noted that, when footprints of a certain shape and size are found, it generally proves that a human being has passed that way. However, it is only because we have been able to ascertain the presence of a person independently of ascertaining the existence of footprints that we have been able to regard the latter as providing evidence of the former. We have found the two to be associated, and that means that we have directly verified the conclusion for which the evidence is evidence. If, however, as is suggested for the case of animal sensations, all we can ever have is evidence, then we have no understanding of what the evidence is evidence for, and hence no justification for speaking of it as evidence in the first place.

This anti-realist objection might involve two distinguishable lines of argument: (i) A cannot be at the same time both evidence for B and the only grounds we could have for B, but before we can advance to speaking of A as evidence for B we must have established B on independent grounds. More accurately, if facts of type

A are what lead us to surmise facts of type *B*, then there is an assumption as to their reliability in the description of them as *evidence* for the latter; this assumption remains unjustified so long as they are the only grounds we have, and if they are the only grounds we *could* have we can never advance to speaking of evidence here at all. (ii) More importantly, the requirement of an independent verification might be made not in order to guarantee the acceptability of the putative evidence, but to guarantee the sense of the conclusion which it is thought to support. In the absence of the possibility of verification we have, according to the anti-realist, no understanding of that for which the evidence is deemed to be evidence. It is no use talking in terms of a *hypothesis* or an argument resting on *analogy*, or, generally, to try to avoid attack by restricting the conclusion to a statement of a mere probability. The problem concerns the meaningfulness of a conclusion, *B*, and is just as acute if *B* is qualified by the clauses 'we may hypothesize that' or 'it is probable that' as it is when *B* occurs unqualified, as a simple assertion. If we do not know what would count as establishing *B* then we do not know what it would be for *B* to be true, and if we do not know that then we have no understanding of what it would be for *B* to be probable either, let alone what it would be for *B* to be an 'explanatory hypothesis'. Nor will it help to say what *B* comes to in other words, to try to establish its meaningfulness by appeal to a paraphrase; this is just to give the problematic conclusion a different verbal clothing; it does nothing to establish the connection between words and reality which the anti-realist demands.

The anti-realist has much to complain of in the realist's uncritical position. However, if the realist ignores a genuine problem, the anti-realist appears to be unable to solve it. It would be a drastic step to reject as unintelligible our ascriptions of sensations to animals, and it is surely impossible to speak of identifying their sensations with anything that observation can reveal to us. This step offers a way out consistent with his principles, but if some form of behaviourism or crude physicalism is the price he must pay, many would feel the sacrifice of his principles to be a more reasonable course to take. For the anti-realist, it would seem, the question should be one of how we can *fail* to know what goes on in the mind of another, but so far from this being a difficulty it would appear that the logical consequence of his reasoning is to confine the individual to assertions relating to events falling within his own experience and to prohibit him from even forming conjectures about the mental lives of others, whether animals or men. In other words, if behaviourism is rejected, solipsism appears to be the only alternative which the anti-realist's reasoning allows him to embrace.

The above illustration of the dispute involves a number of unclarities and ambiguities in the positions of both parties, but the nature and extent of their opposition should, in general terms, be plain enough. In practice, however, philosophers tend not to adopt a standpoint which is exclusively realist or anti-realist, but they generally yield to pressures from both sides, being anti-realist as far as possible, but abandoning this position when it becomes difficult to defend. Indeed, these shifting allegiances are perhaps typical of contemporary treatments of the other minds problem and account for their elusiveness on the crucial question of the nature of the solution being proposed.

Let us consider one such compromise. Analogical reasoning of the kind mentioned is not acceptable to the anti-realist; that has been made abundantly clear in recent discussions of the problem. However, it might be thought that we can meet both parties half way by allowing analogy a part to play at the level of description rather than proof. We may certainly say that the behaviour of animals is analogous to the behaviour which we exhibit when in pain; we differ on certain important points—notably, and perhaps crucially, on the question of verbal 'behaviour'—but that there is a likeness or analogy between us and, for instance, dogs and monkeys is beyond dispute, and on such a basis we might reasonably decide to speak of an animal as being in pain when it exhibits the appropriate behaviour and/or when its nervous system is in a state similar to ours when we feel pain; though no doubt with some creatures, e.g. insects, we might well feel that there is insufficient similarity for an extension of the word 'pain' to be justified.

If the holder of this view also advocates a 'reduction' of pain to behaviour, so that being in pain is just a matter of making certain behavioural responses, or if he thinks there is no more to pain than what can be found by examination of the creature's physiological condition, then we have a position which does not conflict with any specifically anti-realist principles. However, a more interesting possibility is that this view should be part of a form of compromise with anti-realism, a view which for convenience I shall speak of as 'partial' anti-realism. A supporter of the position I have in mind would hold that we attribute pain to both men and animals on the basis of their behaviour or their bodily state as observed, but that we cannot spell out in purely behavioural or physicalistic terms the content of such an attribution; there is no deductive or analytic connection between the two kinds of proposition. Nor, on the other hand, is there any inductive link. To suppose the latter would be to suppose that we learn from experience that certain forms of behaviour go along with the sensation of pain in others, but how could we establish this connection if all we had to go on was the behaviour? This same consideration rules out the use of analogy as a means of proof, since proof requires an understanding of the proposition to be proved which analogy is powerless to give; indeed, to suppose that we had that understanding is, from the anti-realist's viewpoint, tantamount to supposing that we had some means of recognizing when that proposition was true, and could accordingly dispense with the argument from analogy.

The partial anti-realist yields as much to the anti-realist as possible, short of conceding that an ascription of pain to another person or to an animal is conclusively verifiable in behaviour or in any other data which observation may furnish. Since it might not seem possible that, relying solely on observation, we should be able to tell with certainty that a creature is in pain, this position is not unreasonable; it does leave us with the problem of making sense of the possibility that a proposition should be neither inductively nor deductively based on its supporting evidence, but perhaps it is just a prejudice that these exhaust the possibilities: a persistently recalcitrant problem might well be expected to call for a possibility which is normally passed over. Such a view appears to be implicit in a certain amount of contemporary philosophical writing, particularly where an attempt is made to exploit Wittgenstein's notion of a *criterion* to throw light on the problem. Thus, on one interpretation a criterion is held to be a direct, non-inductive ground for the ascription of a mental state or episode, and certain forms of behaviour are held to have criterial status. A behavioural criterion does not furnish a deductive ground for such an ascription, but it is by reference to behaviour that we come by an understanding of mental predicates, so it is not merely contingently tied to that for which it is a criterion.

Another related position is that which emphasizes the need to give substance to any sceptical claims which purport to find it possible that a person should be feeling nothing even though, to take an extreme example, his behaviour is as of one in great pain. Since an ascription of pain is not entailed by any description of the behavioural or physical evidence on which it might be founded, the sceptic considers himself justified in casting doubt on the truth of any ascription so based, and in doing so he might well argue that he is appealing to no more than his opponent is in any case prepared to grant: unless we are to succumb to behaviourism, we must always allow that a person need not be in the state which his behaviour would seem to indicate. To this it is replied that the sceptic must fill out in greater detail the possibility which he is advancing; possibilities stand in need of substantiation just as much as plain, unqualified statements of fact. If the sceptic is prepared to suggest a particular form that the possibility might take, that the 'sufferer' should be feigning pain, for instance, then we can put this suggestion to the test; this is a real possibility, one which may issue in a detectable difference. If, however, he simply stops at the bare assertion of a possibility then we have so far no reason to consider our claim threatened; the doubt remains groundless, we have been given nothing which we might investigate in the hope of confirming or refuting our original conjecture.

The affinity between this rejoinder to the sceptic and the other version of partial anti-realism is fairly obvious. On the one hand, it is not being maintained that the ascription of a mental state or a sensation is conclusively verifiable by behavioural findings, and on the other hand, it is insisted that any suggestion that the ascription might be false should be elucidated in terms of a real or detectable difference. Once more the tension between these two conditions, with the requirement of verifiability being imposed at one point and relaxed at another, may make us wonder whether there can be any consistent basis to the position, and in fact certain difficulties are soon apparent. In the first place, the various possibilities which we should normally regard as real enough, possibilities such as that of pretence, might well prove to be on a par with the proposition with which they conflict. They might, that is, be possibilities which do not allow of conclusive verification, in the sense that they are not logically implied by the verifiable data. However, since this was not held to be a ground for rejecting the original proposition, it is presumably not going to rule out these competing possibilities; and yet, if the latter are countenanced, then it is not the case that we can put to rest any doubts we may have by establishing that the possibility which has been advanced has or has not been realized. Verification may be equally problematic in either case—and that, the anti-realist urges, means that the meaningfulness of each is threatened.

In the second place, if it is held that, however much we may accept in the way of behavioural evidence, we are not logically compelled to accept the original ascription, this would appear to constitute an admission that the ascription could be false even when the evidence is as described, and this, in terms of the view being put forward, calls for the specification of a real possibility. It would seem, that is, to show a misunderstanding of the situation if one were to insist that the sceptic should give sense to the possibility which he is advancing before one considered there was a case to answer, since in allowing that the ascription is not entailed by a statement of the evidence one is already committed to the acknowledgement of such a possibility and hence, on the premises accepted, to giving sense to it oneself.

This last point may be queried, since it is possible to interpret the notion of non-entailment differently. I have assumed that to say that P does not entail Q is to commit oneself to the claim that the conjunction of P and not-Q expresses a possibility, but it might be argued that we can put this more negatively, avoiding any reference to such a possibility. For instance, we might read 'P does not entail Q' as, roughly, 'we are not entitled to pass from the assertion of P to the assertion of Q solely on the basis of logical or linguistic considerations'; or, more simply—though not equivalently—as 'the conjunction of P and not-Q is not contradictory'. I shall not go into the question whether these formulations do or do not enable us to avoid the objection, since I do not believe that the objection is one which we should try to avoid. On the contrary, it gives one version of the very problem which is troubling us. Thus, it is often supposed that behaviourism is obviously false; furthermore, the falsity of behaviourism is or may be interpreted in line with our first interpretation of non-entailment: it is possible that a person is not in a given mental state despite the fact that he is in a certain behavioural state. However, to establish this possibility in a way which accords with anti-realist principles we must show

how we could give sense to the ascription of the mental state; and if not in terms of behaviour, how otherwise is this possible? To the extent that this problem has not been resolved, to that extent the challenge of behaviourism has not been fully met.

A similar problem arises whenever the sceptic exploits a 'gap' between premises and conclusion; for instance, when what is currently observed is invoked in support of a statement about the past or the unobserved or the unobservable. In these and other cases the sceptic's opponent may have every right to demand that an expression of doubt be made specific before it can reasonably be said that his conclusion may be in error. However, if a non-sceptic of the kind we are considering is prepared to agree that the evidence E which he has does not allow a logically valid deduction of the conclusion C, then he must on his own admission explain how E falls short; he must specify at least one possibility which stands in the way of a logical connection between E and C. Note that to specify a way in which E is deficient does not mean stating what, in conjunction with E, is logically adequate for the assertion of C. The anti-realist's position requires that a specification of adequate truth-conditions be possible—and necessary for a complete refutation of the sceptic—but only one falsifying possibility need be advanced in order to merely reject the entailment— though of course the negation of such a possibility conjoined with E will give rise to a repetition of the problem if the possibility does not suffice to make up the difference between E and C.

We might sum up the difficulties as follows. The problem of other minds is typically seen as calling for a third way between two singularly unattractive alternatives. On the one hand, there is the possibility that we have a straightforward logical connection between behavioural evidence and mental state; the strength of such a reduction lies in its compatibility with anti-realism, but it seems not at all to square with our concept of a mental state. On the other hand, there is the possibility that behaviour provides no more than evidence for a conclusion about the mental; this alternative preserves the integrity and independence of the mental, but at the price of leaving unanswered the anti-realist objection: how can we speak of behaviour as *evidence* for a conclusion if we have no independent means of arriving at that conclusion, no way of establishing that for which the alleged evidence is evidence? A

feeling for the virtues in each alternative may then lead us to put
forward a compromise, or to argue that there just *must* be an intermediate position. However, although we are clearly not in a position
to reject any of them, we have seen a common pattern of difficulties in the intermediate positions considered, and however
persuasive an argument to the effect that there must be a third way,
we cannot be satisfied until one such is specified in detail. *Reductio
ad absurdum* arguments directed to such a conclusion generally
have a transcendental flavour: for instance, we could not have our
concept of a person unless some way of avoiding the two alternatives were possible. However, to know that there must be such
a way without knowing what it is or what it is like is surely not a
final answer, and indeed the misgivings which we feel about the
lack of information yielded by such a *reductio* proof are worked up
by the anti-realist into grounds for a more emphatic rejection of the
argument: on his principles an existence assertion is without content until it is backed up by knowledge of a specific instance, so,
however persuasive we might find a *reductio* existence proof, it
does not meet the terms for an answer which the current conception
of the problem imposes.

One possibility is, of course, simply to reject the conditions
which the anti-realist lays down as determining a satisfactory answer. After all, we do not have strong enough arguments in support
of his theory of meaning to be confident that it will be consistent
with the facts about our knowledge of other minds which have to
be reckoned with; still less could we appeal to this theory to determine what these facts are. However, we have a right to reject the
framework within which the other minds problem is posed only if
we can rebut the anti-realist's objections in detail. It is no doubt
true that his doctrine calls for modification at a number of points,
but it is surely difficult to know how what we say about the mental
lives of other people, and possibly of animals, can make sense, even
only as hypotheses, if the possibility of verifying such hypotheses is
totally ruled out. Perhaps the main anti-realist tenets will have to
be abandoned eventually, but it is appropriate, at least initially, to
regard them as laying down the conditions for a successful solution
to our problem.

I

TRUTH AND VERIFIABILITY

EXISTENCE assertions based on *reductio* proofs represent a step which we might innocently take without realizing that we were running foul of the anti-realist, and there are other more or less obvious ways in which a position presumed to be consistent with his principles might prove to be vitiated by an unjustified use of the Law of Excluded Middle. For instance, we can soon arrive at a point where we can say 'either he really is angry or he is feigning anger', and each disjunct here could be held to have mentalistic implications, but if neither disjunct is decidable then the disjunction as a whole is unacceptable to the anti-realist. Again, it is often argued against the sceptic that it makes no sense to suppose that, for example, we are always dreaming, since such universal error would destroy the contrast between dreaming and waking life. For the anti-realist, however, this rejoinder is not completely satisfactory, since as long as we are not able to tell in a given case which of the two alternatives hold, but can only say that we must at least be awake *sometimes*, we have not provided an adequate basis for the knowledge needed to counter the sceptic. (This illustration is of course much more problematic than I have made out, but I use it merely to demonstrate the *kind* of objection which can be expected from the anti-realist.)

There are a number of other general observations worth making at this stage about the anti-realist position. The doctrine is not, as I understand it, to be thought of as a theory about language learning. I should stress that this is my understanding of the position and not necessarily the interpretation which is generally at stake—though I suspect that it is by oversight rather than intention that the language-learning interpretation tends to hold sway in discussions of the other minds problem. It is sometimes held that our use of language is the outcome of a training which has brought about an association between verbal utterances and corresponding states of affairs, and from this it may seem a short step to the anti-realist claim that, in order for us to have grasped the sense of a declarative sentence, we must be able to recognize circumstances which would warrant us in asserting it; sometimes, even, it is argued as if the problem were no more than one of how we might teach a child the meaning of a word such as 'pain'. Certainly, it is not uncommon to find the problem represented as one of reconciling the recalcitrant facts with the demand that there be public phenomena by reference to which we can teach and learn the meaning of such words.

I do not wish the theory of meaning which is at issue to stand or fall depending on the cogency of speculations concerning the acquisition of language. Such speculations may be suggestive and they may legitimately be used in giving a more concrete illustration of a logical point concerning the meaning of mental predicates, but if actually incorporated into the theory they can only be to its disadvantage. The principal problem which faces us would be no more and no less acute if human beings were born with a command of language, or if at some point in their development children were to start talking coherently without the benefit of exposure to a linguistic community—let alone to actual *training* at the hands of adults. Our tests for understanding are logically independent of any facts about how that understanding was acquired, and the question is not: how could I come by an understanding of what it is for another to be in pain if the possibility of conclusive verification is ruled out? but: supposing this possibility excluded, how then can ascriptions of pain to others be treated as factual propositions, as propositions which can be significantly spoken of as true or false?

Its being a question of the content of a form of words, and not of the way in which understanding of these words is acquired or imparted, is important in determining our attitude on certain questions which naturally arise here. For instance, if it is a matter of the genesis of our understanding, then it may appear unsatisfactory to try to resolve doubts concerning a problematic proposition by suggesting an artificially contrived and complicated test situation. Surely the acceptability of the proposition cannot wait upon such a discovery, given that appreciation of the possibility in question played no part in the development of our understanding of the proposition? If, on the other hand, the claim is that it must make a recognizable difference whether or not the proposition is true or false, then it is appropriate to specify how that difference could show itself, even if this requires us to think up a totally unnatural and improbable state of affairs. Similarly, an emphasis on the genetic account points in the direction of a theory which cannot find room for the notion of *verifiability in principle*. If actual familiarity with circumstances warranting the assertion of *P* is what my understanding of *P* must rest upon, it becomes difficult to see how I can find a totally new proposition intelligible. It would seem of little use to appeal to the *possibility* of verification, since circumstances which can only be imagined did not figure in my training; my understanding of *P* owes nothing to such fantasies. But once more, if our concern is with extracting a recognizable difference between the two possibilities, *P* true and *P* false, it is only the possibility of verifying the one or the other that need concern us.

The preceding clarification does not show up anti-realism as an illiberal theory of meaning, but there are other considerations which reveal it as more restrictive than might be supposed, as soon emerges from a comparison with Logical Positivism. In expounding the anti-realist's position I claimed that he would not allow the acceptability of 'it is probable that *P*' unless assertibility conditions for the simple *P* could be specified: if no conditions sufficient for the truth of *P* can be recognized then we do not know what is asserted by *P*, but since what is asserted is the same as what may be said to be merely probable, any doubts affecting the content of the assertion *ipso facto* affect the content of the probability judgement. Positivists, however, were sometimes quite happy to allow that a proposition could be true even though knowledge of its truth was forever out of our reach. In Ayer's view, for instance, general propositions and propositions about the past are of this kind, but they are saved from meaninglessness by the consideration that observation is relevant to a determination of their truth or falsehood, in the sense that observation can render them highly probable, though not certain—see the Introduction to the second edition of *Language, Truth and Logic*. The question, but *what* is being said to be probable? did not, curiously enough, trouble the Positivists as much as it should, but their conception of truth was firmly realist on a number of central issues. On the other hand, Ayer did feel constrained to argue for the meaningfulness of statements about the past by appealing to the logical possibility that he should have been living at the time in question, and in similar vein he dallied with the view that 'it is not logically inconceivable that I should have an experience that is in fact owned by someone else', a possibility which he thought might justify an argument by analogy for other minds; though if he thought that probability was sufficient there was no need for such manœuvres, since there assuredly are observations which are highly relevant to a determination of the truth or falsity of propositions of the sort in question, without going so far as to settle their truth-value. (See Ayer's *The Foundations of Empirical Knowledge*, pp. 166–70.)

Verificationist theories of meaning threaten to come to grief over—among other things—the notion of *conclusive verification*. This notion proves troublesome if, as is commonly done, it is linked to that of indubitability, especially if it is felt that for verification to be conclusive it must be the case that doubt is somehow *logically* excluded. This proviso does not appear to allow of any coherent interpretation, since whenever it makes sense to speak of verification it would appear that the logical possibility of error must always be acknowledged. However, one of the anti-realist's central claims is that if *C* is assertible on the basis of evidence, then it must be possible to assert it without such a basis, and in terms of this thesis the notion of conclusive verification allows of a comparatively straightforward interpretation: it is a matter of direct verification, not mediated by mere signs of whatever it is we are trying to establish. Such verification is conclusive in that there is no presumption as to the continuing evidential value of the data, and so no possibility of a breakdown at such a point. If this allows us to speak in terms of the exclusion of doubt, well and good, but any appeal to the possibility of certainty which the anti-realist might make is to be understood in the first instance in terms of the possibility of such a direct verification. (I understand *evidence* as something less than that for which it is to be accounted evidence: if *A* is to be a statement of the evidence for *B*, the inference from *A* to *B* is not to be deductively valid. A creature's having an organ which circulates blood through its body is not *evidence* for its having a heart; that is just what it is for it to have a heart.)

One final point is worth making on the comparison between anti-realism—as I am interpreting the doctrine—and Logical Positivism. What the anti-realist finds senseless is primarily the suggestion that a proposition may be true when there is no question that we should ever be able to appreciate its truth. There is no immediate inference from 'unverifiable' to 'meaningless' with respect to the particular form of words in question, since these could be acknowledged to express something which might be recognized to be true in other circumstances, or they could have some other role in the language and a meaning which could be explained without reference to any fact-stating function. Thus, if we have a well-formed arithmetical formula which is shown to be undecidable we are not to conclude that it lapses into meaninglessness. What we cannot meaningfully say is 'for all that, it may still be true or false'; we cannot grant that the facts are as shown by the proof of undecidability and at the same time contend that things may be as the formula asserts them to be. Of course, given the nature of the propositions which concern us, it is unlikely that we should be interested in any other role they might be deemed to have should it prove that it makes no sense to suppose them true; it would be little solace to find that they had a function quite other than that of stating how things are.

As far as possible I am concerned with the dispute between realist and anti-realist as it bears directly on the problem of the meaning of psychological predicates. I am less interested in difficulties, real though they may be, which the anti-realist must get to grips with over such ubiquitous trouble-makers as general statements and statements about the past. Just as the latter pose a problem for the anti-realist, so past-tense ascriptions of mental states will pose that problem, but this is only accidental to their character as ascriptions of mental states. However, there is one species of proposition, namely the subjunctive conditional, which, although falling within this broader category, has—or has been thought to have—a special role in the description of mental states, and I propose to single this out for more thorough discussion.

Only a very crude version of behaviourism would require that statements about a person's state of mind at a given time be translatable into statements about his actual behaviour at that time; what the person *would* have done may be as relevant as what he actually did. The subjunctive conditionals involved here are compatible with any liberal behaviourism, but it may be doubted whether they can be handled by the anti-realist. How, after all, could such a conditional be verified? To take one among many possible examples, suppose we conjecture that a certain man was worried. Given there was no behavioural manifestation of his state of mind, it might be held that we can support our conjecture only to the extent that we can sustain a conditional specifying how the man would have acted if certain things which did not happen had happened—circumstances chosen for their supposed capacity to elicit the man's mental state. In most cases there will be considerable difficulty in devising a hypothetical which we could say with any confidence was implied by the original categorical assertion, but aside from this there is the problem of determining how the man would have acted in the circumstances contemplated. And, if there is no way of telling, what use can such conditionals be to the anti-realist?

The problems posed by subjunctive conditionals have made some philosophers sceptical of the value of a programme of analysis of psychological ascriptions which places any weight on the possibility of translations into this form. From one point of view, however, the controversy does not have quite the significance it would seem to have, but there is a sense in which such conditionals can only be of secondary importance. Let us grant that to say a man was worried, although he did not show it, is to commit oneself to a statement about how he would have acted had the circumstances been different. As I say, it is difficult to state any definite committal which the categorical can be held to bring with it, but for the sake of argument let us opt for something along the lines of 'if he had been drawn into conversation his speech and manner would have been distracted'.

Two points are noteworthy about this example: we have chosen to analyse 'was worried' rather than 'is worried', and we have envisaged the particular circumstances in which it is known or believed that the man did not engage in conversation with anybody. It is surely more natural to begin with the conditional corresponding to the present-tense version, namely, 'if he is drawn into conversation his speech and manner will be distracted', and to modify this in ways appropriate to the facts as the occasion requires. If in a given case we think it unlikely that the man will be drawn into conversation the appropriate formulation will be: 'if the man were to be drawn into conversation his speech and manner would be distracted'; for the simple past, assuming no special knowledge or beliefs, we have: 'if he was drawn into conversation his speech and manner must have been distracted'; and, if the time for engaging him in conversation is believed by us to have passed, we have: 'if he had been drawn into conversation his speech and manner would have been distracted'. The present-tense version has a central place and is the one to be tackled in the first instance; if it should prove that all present-tense statements about other minds are capable of verification, that will surely represent a solution to the main problem, irrespective of the complications which arise with a transposition of these statements to other moods and tenses.

These observations perhaps dispense us from further examination of subjunctive conditionals. However, given the frequency with which such conditionals crop up at crucial points, and given the extent of the damage to anti-realism if it breaks down on this question, I think it is better not to take the easy way out just offered. This topic also gives us the opportunity to look further at certain notions of general importance to the anti-realist, and I shall begin with some preliminary remarks on one such notion, namely that of *verification*.

Consider the future-tense statement, 'It will snow tomorrow'. It could surely not be held that our ordinary understanding of this statement requires that we know when we should be warranted in asserting it, if by this were meant—as is most natural—that we should be able to recognize such conditions before the time at which the statement might come true. I could certainly tell that a person had been right or wrong in making such a prediction about the weather, but I may not know what would warrant its assertion prior to the event—of course, nothing would, if it is a matter of conclusive verification, but if it is less than that, a question of possible evidence, then I need not know what thus qualifies. Clearly, what is essential to anti-realism is that we should be able to appreciate when such a prediction has been fulfilled; it is not necessary that we should be able to recognize as such signs or evidence on which the prediction might be based. And, of course, according to the anti-realist we have no right to regard present signs as evidence for the future snowfall unless we can directly verify its occurrence at the appropriate time.

Similarly, in order for a person to understand the indicative conditional, 'if you press the button the light will shine', we cannot insist that he be able to recognize particular evidential conditions which would warrant him in asserting this in advance, but all we require is that he should know what is involved in its eventual fulfilment or verification. The appropriate sense here of 'verify' is, I maintain, such that in order to speak of the conditional as *verified* we need no more than knowledge of the truth of the consequent, given (knowledge) that the antecedent has been fulfilled. Thus, given that the button has been pressed, this conditional is verified or falsified accordingly as the light is found to shine or not to shine. Or, taking 'verify' in the wider sense, where it covers the case of finding false, we can say that verification waits upon ascertaining the truth-value of the consequent of the conditional, given that the antecedent has been fulfilled—or, for the antirealist, given that it is known to be fulfilled—and this we may sum up in the formula: the truth-value of 'B, if A' is the same as the truth value of B, if A.

I say we need no more than knowledge of the truth-value of the consequent, given that the antecedent has been (found to be) fulfilled, but it may be argued that we need even less than this, depending on how we treat those cases in which the antecedent is not fulfilled. I am not concerned with this complication, but the main point I wish to make is this negative consideration: in order to speak of a conditional as *verified* there is no call to establish in addition any connection of meaning, relevance, or whatever between antecedent and consequent. It could be that fulfilment of the one has nothing to do with fulfilment of the other: by sheer chance the light goes on when you press the button. But that is of no account. If all I said was that if you press the button the light will shine then it has come to pass as I predicted, and the fact that any reasoning which I might have advanced in support of this conclusion might have been fanciful in the extreme does not detract from the correctness of the prediction which my muddled thinking led me to make. (Some of the gaps in this discussion are filled in in my 'Is Natural Deduction Natural?', *Proceedings of the Aristotelian Society*, Supplementary Volume XLIII (1969).)

The belief that something more in the way of a connection is needed is probably an instance of the common confusion of meaning with grounds, here in the form of a confusion of a conditional's being verified with its being 'well-founded', as we might put it. Nothing more is needed for the verification of the conditional when

the time comes to put it to the test, but something more *is* needed
to persuade someone prior to that time that the conditional will
turn out the way you claim. If I can cite no reason why my pressing
the button can be taken to be relevant to the light's shining, then
you may well disregard my prediction as without foundation.
Exceptions to this are possible—I might establish to your satisfaction that the light was going to go on anyhow, irrespective of your
pressing the button—but generally speaking support of a conditional prior to knowing the truth-values of antecedent and consequent requires some connection to be traced out between the
two.

The notion of a conditional's being *well-founded*, of its being
strongly supported by argument or evidence, takes second place
to the notion of its being *verified*, at least for the anti-realist, since
in his eyes a person who did not know what would verify a conditional would lack an understanding of the meaning of the consequent—if not the antecedent—and so would have no knowledge
of *what* had been established, no appreciation of what the evidence
for the conditional was evidence for. And, to repeat the analogy
with future-tense statements, as with the simple prediction, 'it
will snow tomorrow', so here it would seem conceivable that a
person should be able to recognize when a conditional was verified
without having any knowledge of how, prior to the event, he could
have been in a position to advance the conditional with substantial
supporting reasons.

But what are we to say about subjunctive conditionals? When
you say 'if you press the button the light will shine', we shall expect you to be able to give some backing to your claim, but whether
or not you do so, final confirmation of your prediction awaits the
outcome of the button's being pressed. On the other hand, with
the subjunctive conditional, 'if you had pressed the button the
light would have shone', the possibility of final confirmation or
verification—which is precisely what the anti-realist requires—
would appear to be ruled out. I say 'would appear', since it is not
entirely clear in what sense this is so. The reason why verification
is taken to be ruled out is usually stated in terms of the implied
falsity of the antecedent, but this cannot be quite right—an
indicative corresponding to the subjunctive could be false, but in
the form in which it actually occurs the antecedent cannot be described as either true of false—and we might begin to wonder what

meaning this missing verification could have in this connection. On the other hand, the assertion or rejection of a subjunctive conditional need not be arbitrary; they can be more or less strongly supported by the evidence, so perhaps we can get by here with a notion of truth understood in terms of well-foundedness. In keeping with this decision it might be questioned whether in the example of the worried man it really is true that there is no way of deciding whether he would or would not have behaved in a certain way. We certainly could have good grounds for asserting one rather than the other of two opposing conditionals, and perhaps we could say that a subjunctive conditional could be known to be true in the only sense in which we can meaningfully speak of it as being true, namely in the sense of being well-founded.

That is one possibility, but another approach points to another conclusion. If we take our indicative conditional, 'if you press the button the light will shine', then, however strong the supporting evidence, there is always the logical possibility of falsification when it is put to the test, and however ill-supported or in conflict with the evidence there is always the possibility that it should prove true, given in either case that we have to do with an empirical proposition. Now if the time for putting such a conditional to the test passes and the antecedent remains unfulfilled, then, to the extent that we have no reason to consider that we were mistaken about the strength of the evidence, to that extent we should be prepared to agree to the corresponding subjunctive conditional 'if you had pressed the button the light would have shone'. However, just as the truth of the indicative conditional was a distinct question from its degree of well-foundedness, so, it would seem, this distinction is to be preserved when we forsake the indicative for its subjunctive version. However strong the evidence, there is still the logical possibility that you should have pressed the button but that the light should have failed to shine, and since we do have this possibility, then if the anti-realist is right, there must be something which would count as verification, and not simply as evidence for the conditional—*if* we are to speak of it as being true. Since well-foundedness falls short of establishing truth, the truth and hence sense of subjunctive conditionals has yet to be explained.

That there is a possibility which keeps them apart and that it would be a mistake to try to close the gap between well-foundedness and truth is further suggested by the consideration that, however well founded 'if you had pressed the button the light would have shone', it is quite possible we should discover that the person actually *did* press the button but that the light did not shine. Similarly, however meagre the evidence for such a conditional, or however weighty the evidence against it, it could be found that the button was pressed and the light shone, and indeed this possibility, which is what would count as verification in the indicative case, might be offered as providing verification in the subjunctive case as well. As mentioned above, it is commonly supposed that the presumed or implied falsity of the antecedent stands in the way of verification, and it can at least be granted that a subjunctive antecedent is generally used in deference to a belief—not necessarily the speaker's—that the corresponding indicative is false. To allow this, however, is not to go so far as to maintain that one who asserts 'if you had pressed the button the light would have shone' is logically committed to 'you did not press the button'. If the subjunctive is used there is a strong presumption that the speaker does accept this indicative, but it is conceivable that this presumption should fail. In this event we might refuse the conditional a truth-value, but it seems also possible to regard it as showing the removal of the obstacle to verification.

A parallel conclusion holds for the form of subjunctive conditional illustrated by the sentence 'if you were to press the button the light would shine'. The subjunctive is appropriate to the belief that the person addressed will not press the button, or at least is unlikely to do so, but if, contrary to expectation, the person does press the button, the conditional is verified or falsified accordingly as the light does or does not shine. In the case of the past subjunctive, 'if you had pressed the button the light would have shone', there may be a presumption of knowledge rather than belief that the corresponding indicative is false, if only because, since it relates to the past, to events which may well have fallen within our experience, knowledge rather than mere belief or conjecture is possible. However, as far as the question of entailing indicatives is concerned, both conditionals are on a par; in either case the conditional is, if unverifiable, only contingently unverifiable.

There are, then, two ways in which the notion of *truth* might be interpreted with respect to subjunctive conditionals, neither of which need be a source of embarrassment to the anti-realist. On the one hand, if it is insisted (i) that we *do* have a notion of truth which has application to subjunctive conditionals, and (ii) that this notion is to apply without requiring fulfilment of the indicative corresponding to the antecedent, then the only conceivable answer would seem to be that such a notion of truth, or such an approximation to the notion, must be characterized in terms of well-foundedness. If, given that verification is disallowed, well-foundedness is the nearest we can logically get to truth, then that is the most we could mean by 'truth' in this context. Such a view would be akin to the current conception of such conditionals as compressed arguments describable as 'true' or 'false' only in the sense of 'valid' or 'invalid'.

This alternative relies on taking the subjunctive antecedent seriously, to the extent that the possibility of the fulfilment of the corresponding indicative antecedent is supposed ruled out; not on the grounds that the subjunctive conditional *entails* the falsity of this indicative, but in the belief that the notion of truth should be explicable against the assumption of its *de facto* falsity. On the other hand, we advanced an argument which suggested that we might well distinguish between truth and well-foundedness, understanding the former in terms of verification as applied to the corresponding indicative conditional. This move depended on not taking the falsity of the indicative antecedent as an unrevisable assumption which the notion of truth as applied to the subjunctive conditional must respect, but exploiting the possibility that you might after all find the corresponding indicative conditional falsified or verified, no matter how strong the arguments for or against the subjunctive conditional. Clearly, however, if this is the way in which we argue a distinction between truth and well-foundedness, we provide at the same time a notion of truth acceptable to the anti-realist: it is no more than a trivial extension of the notion of truth as applied to categorical empirical statements.

Since well-foundedness allows of degrees in a way which may seem foreign to the notion of truth, there is some reason for preferring this second alternative. However, I am inclined to think that the anti-realist must allow *truth* to cover both verification and well-foundedness if he is to recognize the multiplicity in our everyday conception. Thus, if the only usage of 'true' available were to be expounded in terms of verification, we should be at a loss to know how to handle compound propositions in which a subjunctive conditional is coupled with the negation of the corresponding indicative antecedent. Consider, for instance, 'he did not press the button, but if he had the light would have shone'. Here the possibility of verification is *logically* excluded—assuming that verification would have required us to see what happened on the button's being pressed—yet we should quite readily speak of the whole statement as being true. This being so it would seem that, while we can speak of the first conjunct as being verified, if we are at the same time to speak of the second conjunct as being true, our justification for this must rest upon no more than our ability to establish by *argument* that fulfilment of the consequent would have followed on fulfilment of the antecedent. But, of course, the anti-realist can acknowledge both the distinction and the propriety of using 'true' in either case, and this acknowledgement merely requires him to take greater care in stating his position.

There are other forms of proposition which can give rise to analogous problems. Suppose, for example, that to verify a certain proposition we must verify two conditionals with incompatible antecedents. If we do have a proposition whose truth requires the truth of conditionals 'if P then Q' and 'if R then S', where P and R cannot both be true together, then I do not think it would be enough for the anti-realist to point out that each antecedent, and hence each hypothetical, could be verified separately; that would in no way alter the fact that the original proposition could not be verified, and this simply is contrary to his principles. In this instance, it is not clear that an appeal to the notion of well-foundedness is sufficient; on the other hand, although it is easy to think of propositions which might be taken to involve conditionals with antecedents which in some sense conflict, it is difficult to find a realistic instance where this leads to the impossibility of their joint verification. To describe a ball as 'elastic' no doubt commits one to saying that it will bounce when dropped from a range of different heights; in one sense the antecedents of all the appropriate conditionals imply one another's negations, but this does not mean that they cannot all be true, only that they cannot all be true at the same time, or at any rate verified at the same time. For verification to be logically excluded, P and R would have to be so formulated as to relate to exactly the same moment; we should have to suppose that once P had been fulfilled the possibility of R's being fulfilled at a later time was logically excluded, and this is not a possibility for which I can find a realistic example.

Nor, I suggest, is it realistic to suppose that the truth of an infinite number of such conditionals is ever required for the truth of an empirical proposition. An indefinite number, perhaps, but that is another matter. However, this is to raise the problem of how general statements are to be handled by the anti-realist, and we could not accept this way out without further discussion. Such discussion will not be entered into here, but we might at least state the wider problem more fully, and this I shall now do. We can make sense of the suggestion that a proposition of the form '*f*s are *g*' is true by reference to the possibility that particular *f*s have been found to be *g* in the right circumstances and in sufficient number; or, if something other than an indeterminate totality of individual cases of this sort is required, the truth of the general statement can rest on the availability of a finite number of general procedures to which we may appeal in establishing that an arbitrary *f* is *g*. Each of these alternatives calls for elaboration, but the essential point is that the realist sees a third possibility: that a general proposition should be true, but that its truth should not be discoverable either by accumulating particular instances or by invoking a general argument applicable to the arbitrary case; it may be true that *f*s are *g*, he claims, even though this means the truth of an infinite number of particular propositions, '*a* is *g*', '*b* is *g*', . . ., with no prospect of effecting a finitistic reduction. Which means, replies the anti-realist, no way of interpreting the generalization which makes its truth a genuine possibility. But who is right and who is wrong is a question we shall not pursue.

For our purposes the topic of subjunctive conditionals is chiefly relevant to the question how we can be in a position to affirm the existence of an unexercised disposition, ability, or capacity. In order to defend such an affirmation it may be necessary and/or sufficient to establish what would have happened in circumstances supposed not to have obtained, and to this end we may find ourselves appealing to the evidence of some factor, *F*, whose occurrence is not dependent on fulfilment of the antecedent of the relevant indicative conditional, but which we have found associated with satisfaction of the consequent of this conditional in those cases where the antecedent has been fulfilled. The evidential value of *F* having been established in those situations, its presence can be invoked in support of the corresponding subjunctive conditional on occasions when such a conditional is the most we can assert.

There is a temptation to suppose that a subjunctive conditional, or the corresponding statement of a disposition, say, actually entails such a condition—a 'categorical basis'—on the grounds that the truth of a conditional requires some *actual* state of affairs to make it true: if it is to be the case that the prudent man would have acted in a certain way in certain circumstances, this can only be true in virtue of some actual state of the person at the time in question. This view is likely to involve a misreading of the distinction between the categorical and the hypothetical, but it is not altogether off the mark. It is correct, as far as the anti-realist is concerned, to the extent that we are warranted in asserting the conditional only if we know that such a condition, F, obtains, or at least have some evidence or reasons with which to support our assertion: the supposition of the conditional's being true in the absence of any knowable condition in virtue of which it may be deemed true is, for the anti-realist, quite empty. However, the consequence to be drawn from this is not that the conditional, on the strength of meaning what it means, involves reference to such a condition, but what we are to infer is merely that we cannot be sure that the supposition of the truth of the conditional is a supposition which we can make in all circumstances; the possible gratuitousness of the assertion of the conditional is something which we must simply acknowledge, rather than clinging to the belief that it can be supposed to be true whatever the circumstances.

Problems somewhat similar to those posed by subjunctive conditionals are to be found in connection with other forms of proposition which have been put forward as counter-examples to verificationist theories of meaning. Consider, for example, 'it rained while no one was here', or 'the oceans existed before there was life on earth'. The acceptability of such propositions as these is surely in no way threatened by the impossibility of verifying them; on the contrary, we should be suspicious of any theory which would impose such a condition. It must be allowed that in either case we may be in possession of evidence which is overwhelming; the question is whether the anti-realist can simply maintain that the reliability of F as evidence for the occurrence of rain or the existence of an ocean can be established in those cases where the occurrence of F and that for which it is evidence are jointly verified, and then transferred to those contexts in which direct verification is logically excluded.

An affirmative answer is reasonable whenever the problematic proposition can be resolved into two components, a proposition P for which F has been shown to be evidence by direct verification of both, and a clause which amounts to a denial of conditions which are necessary to verification of P. It is not good enough simply to say that if verification is *logically* excluded then it is no failing of any theory that it cannot show how it is to be achieved in such circumstances, since the theory in question does after all make an unqualified demand of verifiability, but as long as the proposition can be represented as such a conjunction the anti-realist's position would appear to be defensible. To see this, consider by contrast the attempt to solve the problem posed by statements about the past by saying that such statements are only contingently about the past, so only contingently unverifiable: instead of saying what I said with respect to last week, I might have said the same thing with respect to the present, in which case my assertion could have been put to the test. It is surely reasonable to require that any such proposition be verifiable, if that is the demand, without any such drastic revision, and in this instance there is no question of a breakdown into a conjunction containing one proposition, P, verifiable in principle, along with a clause whose fulfilment makes for the unverifiability of P. The reference to the past will surely have to be retained in P itself; a present-tense statement corresponding to P may be readily verifiable, but it will not be part of the assertion contemplated, so will offer no help to the anti-realist.

To take another example, it is of no avail to say that we could in principle have learned what Smith had been thinking on the grounds that instead of thinking his thoughts to himself he might have expressed them out loud. The observation is not mistaken, but it shows verifiability only at the cost of making out the state of affairs to be other than the one we found perplexing. It is not to the point to mention that, had the man done something different, then that would have been something of which we could have known, unless 'something different' means something *in addition* to what we initially said he did, and not something *in place* of that. If the thesis were that we could have known what he was thinking because he might have spoken his thoughts—as well as thinking them to himself first, and not instead of this—then it is not open to our objection; and this is the thesis which the anti-realist can reasonably enlist.

Causal propositions are another class of proposition which will figure prominently in the investigations to follow, bringing with them further questions concerning verification. However, such questions are of particular interest to us only to the extent that causality in the context of the mental is problematic. When establishing that A causes B we are confronted with difficulties posed by universal statements, since to isolate A as a cause we must ensure that *all* the relevant conditions have been considered, and it can be a problem to know how we can recognize when we are done with the totality of such conditions. The problem may be severe enough when the conditions are individually verifiable, but it could take on another dimension of severity in the context of other minds if the existence of possible causal factors, such as sensations, proved impossible to verify, and this is the kind of possibility which concerns us.

This completes my sketch of the theory of meaning which is at stake in the other minds problem—or, I should say, the theory which I believe to be involved. It is difficult to know whether others see the problem quite in this way, since it is rare to find any significant attention paid to this fundamental question. I am well aware that verificationist theories of meaning are at present out of favour, and I grant that the version which I have presented— though not advocated—is highly demanding in the requirements which it lays down and with which it would seek to restrict our seemingly broader conception of the extent of the factual. On the other hand, even for a philosopher who is out of sympathy with anti-realism it is of interest to discover whether statements about other minds are subject to conclusive tests, and if not why precisely they fail in this regard; is it for general reasons affecting a large class of statements, or is it something special to the particular class that makes for their unverifiability? And again, if it should prove that they are outside the limits of what the anti-realist can allow, that will tell us something about anti-realism; we can, that is, use the other minds problem to test and possibly to refine this account of our understanding of factual statements.

2

WANTING AND KNOWING

BEHAVIOURISM in the form of a denial of the existence of thoughts and feelings is not a position calculated to command a large following. None the less, it is generally supposed that the traditionally sharp distinction between the mental and the behavioural has been gradually broken down, with the mental giving way and the behavioural extending its boundaries in consequence. There are at least two ways in which this weakening of the division has been thought to be at the expense of the mental. First, a person's state of mind may, it is held, be more evident to an onlooker than it is to the person himself, and this would seem to indicate that what mental state a person is in can be very much a matter of how he looks and acts; the man affected is not necessarily in an authoritative position *vis-à-vis* the question of his state of mind, but we often know better whether he is in love, is jealous, frightened, worried, shy, and so forth. Second, it is argued that for us to have any understanding of the language descriptive of mental phenomena, such language must relate closely to what can be observed, and this would here seem to mean: to the behavioural.

In both these cases the move towards the grounding of an ascription of a mental state in behaviour is likely to be partly in response to anti-realist pressures, but in both cases there is an equally strong contrary pressure from the direction of common sense: there surely can be no question of an *identity* between the mental and the behavioural; any theory which requires that for its validity must be in error. And yet, if we wish to satisfy the anti-realist, is there any possibility of stopping short of this identity? First, however, we might query the significance of these two standard arguments. The second runs the risk of being misdirected towards the irrelevant pedagogical issue, and calls for a restatement in something like the following terms: if we suppose psychological ascriptions to be unconnected with behaviour, what would fail is our understanding, not in the sense that understanding could not then be acquired, but in the sense that there would be nothing *to* understand. However, granted that the logical point is prior to the genetic point, it is still not clear that it is correct. That there should be an intimate relationship between a man's mental life and what he does or would do is no doubt more than conjecture; the whole difficulty lies in making clear how precisely the two interconnect, and until this is done there is no reason to believe in the possibility of an actual behaviouristic reduction.

Nor does the first point, that we may be as well placed to judge of a person's mental state as the person himself, have sufficient scope to take the behaviourist very far forward. It is plausible as applied to certain moods and states of mind, but it leaves untouched a number of mental phenomena with regard to which there surely is an important asymmetry between the subject and others; just consider, for instance, questions about a man's thoughts, dreams, and imaginings. Again, although we are sometimes able to pronounce upon a person's mental state and to defend our description against his rebuttal of it, merely to see a person as performing *actions* is, on one common conception, to go beyond what a strict behaviourist can recognize. More obviously, our pronouncement may depend on our having discerned a pattern not merely in his behaviour but in what his words reveal to us; what he says, as much as what he does, may be required for us to infer that he is jealous or in love, yet in basing our interpretation on his utterances we once more go beyond a behaviourist treatment of them. For such purposes we may have to accept what he discloses about his hopes, fears, wishes, and desires, with no guarantee that such reports will or can be rendered superfluous by his subsequent behaviour, properly so called.

It is also worth mentioning that, although we can at least allow the possibility of mental predicate which may in some circumstances be verified solely on the basis of a person's behaviour, such predicates would, by that fact alone, be unlikely to be regarded as *mental*, and certainly not as paradigmatically so. We might even suspect that the support which behaviourism still enjoys derives from its unwarranted extension of the realm of the mental beyond its normal confines to embrace phenomena which it can handle with some degree of success, such success diverting attention from the failure of the theory on the topics which should be its major concern.

Let us consider the overall strategy which the anti-realist might be led to adopt. The data to which he can appeal for an understanding of the mental are those of behaviour, language, and physiological and physical conditions. For the present we may pass over the latter, which are secondary in connection with problems of meaning, and concentrate on the similar problems surrounding behaviour and language. With regard to the former there is the point, just alluded to, that merely in describing someone as doing certain things we are often going beyond what a description of his bodily movements alone would entitle us to assert. It is no comfort to the anti-realist to be told that the very notion of behaviour carries implications of a mentalistic kind which render behaviourism more plausible, if it then becomes questionable whether he has any right to make use of such a notion; from his point of view the implications might stand in need of elimination, or at least of a justification which he might have difficulty in providing.

The problem with regard to language is analogous. On the one hand, we can think of speech in terms of mere behaviour: a man's uttering of words is something which, like eating and walking, he does, and there is apparently the same logical gap between the uttering of words and the having of a thought or feeling as there is between other forms of behaviour and mental states. On the other hand, this is not the only way in which we can conceive of speech; there is, after all, the obvious consideration that *what* a man says, as opposed to his uttering of certain words, is not to be reckoned along with his behaviour, and a moment's reflection suggests that if we are going to make any sense of the mental we must have regard to a person's words as, by virtue of their meaning, indicative of his mental state. But *how* indicative? By providing *evidence* of that state? But then, surely, a more direct verification must be theoretically possible, at least for the anti-realist. Words, together with behaviour, seemingly provide us with a wealth of evidence, but, to repeat, if all we ever have is evidence, we are never in a position to check that it really is correlated with that for which it allegedly is evidence, and hence our right to speak of it in these terms has not been secured.

There is a natural assumption that direct verification would have to involve somehow looking into the man's mind, sharing the experiences whose existence we can otherwise not know of with certainty. The way I have presented the anti-realist position, with its requirement of an independent check, suggests something of this absurd interpretation, but what is essentially involved in the requirement of direct verification is, I maintain, the possibility of excluding the kind of error which could result from the break- down of an inference based on evidence. If this is accepted, it seems clear that the subject's word can be held to provide final confirma- tion of any speculations we may entertain as to his inner life. What *he* says is not based on evidence, and provided his words can be taken at their face value, we surely have here the conclusive verifi- cation which we seek.

This proviso, that the man's words involve no distortion, is not a minor detail. However, although there are obvious difficulties, the approach just sketched appears to offer some hope to the anti-realist. Certainly, even if it does not wear its truth on its face, the hypothesis that between them language and behaviour can somehow provide the data on which mental ascriptions can be satisfactorily based is a hypothesis which is worth pursuing further. But, we may note, if we do have an instance where an appeal to what is or might be said is indisputably ruled out, then, if the hypothesis is not to be abandoned, the implication that we need consider no more than behaviour must be vindicated. Further, it is clear that just this possibility is realized in the case of creatures other than men. There are a variety of psychological predicates which we apply readily enough to animals, and while some may be dismissed as mere metaphor, others—e.g. 'sees', 'hears', 'wants', 'fears' and 'knows'—cannot be disposed of so easily. And yet, can it possibly be held that a thoroughgoing behaviourism will be adequate to these and all the other instances which arise? Not only do we have the obviously troublesome notions relating to percep- tion and sensation, but the simplest descriptions of animal be- haviour—saying that the dog is looking for his bone or trying to get into his kennel—seem to embody presumptions of a broadly mentalistic kind every bit as much as similar locutions which, in their application to human beings, present an obstacle to an analy- sis in terms of the only behaviour which the anti-realist can ini- tially recognize, namely mere bodily movements. The anti-realist is not, of course, obliged to confine his attention to behaviour, but have we allowed him enough for the task in hand even if we allow him the use of all verifiable data?

To show in detail that a behaviourist approach is in fact adequate to the animal kingdom we should have to investigate a forbiddingly large range of phenomena. I do not propose to go to such lengths, but I shall consider a selection of predicates which give rise to the difficulties facing the theory in as sharp a form as any others, concentrating for the remainder of this chapter on the key notions of *wanting* and *knowing*. The former connects with the problem of characterizing bodily movements as actions, or, what is much the same thing, the problem of analysing purposive behaviour, and I shall consider this topic in detail in the next chapter. The latter is necessary to an investigation of perception, and this too will subsequently be pursued at length.

Provided we are not talking nonsense or in hopelessly vague or metaphorical terms, there is an enormous presumption that our use of psychological predicates with respect to animals is consistent with some form of behaviourism. After all, there are many occasions when we regard it as obvious that a dog can see us, say, or that he is hungry or wants to go outside, and we do not have to do anything more than watch him to come to such conclusions. Admittedly, the use of a particular description may sometimes be questionable— think of the way old ladies personify their pets—but there are many cases in which no material dispute is possible, and this surely speaks for an intimate connection with behaviour and other observable phenomena. It is worth stressing this presumption in favour of behaviourism, since there is a tendency to reject behaviourist analyses at the first signs of difficulty in carrying them through; and yet critics of such theories leave it totally unclear how, if the behaviourism they reject is not simply to be modified, we can possibly have any understanding of our familiar characterizations of animals. If behaviour, supplemented perhaps by other observable data, does not suffice, what are the additional assumptions which we require? To judge by the extent of our agreement in describing animals, they are assumptions which are readily grasped and commonly accepted, but what they might be and how they could help has not yet been made plain.

A short space back I mentioned doubts we might have as to the possibility of a behaviourist analysis; now I am suggesting that there is an enormous presumption in favour of just such an approach. This latter claim still stands, but the grounds for doubt are soon appreciated when we turn from this general presumption to consider how the behaviourist might proceed in particular cases. For the most part, his difficulty takes the following form. We have an expression, such as 'wants', 'knows', or 'sees', for which there appears to be no corresponding behavioural description. It is because of the way it behaves that we speak of the animal as wanting, but no item or combination of items from a recognizably behaviourist vocabulary provides a match for the psychological predicate; seeing, wanting, and so forth begin to emerge as phenomena underlying the behaviour and in no sense constituted by it; no other verifiable data appear adequate to close the gap, but we are left with a hazardous inference from what can be observed to inaccessible mental states. In short, *either* the verb signifies something which must be equated with behaviour, *or* it relates to some underlying, merely conjectural mental phenomenon.

Let us now consider how this unpalatable dichotomy fares with respect to the particular example of *wanting*, one of the commonest and most central notions which we have occasion to apply to animals. What item of behaviour can plausibly be singled out as what is referred to when we speak of the animal as wanting something or as wanting to do a certain thing? If a dog is whining and scratching at the door we shall doubtless say that he wants to be let out, but we should not wish to identify his wanting with all or part of what he is observed to be doing. The connection between the two is no doubt very close, but it would surely be wrong to say that the animal's wanting just *is* his whining and scratching, or anything else he may be said to *do*.

If proof is sought for this contention, we might enlist the following argument. On the strength of what we observe the dog to be doing we say that he wants to go out. If, now, he makes no move to go out when the door is opened, doubt is cast on our claim. We are not compelled to admit we were wrong—a large threatening dog standing outside the door could provide us with a saving hypothesis—but the onus is on us to explain how it could be that the dog wanted to go out but did not do so when the opportunity arose. And now we come to a crucial difference between 'want' and verbs such as 'whine': since the dog's failure to go out throws doubt on our description of him as wanting to go out, and since it does not throw doubt on our description of him as whining and scratching, the statement 'the dog wants to go out' does not in any sense simply give a redescription of this behaviour.

In one form or another this style of argument can be effectively directed against a variety of reductionist theses. However, although it counts against a simple-minded conception of the connection between wanting and behaviour, it need not be inconsistent with a less crude behaviourism: it is in virtue of the dog's present be-haviour that I say he wants to go out; this present behaviour provides the evidence on which I base the assertion, which is at this stage no more than a hypothesis, but its verification must wait upon the *future* behaviour of the dog: does it go out when the door is opened, or, more importantly, does its distressed state cease once it is out? These are the questions to be asked. One consequence of this account is that if the dog is destroyed, say, before the occasion for his engaging in the appropriate future behaviour has arisen, the possibility of verification is ruled out: I say the dog wants to be let out and he dies before we can put this to the test. Still, in such a case verification is only accidentally precluded, so the anti-realist would not seem to be faced with a real difficulty.

Extending our consideration of the animal's behaviour beyond its current activities helps to show how want-ascriptions can be veri-fied in behaviour, but to see more clearly how wants and behaviour connect we must get closer to a definition of the former. It is noteworthy that in many of its uses 'want' is not far from the notions of *lacking* or *being without*, as when we say that something was found wanting in a certain respect, and it is helpful to bear this connection in mind. Of course, not every case of lacking or being without is one of wanting: a pig lacks wings, but it does not want them. To make the step from lacking to wanting it must be added that the creature finds the lack distressing or unpleasant, or at least that not having what it lacks is in some way bad for it. As an illustration of the latter condition, we may remark that when we say that an animal wants more iron in its diet it is supposed that the health of the creature would be improved if the deficiency were made good. In such a case there is no necessity that the creature should be in any way conscious of the lack or of what will remedy it, and this makes it rather a peripheral case of wanting from our point of view. More typical are those cases in which there is a connection with sensibility, where the lack at least gives rise to distressed or frustrated behaviour. Witness the example of the dog whining or that of the howling animal or baby which wants to be fed.

It is evident that a want can exist independently of any ability to direct actions towards the goal of getting what is wanted, and in one way this appears to be the basic case. So let us look at the question of verification in this case, as when we have the crying baby which wants to be fed. There would appear to be two possibilities here. A variety of reasons could lie behind the baby's crying, and if it is to be true that it is because it wants its milk that it is crying, then it must of course be the lack of milk that is responsible for its crying. The difficulty arises with the question whether or not the fact that feeding the child results in relief of its distressed state is by itself sufficient for proof that that is what it wanted. After all, it might be that a number of quite different things could have brought about this same effect, but should we wish to say of all of them that they were what the baby wanted? Well, if feeding *or* tickling the baby has the same effect, and is in either case equally long-lasting in its effect, then I should be happy to say that the child wanted the one or the other, it didn't matter which. It is misleading to characterize a want very specifically when a more general description will do, and we must take care to exclude actions which momentarily distract the child from its miserable condition; but given that both x and y have comparable, lasting effects in alleviating the distress, then it would seem that it is arbitrary to select the one rather than the other as being what was wanted. It is not like the case of an older child's want, where we do have another criterion to allow us to make a choice in such cases, namely the criterion provided by the child's avowal.

There would appear to be no serious problem here with verification, nor does the notion of distressed behaviour seem to harbour any particularly stubborn difficulties for the behaviourist. Inevitably there is something of a problem about exactly what is to count as distressed behaviour or a distressed state, but it is precisely behaviour or an observable state that we are concerned to characterize. Yet somehow we may feel that there must be more to it than this. If it is *only* a question of behaviour or a physical state, have we any right to regard the animal's distress as having the significance it has in a fully conscious human being? We normally regard distress as calling for a particular response from us; we think it appropriate to alleviate a person's distress, it is not an indifferent event like a mere change in colour. But, surely, if the behaviourist account is right there is not the difference in kind between distress and a colour change which could support a difference in attitude on our part.

The main point to be made in answer to this is simply to allow the possibility of such a consequence, or at least to insist that the analysis which we arrive at on other grounds takes priority to the extent that it may determine, but is not to be determined by, the attitudes we have towards the phenomena. However, I also believe we can challenge the objector's choice of a dividing line between what does and what does not merit a sympathetic response from us. Even if behaviour alone licenses such descriptions it is true to say that animals and babies dislike certain things, find them unpleasant, disturbing, and so forth, and if one believes in not treating creatures in a way which they do not like, then that belief retains its relevance here. What of course has no application is the belief that only beings with a fully developed consciousness need be treated humanely, but it just is not the case that all our descriptions in the categories of distress, dislike, fear, shock, and so forth, are reserved for application only to older children and adult human beings.

Returning to wanting, we may note that one reason for the complexity of examples such as that of the dog wanting to be let out is to be found in the coupling of the want with certain abilities and a degree of intelligence. A want can exist in the absence of an ability to engage in purposive behaviour, but when it combines with the ability to sense, move around, and manipulate the environment, there arises the possibility of a situation in which the want as evidenced by the deprived behaviour is apparently denied by the creature's failure to take steps, well within its proven ability, to satisfy the want. However, whether or not the animal does take steps to get what we conjecture it wants is a secondary matter as regards the correctness of the conjecture. In the example of the dog wanting to be let out, what gave final proof that this was what he wanted was not so much that he went out when the opportunity offered, but that once out his distressed behaviour ceased. If the dog had not gone out of his own accord but had been carried out, and if he had stopped whining or otherwise fretting, that would be enough for us to say that he wanted to be let out—given that his being out is in fact what puts a stop to his fretting.

The notion of wanting is not inseparable from that of a distressed state. If the dog starts to go out once the door is open we can say that he wants to go out even if there has been no preceding distress, and even if any such distress continues when he is out; the only requirement is that we should be able to describe going out as the animal's *purpose*. I am inclined to think that 'want' connects primarily with the presence of a distressed state, but there is this broader usage in which it applies whenever a creature is engaged in purposive behaviour: if the cat can be said to be climbing the tree in order to get the bird we can say that it wants to get the bird, and we can say this without committing ourselves on the question of actual or hypothetical displays of distressed or frustrated behaviour on the part of the cat. Examples such as this are the source of a range of intricate questions, both practical and theoretical. For instance, how do we know that x is what the animal wants and not just something which it likes and which has distracted it from the goal it was pursuing? This is not a problem in the cases which we have so far been concentrating upon; here anything which remedies the defect or puts an end to the distressed state—by satisfying the creature in this respect—can be described as what the animal wanted. However, an animal which has set off apparently in pursuit of x may desist when face to face with y; y could certainly be something which it wanted in either of the less troublesome senses just indicated, but it need not be what it wanted in the sense of what it was aiming at. The problem of determining the animal's goal can be particularly vexing when a course of action regularly terminates in a number of end-states; just which of them did it really want? When we attribute a want solely on the basis of the purposiveness of the behaviour, then we can hold that the creature wanted x even if, when it gets it, this results in no satisfaction to the creature, whereas in the other uses of the term we should be forced to say that it had not really wanted x after all. This double usage is familiar from the human case: if I sincerely say that I want to go on holiday and make efforts to bring this about, then, at least in one sense of the term, I really do want to go on holiday, however the experience turns out. On the other hand, there is such a thing as finding that what one thought one wanted was not really what one wanted after all.

Returning to the animals, I suggested that to speak of a creature wanting, in the sense in which this connects with purpose, is to say no more than that its actions or efforts are directed towards the attainment of a thing or a state of affairs which it lacks; no discontent or distress need be implied. On the other hand, I have also indicated that wants are to be recognized not so much in the successful pursuit of a goal, but primarily in deprived, frustrated, distressed, or at least persistent behaviour. We 'measure' the extent to which an animal wants something by its persistence in following a course of action which will lead to the attainment of its goal, despite our attempts to interfere with it, and by reference to the extent to which when thwarted its frustration is manifested in its cries and growls. An animal which desisted from a course of action as soon as we made things difficult for it, and which displayed no signs of frustration even when not diverted by something which it liked, but which set about some other goal-directed behaviour, would not be said to have wanted the goal very much.

Still, whether or not the use of 'want' with respect to purposive behaviour may sometimes be rather attenuated, it is clear that the main problems which arise here have to do with goal-directed behaviour and not with wants construed in terms of distressed states—with the 'cognitive' rather than the 'affective'—and I hope to try to sort out in the next chapter some of the complications which abound in this area. To conclude this section, let us just look back at the behaviourist's dilemma with which we began. The behaviourist is convinced that logically adequate grounds for ascribing a want to an animal can be formulated in behavioural terms, with perhaps a reference to the causality and circumstances of the behaviour. However, there appears to be a total mismatch between the psychological description—'wants to be let out'—and any phrase descriptive of the creature's distress at not being out, its efforts to get out, or any other relevant behaviour. None of these states or activities can be described as the animal's *wanting* to go out. The traditional explanation of this lack of correspondence would be that the verb signifies something non-physical and non-behavioural, some mental state which is manifested in, but not exhausted by behaviour. By way of rebuttal the behaviourist might be tempted to try once more to find the match which has so far eluded him, but what instead he must do is exploit the implications of the fact that behavioural data can be logically adequate for the ascription of a want. Behaviourism sounds absurd if we insist on taking it to require a simple one-one correspondence between psychological and behavioural terms, but the failure of a straightforward fit between 'wants', say, and any item or items of behaviour is of no significance, since if a description of behaviour can entail a want-ascription then we are assured that the condition which is thus guaranteed, and which is signified by 'want' in the conclusion inferred from the behavioural evidence, allows of some minimal but adequate construal in which it has no mentalistic implications. This is not to say that 'want' could never signify some mental state; it is just to put forward the triviality that, if the want-ascription is deductively based on the behavioural evidence, then any inferences which the former licenses, inferences about the kind of state which has been shown to obtain, must be derivable from the behavioural evidence itself, and hence do not transcend this evidence.

This strategy can be adopted by the behaviourist prior to actually giving an account of a particular psychological notion, provided only he is correct in maintaining the verifiability of the statements in which it occurs; that by itself dispenses him from any concern with conjectural inner states of the animal. On the other hand, the analysis of *wanting* which has actually emerged could be accounted behaviourist only on a rather liberal interpretation of this often illiberal doctrine. Thus, leaving aside the use of 'want' where it relates to purposive behaviour, to say that *x* wants *y* is, roughly, to say that *x* lacks *y* and is distressed by the lack; to lack something is not to *do* anything, nor can a lack be correctly described as a 'disposition', another of the behaviourist's favoured categories. Still, this is unimportant. Essentially it is anti-realism that is at stake here, not any narrow behaviourist doctrine, and so far the more general position has not met with any serious difficulties.

The preceding discussion points to purposive behaviour as a topic requiring the anti-realist's attention, and we come to the same conclusion if we examine the use of 'mean' as applied to animals. This verb is not used here as readily as is 'want', and there may be a strong feeling that we are indulging in metaphor in speaking of an animal as meaning to do something; still, the term can be used with sufficient seriousness for there to be at least the possibility of a problem. First, though, consider the analogous verb 'intend'. We can say that the dog is going to bite you, but can we say that he *intends* to bite you? Perhaps. But use of 'intends' does bring with it the inappropriate suggestion that the dog has given some thought to the matter and opted for a particular course of action. Of course, the dog *is* set upon a course of action, even if not as the result of formulating an intention to himself, and that much of an implicit reference to purpose is perhaps enough to make *some* talk in terms of intention applicable—though I imagine we should use the verb only with considerable hesitancy.

What about 'mean'? Does the dog *mean* to bite you? There is still something of the unwanted suggestion conveyed by 'intends', but 'means' surely is more acceptable in this context. This distinction is not to be given too much weight, but it would seem that many of the things we do are things which we mean to do, while not exactly things which we intend to do; to speak of intending to ϕ suggests giving some thought to the matter of ϕ-ing and making up one's mind prior to the event, whereas 'means' is not always so explicit in this respect. Admittedly, 'means' does sometimes carry this suggestion, and it is sometimes even more than a suggestion, namely, when saying that x meant to ϕ implies, with the help of the surrounding context, that he did not ϕ: I meant to call you, but unfortunately I did not have the time; here *meaning* is a matter of formulating an intention prior to the period within which the event would have taken place if the intention had been fulfilled. However, the possible difference between 'mean' and 'intend' can be detected when I say of some action which I actually engaged upon that I meant to do it: I mean to do many of the simple things which, like turning the page of a book, I do without much thought, if any; perhaps it can be said that such actions are done *intentionally*, but it seems unreal to suggest that I *intend* to do them. That seems to refer to a time prior to the action, to have the force of 'I *had* meant to'; both set a distance between a time of resolve and the moment of acting, whereas meaning to do something need not precede the doing of it; often it is no more than a matter of going along with, not resisting the natural tendency of one's movements, together with some minimal awareness of these movements.

Returning now to our dog, we find a corresponding pair of possibilities to consider. In the first place, if we say that the dog meant to go outside but was prevented from doing so, we have to make sense of his meaning to act as something which occurs prior to the time at which the action might have been executed. In so far as we can make sense of 'meaning' here, it would seem to come to saying that the dog's movements were directed towards going outside; but, of course, we shall have to understand this in such a way that for the ascription of meaning to be true it is not sufficient that the dog's actions should have had a certain outcome, viz., bringing him outside, if they had not been interfered with. It may happen to be the case that the dog would have ended up outside if it had been allowed to keep going in that direction, but however extended the use of 'mean' in this context, it could not be applied merely on the strength of that supposition.

This same point arises with the second possibility, when we say that the dog meant to do something which he actually did: the dog meant to go into his kennel—he did not do this accidentally, just by chance. The movements of the dog which brought him to the kennel must have been purposive, directed at bringing him there, and it cannot simply be that his movements accorded with a possible purpose; it must in some sense be *because* they fulfilled that purpose that the dog engaged upon them. For human beings, the condition that we should know what we are doing seems to be necessary for our meaning to do what we do; 'I hadn't realized that I'd knocked it over' serves to rebut a condition necessary for its being the case that I had meant to knock an object over. A similar condition would seem to be necessary for animals as well: the dog must be sensitive to the relevant features of his environment, able to recognize or at least to perceive his kennel and its surroundings if we are to be able to speak of him as meaning to do what he did.

Thus, for the dog to mean to do what he is doing he must be engaged in his actions for the sake of their consequences—however this is to be interpreted—and he must be aware of the effect of his actions on the environment in the respects required by the given characterization of his meaning. If now we say that he meant to ϕ but was prevented, this 'meant' is to indicate that he was by then set upon such a course, that that direction had already been given to his actions. Just what this comes to is a matter of some obscurity, but there is not in addition a problem of ascertaining the thoughts which the creature had in formulating an intention to himself at this point of time.

This discussion does not take our problem much further forward, but it is worth linking the notion of meaning to that of purposive behaviour explicitly, since if the subsequent treatment of the latter topic is successful the anti-realist can claim that 'means', a most unpromising candidate, can be readily handled by his theory. The achievement which that represents is slightly diminished by the acknowledgement that the use of the verb is frequently if not generally strained in this context, but it is worth establishing that what use we do have for it can find a place in the anti-realist scheme of things.

The most perplexing examples of animal behaviour are those in which an unexpected degree of intelligence is manifested, or where we appear to have evidence of thought in some form, and I want now to consider such phenomena, approaching them via the concept of *knowing*. The issue with respect to *knowing* is very like that with *wanting*, in that the behaviourist is hard put to explain how 'knows' latches on to the observable data, and it is also like that with *meaning*, in that it is not always clear to what extent a usage or proposed usage is sufficiently non-figurative to allow of well-defined truth-conditions.

To begin with the latter difficulty, we may observe that there are at least some uses of 'know' which give rise to no qualms: the cat knows its way through a maze, it knows its home, it knows where its saucer of milk is and it knows when it is fed. If the knowledge is a matter of recognition, of knowing how to do something, or of some other species of practical knowledge, it is not difficult for the notion to find application, but where we are more likely to hesitate is at the suggestion that the animal knows *that* such-and-such is the case. The cat can see the grass, it can, let us suppose, discriminate green from other colours, but we should not be inclined to say that it knew that the grass was green; that would seem to call for propositional knowledge, knowledge of a kind which is beyond the capabilities of a creature lacking a language sophisticated enough to record such facts. It can be said to be aware of the green grass, but such awareness does not require the ability to formulate a judgement, to categorize the grass as green. Similarly, the cat can be aware of the rain without knowing that it is raining; to assert the latter on the strength of the former would be unwarranted.

However, this way of viewing the question is not entirely fair. First, it would be wrong to generalize from these examples and conclude that there is no scope for speaking of knowledge in such contexts. After all, we can and do say such things as that the dog knows that his master is outside the door. This surely is perfectly intelligible. What, then, makes for the difference? Why do we readily say that the dog knows that his master is outside, but not so readily that it knows that it is raining? The answer is, I believe, that it is largely a matter of whether the creature indulges in behaviour which is characteristic of a creature having the *specific* knowledge in question. There does not seem to be any familiar pattern of behaviour which is sufficiently specific to knowledge that grass is green or that it is raining, so we have no cause to speak of an animal as having such knowledge. The cat may react in a certain way to rain falling on it, but it is likely to act in the same way if the water comes from a hose; given that its response is the same in either case, we are as yet without justification for saying in the former case that its knowledge is precisely knowledge that it is raining. On the other hand, I am supposing that the dog engages in a form of behaviour which is reserved for the presence of his master; this supposition allows talk of knowledge to get a grip, but if we were to find that the dog reacted indiscriminately to the sound of approaching footsteps, not just those of his master, then we should have lost the right to speak of knowledge that his *master* was coming—though some more general characterization might now be applicable.

The over-simplified view which I am criticizing makes a sharp distinction between 'knows' followed by 'that' and 'knows' followed by 'how', 'where', 'when', and so forth. This separate treatment of the conjunction 'that' strikes me as artificial. It is not that if we can speak of the creature as knowing that P, we can say it has knowledge of a propositional kind, whereas in other cases the knowledge is only 'practical'. In all cases the knowledge is of the kind deemed 'practical', in that it is manifested only in behaviour; it is just that with 'how', for instance, the appropriate behaviour is more obvious. This observation repeats the kind of point made earlier with regard to distress. Given a psychological predicate we are inclined either to deny that it is applicable to animals, or to make its applicability contingent upon the occurrence of some totally elusive mental event; thus the question whether an animal can really be distressed and the present question about the possibility of knowledge that such-and-such is the case. However, our actual understanding of most such predicates favours drawing the line at a different point, a point which does not lead to the exclusion of animals from under the concept, nor to the necessity of invoking an impossible condition for its application to them. Locating that point at the right place is obviously crucial to a proper assessment of the relative behavioural and non-behavioural connections of a predicate, and therewith, of course, to our verdict on behaviourism.

Specificity of response appears to be a requirement if our statement of what the animal knows is to be upheld, but it clearly does not by itself entitle us to speak of knowledge. What is required in addition is some sort of *appropriateness* of response. The precise way in which a response may be appropriate varies from case to case, but in the more complex examples it is to be understood in terms of the relevance of the behaviour to the attainment of something wanted by the creature. For instance, the dog does not walk straight into the log which blocks his path; he walks around it. Not just anything which the dog might do here would give proof of knowledge of the log's presence, but the dog's action can be deemed to be appropriate in the light of his desire to avoid the log, and it is because it allows of this characterization that his behaviour can be said to manifest knowledge.

This contention raises a topic for discussion rather than putting an end to the question which led to it, and it will eventually receive more of the attention which it deserves. Continuing with our outline of an account of knowledge, we may note that a third factor of importance must be introduced to supplement specificity and appropriateness of response. With human beings the question how we come to hold a belief may be important in deciding whether that belief is to count as knowledge, and a corresponding question arises with respect to the behaviour which, because of its appropriateness, is thought to warrant the attribution of knowledge to the animal. For example, from the way the dog is trembling I might infer that he knows he is going to be beaten, but we should have to add further details—he is trembling at the sight of the stick, say—for there to be any question of ascribing knowledge, however metaphorically, to the animal. If the trembling were caused by cold, for instance, or if it were attributable to fear, but not fear of anything which presaged a beating, the interpretation which I put on the dog's behaviour would be unwarranted, however apposite that behaviour might happen to be in the circumstances.

When the use of 'know' is roughly dispositional there is comparatively little for the behaviourist to worry about; as with wanting, so here we require only that behaviour should provide logically sufficient grounds for the attribution of knowledge, and this can be made without further requiring that *knowing* somehow be one of the creature's activities, there for the behaviourist to observe. The real problem arises when 'knows' is used in such a way that it does make some sense, at least initially, to construe it as signifying some episodic event, for then the behaviourist can be challenged to find an appropriate occurrence among the data which he recognizes, and it would seem more difficult for him to turn aside this challenge by arguing that it represented a misconception of the nature of the identity which his theory required him to establish. Both a man and an animal can know how to get from A to B, but I can also suddenly come to know or realize something, and this use of 'know' would seem to mark a particular datable occurrence. Just what occurrence is enough of a problem to decide when we are speaking only of human beings, but if we can speak in the same way with regard to animals the behaviourist's difficulties would appear quite insuperable.

So, I notice a chimpanzee shaking a branch and eating the fruit which falls off. If its present action is the outcome of past experience with such trees then it can be explained in such terms, and there would seem to be nothing very perplexing in a description of the chimpanzee as knowing that if it shakes the branch the fruit will fall off. However, without the benefit of any past experience of any directly related kind it might suddenly dawn on me that if I were to do x then y would follow. Might not an animal's knowledge arise in a similar way? Other examples which come to mind are those of Köhler's apes fitting together sticks and using them to pull in bananas which had hitherto been out of reach. Here again we have knowledge which seems to involve thought, insight—some kind of inner mental event.

As another example, consider the ability of pigeons to respond differentially to sequences containing different numbers of sounds. The bird seems able to 'count' the sounds in some sense, and that, it is suggested, means that it engages in some form of mental activity in the genus of thinking. Again, an animal may be trained to run a particular sequence of right and left turns in such a way that on first reaching a certain point it turns right and the next time it reaches the same point it turns left. Since cues to the appropriate responses are not to be sought in the environment, it has seemed to some that the animal must 'bear in mind' its position, and that its behaviour at the turning-point is determined by internal representational stimuli.

These last two examples would seem to be the least impressive, since there appears to be nothing in either which calls for any specifically *mental* capacity. The 'counting' can easily be referred to a capacity of the pigeon's brain, and it is no problem to define a function whose values for a given argument are dependent on the values which it took for earlier arguments; nor are there any theoretical difficulties in the notion of a physiological realization of such a function. And, after all, it is rather obviously not the case that the only alternative to stimuli being in the environment is that they should be in the animal's mind. There are such things as nervous systems. Finally, there need be no 'cues' in any sense based on an analogy with 'sensory cues', items of which the creature can be said to become aware, only here not to be located externally to its body; neurophysiological connections are all that are required to mediate input and output.

The mentalist would not, I imagine, set much store by these examples. On the other hand, he might well have misgivings about the general thesis which appears to underlie my rejection of them. If, that is, I refuse to allow an appeal to the mental whenever there is the possibility of a physiological explanation, then surely I shall *never* be in a position to assert the existence of thoughts (other than my own), even with human beings. I shall take up this objection at a later stage, but to continue with the mentalist's own case let us return to our discussion of the episodic use of 'know', the use which does seem to imply thought more than any other. Here, when we can speak of realization dawning, insight attained, a sudden appreciation of a solution, the anti-behaviourist appears to be defending a sympathetic commonsense view against an un-imaginative and soulless picture of the animal kingdom.

It is, then, perhaps something of a pity that a more sober assessment of the facts calls for a much less exciting interpretation. But that is how it seems to be. For consider a typical situation. We have an ape which, having contemplated the bananas out of reach of his grasp, for a while frets and looks unsettled and then suddenly ceases his troubled manner and proceeds to pick up the sticks lying in the cage, fit them together and manœuvre the bananas to bring them within his grasp. Two points may be agreed upon all round: the animal has acquired a certain ability, the ability to fit the sticks together and to use the resultant longer stick to bring the bananas to a position where he can reach them, and this is an ability which he lacked before his fretting and generally troubled state had ceased. This latter is, I should say, an assumption which we are to make in the interesting cases. The moment at which, it is suggested, the solution struck the ape is the moment at which this ability can be said to have been acquired, and as far as I can see that is all that this particular moment can be held to mark.

The difficulty of verification here is the difficulty of determining precisely when the creature acquired this ability. Given advance warning, one could in theory test to see if the ape had the ability at this time rather than that, but given that the episode is now over and done with, verification is precluded for us. However, the central question is whether no more than this difficulty is involved, the difficulty of ascertaining when the ape acquired a new competence, or whether we have any right to say that something further took place at this point of time. Certainly, we may suppose that the transition to this new ability is matched by changes at a neurophysiological level, but such changes are remote from anything that the everyday descriptions might imply, whether coming from me or coming from the mentalist. And what, in any case, is it reasonable to postulate? The ape has acquired an ability, an ability which is surely manifested only in what it does; there is no call to regard it as an ability which requires anything more than a reference to action in its characterization. More fully, one reason why knowing in advance of doing has meaning for men consists in the possibility of giving verbal expression to this knowledge, and to that extent the knowledge or ability acquired is broader in kind than it is with the animal. We cannot say of the ape that it does not know prior to acting, since its acquisition of the ability—which is the form knowledge here takes—could be said to antedate the exercise of that ability. However, the knowledge is manifested only in this way, and there is no necessity to conceive of the creature's performance or performances as manifestations of anything more than the ability to perform thus, no call to speak of an additional 'inner' realization of such knowledge.

This answer will not be complete until more has been said about human thought, and at present it appears to invite the same objection as did my treatment of the other examples. Let me conclude by stating that objection more fully. The anti-realist requires that it be possible to establish as something more than a plausible hypothesis any ascription of mental events which animal behaviour may tempt us to make, so he will be unimpressed by arguments which merely lead us to advance such a hypothesis without giving any indication as to how it could be conclusively verified. This may seem rather a short way with his opponents, but he is surely entitled to adopt this position until someone can come forward with an example in which (a) the only acceptable explanation of certain behaviour can be given in terms making essential reference to thought, and (b) such thought could never be proved by behaviour or other observable phenomena, but must for ever have the status of a hypothesis. On the other hand, the more successful we are in showing the availability of physical explanations in the animal case, the more the anti-realist runs the risk of having this success turned against him when he considers human beings. Thus in their case he cannot appeal to the greater simplicity that the supposition of thought or other mental phenomena contributes to an explanation; this explanatory role met with theoretical objections in the animal case, objections which retain their full force when we turn to human beings. But if in the former case he was successful in providing adequate explanations without making any appeal to the mental, then he might well meet with the same success when he considers people: from this point of view, considering what is required by an acceptable explanation, the supposition of thought may be a dispensable luxury. We have a physically definable input in the form of the stimulus energies which impinge upon the subject's organs of sense, and an output in terms of bodily movement, the production of sounds, and other observable phenomena. Intermediate between these are the complex physiological events in the man's nervous system; surely there is never *logically* a demand to interpose a non-physical state or process as mediating and explaining the relation between input and output.

Essentially, of course, it is not that the anti-realist is trying to supplant an explanation in terms of mental phenomena by an explanation couched in physicalistic terms. He might agree that the two are perfectly compatible. It is rather that the mental cannot have a role *only* in explanation, if that means it can enjoy no more than an inferred existence, but it must be susceptible of direct verification. Accordingly, if the existence of thoughts is going to be proved, then it will have to be by reference to behaviour and other observables. And that does not look to be a simple task.

3

PURPOSIVE BEHAVIOUR

A ROUGH characterization of the kind of situation in which we might speak of an animal as acting purposively, as directing its actions towards some goal, or simply as wanting something, could run as follows: the animal is engaged in an activity which, if allowed to continue without hindrance, will culminate in a certain end-state; if we interfere with the animal and prevent it from doing what it is doing, then either it will modify its behaviour accordingly, i.e., set about another activity— as far as it is able—which will lead to the same end-state, or it will display undirected, 'frustrated' behaviour: jumping up and down on the spot, chattering, and so forth. This characterization is of a familiar enough phenomenon, but there are a number of knotty problems lurking here, the most crucial of which concern the notion of the animal's behaviour as *leading to an end-state*. It is only too obvious that not every end-state of a series of movements will be a state which is wanted or aimed at. The cat's mewing may be terminated by stuffing a rag in its mouth, but we should not necessarily wish to say that that was what the cat wanted, and if we care to characterize the animal's activities in broad enough terms we can truly say that their end-state will be death. Even if we consider only the immediate and invariable consequences of a course of action we find end-states which are in a sense the culmination of the creature's activity, but not, one would suppose, states which it had been aiming at. For example, discussing Russell's definition of animal desire, Kenny instances the following possible accidental consequence of a series of actions: in a sunny climate a bird's movement from place to place will be matched by a corresponding movement of its shadow; we might say that the bird wanted to be at the point where it arrived, but not, surely, that it had flown there in order to have its shadow located thus (Anthony Kenny, *Action, Emotion and Will* (1963), p. 107). We might take a step towards eliminating such accidental consequences by requiring that the end-state be causally effective in terminating the actions which led to it: if the bird watched the position of its shadow as it varied its own position and only stopped once its shadow was in a certain place, and could be seen by the bird to be so, then we should be less reluctant to allow that the position of its shadow was what the bird had been aiming at. However, this still does not rule out the possibility that the bird happened to be somehow attracted by the sight of its shadow in that position and that it stopped moving when it saw it there, even though that was not what its movements had been directed at originally.

With human beings the situation is simpler in two respects: what he says as well as what he does helps us determine what it is that a man wants, the goal he is aiming at, and the fact that he knows or believes that what he is doing will lead to that goal explains why he is engaged in that action. With an animal it would seem that we may be unable to tell whether its goal was what it happened to end up with, or something else, or even whether it could be held to have had a goal at all. The problem is not always that severe, since we can find out what a creature wants to the extent that we can find out what it is the lack of which is causing it distress, but if there is no question of distress, if the only evidence we have for its wanting such-and-such—or, rather, the only sense in which it can be said to have this want—is to be given in terms of its putative purposive behaviour, then we are bereft of an independent identification of its want. Nor, in most cases, can we say that the creature knew or believed that its actions would lead to the attainment of its ostensible goal. Such knowledge or belief is possible in some cases, and tempting to suppose in others, but often it only needs a change in the circumstances in which the creature engages in the relevant goal-directed activity for us to recognize that the seeming knowledge was nothing of the sort. To take a typical example, a digger-wasp is capable of laying an egg on a caterpillar which she has taken into her burrow, and proceeding to close up the burrow with twigs and pebbles even when the caterpillar has been extracted from the tunnel and placed right outside before her eyes. Before witnessing such a futile performance we might have been inclined to say that the wasp knew or believed that if she blocked the burrow she would be able to protect her egg, but this uncomprehending behaviour will surely lead us to retract any such account. In order to regard the wasp as having such knowledge we should insist that she have some conception of what she was doing, to the extent that she act differently accordingly as her actions did or did not result in a certain observable outcome.

In the difficult cases we have no way of identifying what it is that the creature wants, the goal which it has, apart from considering its problematic, apparently purposive behaviour, and we have no grounds for speaking of it as knowing or believing that what it is doing will have a certain outcome. Our problem is thus twofold: how do we know what goal determines the action, and how can we even speak in this way without supposing either knowledge or belief as to consequences or causal efficiency of the goal to be attained? In order to extract ourselves from these difficulties we must enlist something like the following formula:

(A) *it is because ϕ-ing leads to g (or enables x to g) that x is ϕ-ing.*

To see what (A) involves consider it first as a translation of the schema: 'x is ϕ-ing in order to g'—or in some contexts, 'x is ϕ-ing in order that g', or 'x is ϕ-ing for the sake of g'. ('g' is to be thought of as doing duty for different parts of speech even in the same context.) Thus, instead of saying 'the bird is collecting twigs in order to build a nest', we might say, according to (A): 'it is because collecting twigs leads to building a nest—or enables the bird to build a nest—that the bird is collecting twigs'. Again, to establish that the birds are flying south to get away from the cold, it suffices to establish that it is because flying south gets them away from the cold that the birds are flying south.

(A) can be compared with the more obvious characterization of purposive activity as activity which is engaged upon *because of the consequences which it has*. This characterization has certain ambiguities or indeterminacies which (A) can be thought of as resolving in a certain direction. This places (A) close to an analysis of the notion of action based on reasons, but, we shall see, it is at the basis of a totally different account of behaviour, and one especially geared to the lower forms of animal life, where the ascription of knowledge, and even wants in any full sense, is largely fanciful.

When we say that a person or animal is doing something because of the state or whatever that the action leads to, it sounds as though the future state is somehow the cause of the present activity, and for some it has been just this apparent reversal of causal relations which has set teleological explanations apart as so exceptional, to the point of disqualifying them as acceptable forms of explanation. With respect to human action, it requires no more than a slight reformulation to avoid this objection: it is a matter of action for the sake of what it is *believed* it will lead to. However, it may be thought that (A) has a similarly undesirable implication, and it is worth pausing to show that it need not be read in this way.

To say that the monkey is climbing the ladder to get the bananas is to say that it is because climbing the ladder leads to getting the bananas—or enables it to get the bananas—that the monkey is climbing the ladder. This latter version need not be taken as implying that the future state, the monkey's imminent acquisition of the bananas, is somehow causally responsible for its present activity. The form 'leads' is not to be read as a simple future— 'will lead'—but it is a frequentative or habitual use of the verb in which the future is involved only by implication; this is not an implication which there is any need to cancel, but neither is it an implication which (A) requires us to exploit. Similarly, I can say that the bird is collecting twigs because collecting twigs quite generally enables it—or enables birds—to build a nest, and only by implication am I saying that it will enable it to do so this time. And, of course, the implication involved here is not as strong as logical entailment: the truth-conditions for such statements do not allow of any precise formulation, but if, having gathered its twigs, the bird should for some reason be unable to build a nest, the general statement would not necessarily be falsified. (A) is intended to be the most generally applicable formula; as I shall show, variations upon it are more appropriate in certain circumstances.

It may seem pedantic to guard against the following possibility, but (A) should not be interpreted in such a way that it allows of the reading: ϕ-ing leads to g and g in turn leads to ϕ-ing; ϕ-ing is to be something which takes place because of the consequences which it has, but not in the sense that the consequences on this occasion provide an efficient cause of the ϕ-ing—a generally unlikely but none the less genuine possibility. When in the human case we speak of ϕ-ing for the consequences of ϕ-ing, there is no suggestion that the behaviour is dictated by subsequent events. If I make a joke for the sake of the amusement it will bring, the amusement which does in fact follow is not the cause of my making *that* joke, though it might well prompt me to make another one. This unreality of the consequence g as a causal factor in determining ϕ must be maintained in the non-human case: here too, if there is to be any question of purposive activity we must disallow g as an efficient cause of the ϕ-ing which is taken to have it as a consequence. Far from being an implication of teleological explanations, such a possibility would be inconsistent with the explanation's being of that type. It is of course unreal to suppose that the consequences of ϕ-ing could both be future and yet effective in determining the ϕ-ing, but they can have this latter role once they have started to develop, and this is the possibility which we have to guard against: think of an occasion when scratching leads to irritation which leads to further scratching; it is *because* of the irritation which scratching led to that the animal is now scratching, but it is not scratching *for the sake of* the irritation.

More important is the question of the causal role of consequences which are quite clearly past rather than present. Suppose that an animal has become addicted to a substance which it can extract from certain leaves by chewing. We may then have the pattern of: chewing leading to addiction leading to further chewing; in one sense the animal is chewing because chewing leads (or led) to addiction—in that it is chewing because of the addiction which chewing led to—but it is not chewing *in order* to be addicted. We want to rule this out as a legitimate reading of (A) without at the same time banishing such acceptable possibilities as that the animal is chewing the leaves because chewing them leads to satisfaction of its craving; i.e., the animal is chewing the leaves in order to satisfy its craving. In this, the allowable case, the past satisfaction is not to be taken as itself a cause of the present chewing, as conceivably a sufficient condition when taken in conjunction with just *some* further conditions. The only sense in which, in the allowable cases, the past consequence can be described as a *cause* is the sense in which this is true as a consequence of (A). Thus, just in so far as it is because ϕ-ing led to g that x is ϕ-ing, the consequence g can at least be said to be *part* of a sufficient condition for ϕ-ing, but it is not sufficient by itself, and, more to the point, it is not sufficient in the absence of the particular consideration that ϕ-ing led to it; it is not simply g, but ϕ-ing's leading to g that is the cause of x's ϕ-ing.

One instance where a minor variation on (A) is required is on the question of misapplied or ineffective purposive activity. The digger-wasp provided us with an example of behaviour which is remarkably well adapted to certain circumstances, but in other conditions staggeringly inept, and another example is provided by the squirrel, which, it is said, is capable of gathering its nuts into a pile on a hard surface, scratching away at that surface as if it were digging it, placing its nuts where the hole should be, and going through the motions of burying them in it. If a human being indulges in activities which do not lead to the goal he desires we should say that he was doing what he was doing in the belief that it would lead to that goal, but such a way of describing the situation would be absurd in the above example. On the other hand, the question arises whether (A) too is not inapplicable in such cases, since it may be that, while it is false that ϕ-ing (scratching at the floor, etc.) leads to g (concealing its nuts), it is none the less true that the creature is ϕ-ing in order to g. The animal is engaged in its futile activities, not in the belief that they will lead to g, but without even a chance that they will have this consequence, and neither now nor in general is it true that actions of the *precise* kind which it is engaged upon will lead to g. Still, what is true, and is enough to show the applicability of (A) one way or another, is that a more general characterization of the creature's activities can be invoked both in the description of what it is doing and in the version of (A) which is to correspond to this. It is the activity more broadly construed—scratching at the surface on which it stands—that has had g as a consequence, and it is because it has had this consequence that the creature is currently engaged upon it. I think that in many cases we should wish to say that the appropriately revised version of 'x is ϕ-ing in order to g', the version corresponding to the correct instance of (A), was more accurate as a description of x's purposive activity, but in any case we can easily modify (A) to read: for some ψ true of ϕ-ing, x is ψ-ing because ψ-ing leads to g.

Examples of inappropriate purposive activity do not take us away from the kind of interpretation provided by (A), but they do perhaps cast doubt on the suitability of the term *purpose* in many descriptions of animal behaviour. It has sometimes been held that the 'plasticity' of an animal's behaviour, the creature's persistence towards a goal under varying conditions, is what defines its purposive character. I am inclined to think that such plasticity is indicative of the creature's adaptability and intelligence, but that we can speak of behaviour as 'purposive' even in the absence of flexibility and variety; unvarying, undiscriminating behaviour may often prove futile, but we can still describe it as 'purposive', still say that the animal is ϕ-ing in order to g. On the other hand, it does seem less in order to speak of the animal as having *a purpose*; that is like saying that the creature, a being without thought and language, has an intention to do something. We might say that the cuckoo puts eggs in the nests of other birds so that these birds will hatch and feed its young, but the cuckoo, like the squirrel and the digger-wasp, is totally uncomprehending of the situation, with no conception why it behaves thus, no knowledge, no beliefs, no grasp whatsoever of a purpose in its actions. There is much to be said for refusing the term 'purpose' when the behaviour is quite blind, and even though the adjective does not mislead to the same extent, it could well be replaced by the more neutral 'goal-directed'.

(A) was introduced to enable us to deal with purposive behaviour which could not be satisfactorily explained in terms of what is known or believed and what is wanted. However, even if there is room to speak of both, either (A) or the modification mentioned above retains its relevance in the realistic cases. Consider the example of the monkey climbing the ladder in order to get the banana. This is one of the comparatively simple instances where what is sought is already in existence in the environment and can be effective in directing the creature's behaviour; the difficult cases are those in which it is not possible to identify what is wanted with anything present, anything which might be a stimulus and a guide to action in the same way. But now consider the means which the animal adopts, for even in these simple cases we can raise the question how the animal comes to behave as it does in response to the sight of something it wants. Perhaps we wish to say that it is because it knows that climbing the ladder will enable it to get the bananas that it is doing so, but it could be that such knowledge is dependent on the fact that climbing has had these consequences for it in the past, in which case (A) is still relevant; or, it could be that something akin to climbing this ladder has enabled the monkey to get what it wanted, in which case the modified version of (A) is in place; or, finally, it could be that the monkey had not learned this pattern of behaviour, but that it was ultimately as a result of such actions having had certain consequences for its ancestors that it was now thus engaged, in which case (A) or its modified version would continue to apply.

We were originally faced with the difficulty that not every end-state of a series of movements will be a state which was wanted or aimed at: I put an end to the cat's mewing by stuffing a rag in its mouth, and the final state of the bird's flight involves its shadow being in a certain place; in each case the creature's behaviour in some sense leads to these end-states, but are they states which the creature wanted? In one sense they conceivably could be, in that they could be states which the creature liked to find itself in, but this possibility only adds to the difficulty of distinguishing such states from states which the creature wanted in the sense of *aimed at*.

We might hope to distinguish accidental from non-accidental consequences on the basis of the type of causal chain into which they entered. Thus, suppose that dousing a cat with water serves to silence its mewing; the dousing could be described as the final state in a series of events which began with its mewing, but the relation which this latter event bears to the events which preceded it strikes us as accidental even by comparison with the example of the bird's shadow ending up in a particular position as a result of the bird's manœuvrings, and certainly as accidental by comparison with the relation between an animal's stalking and its consequent capture of the prey, or other examples where a particular goal is obviously being sought. This is all rather vague, but, as far as I can tell, the truth which lies behind it is taken account of by (A), and it is one of the merits of the formula that it enables us to distinguish between what is and what is not correct here. Thus, an accidental outcome of a pattern of behaviour is ruled out as the state which was aimed at by the consideration that if ϕ-ing just happens on this occasion to lead to g then it cannot be *because* ϕ-ing leads to g that x is ϕ-ing. How could this *because* be established if it were quite by chance that g followed upon ϕ-ing?

Note too that (A) does not involve the error of making the non-accidental character of the relation between ϕ-ing and g sufficient for the ascription of a purpose. Let me explain. The cat's mewing may or may not be causally related to my throwing water on the cat; I may act in this way in order to quieten the cat, or the cat may just happen to be passing when I get rid of the water. My action is of a very different kind from the cat's behaviour which led up to it, but the two can be causally related, and it is only in the latter case, when the cat just happens to be passing, that my action is accidentally related to the cat's behaviour. In both cases, however, we wish to rule out the connection required by purposiveness—on the part of the cat—and this (A) accomplishes. Of course, it is conceivable that the cat *should* mew in order to have water poured upon it, and, as (A) prescribes, this would be established if it were established that it was because of the consequences which mewing in my presence had for it in the past that it was mewing on this present occasion. Furthermore, it is not necessary that these consequences should not have occurred nonaccidentally in the past. Typically, the clause 'it is because ϕ-ing leads to g' in (A) will refer to a non-accidental relation, but it is sufficient for the truth of 'x is ϕ-ing in order to g' that this clause should be weakened to 'it is because ϕ-ing once led to g', and that g should have been no more than an accidental consequence of ϕ-ing. (It is interesting to speculate on the matter of how, out of a chance combination of events—ϕ-ing happens to be followed by g on a number of occasions—a regular pattern of behaviour might arise, and order be generated from chaos.)

The more obvious causal condition, that g be effective in terminating the preceding ϕ-ing, and not merely the upshot, possibly accidental, of the earlier sequence of events, is generally too strong in one respect, the respect just mentioned, to do the work of (A), and in another respect too weak: it is relevant to determining whether x wants g only in the non-purposive sense of 'wants'; even if its efforts were not directed towards the goal of being soaked, the animal in this sense wanted to be soaked if soaking it was in fact effective in terminating a distressed state it was in. Note too that (A) is required when we have a pattern of activity which leads to more than one end-state, as when, say, running around leads to both tiredness and being rewarded. If the two outcomes are causally inseparable from one another it might be practically impossible to perform the eliminative experiments aimed at determining what precisely was responsible for the behaviour, but (A) at least prescribes what we are to try to establish. The two states come about at roughly the same point of time and as a result of the same activity, but it is because the animal's activity has the one rather than the other as outcome that it is running about.

Animals often engage in activities for the consequences they have; that surely is in some sense true. For it to be true, further-more, it is not necessary that the animal should act in the belief that its actions will have the relevant consequences. However, do we not require that the animal be aware in some way of the conse-quences of its actions before we are prepared to speak of purposive behaviour, even of the animal as ϕ-ing in order to g? Suppose that an animal was eating a certain plant because of the beneficial effects which consumption of that plant had upon its health. The animal need not in any sense know that the plant has this effect, let alone know that that is why it is eating it; but should we in such a case wish to say that it was eating this plant in order to improve its health, or in order to bring about some other physio-logical effect which the substance had but which the animal was incapable of recognizing? It is one thing for the animal not to know why it is acting, quite another thing for it to be totally unaware of the consequences which it is allegedly acting in order to bring about—unaware of them when they happen, that is. More generally, there are surely many cases where it is true that it is because ϕ-ing leads to g that x is ϕ-ing, and where g relates to the survival of the species rather than to anything which falls within x's experience, yet we should not wish to say that the animal wanted or was aiming at the survival of the species—though its action *was* aimed at this; nor, I imagine, should we wish to say that the animal was ϕ-ing in order that the species should survive. In such cases the clauses are clauses of result, not clauses of purpose.

No sharp line is to be drawn here—where are we to put the digger-wasp?—but we are on the borderline between two divisions within the category of the teleological, namely, the subclass com-prising *purposive behaviour*, in which some connection with con-sciousness is required, and the more general subclass relating to *functional* activities which in no way presuppose consciousness, either at the level of knowing what the activity will lead to, or at the level of recognizing the consequences of the activity when it has come to fruition. This distinction is sometimes drawn in terms of an animal's *goals* on the one hand, and on the other hand certain *biological ends* which its actions serve. Both may exist together in a situation, the goal often in the form of satisfaction, or the acquisition of some object which acts as a stimulus prompting the creature to pursuit or other action—in any event connecting with the creature's experience or powers of detection—the end as the condition which is often ultimately responsible for the object being effective as a stimulus to that action. Thus in the example of the nutritious food we should expect it to be the case that we have both a goal *g* and a biological end *e*, and that it is true that *x* is eating because of *g*, and also because of *e*, though it is only with respect to a description of the action as performed for the sake of *g* that we can speak of purposive behaviour. To restrict (A) to this subclass we must then add the proviso that the creature be able to recognize the end-state of its actions, but while this emendation is appropriate to our immediate purpose, it is the more general unqualified version of (A) that appears to hold the key to a solution of the problems peculiar to teleological phenomena.

Philosophers often treat of biological function and purposive behaviour more or less indifferently. In doing so they risk overlooking a genuine distinction, but, as already observed, it is true that the terms 'purpose' and 'purposive behaviour', and to some extent 'in order that', suggest connections with thought and consciousness which talk in terms of 'function' succeeds in avoiding and which in the vast majority of cases it is right to avoid. To illustrate, we may say of the markings on an insect that their function is to frighten away predators; this is slightly preferable to speaking of their *purpose*, which suggests design or intention, or to saying that the insects have these markings *in order to* frighten away predators, which suggests that they can manipulate the markings to this end; and, of course, the possession of such markings in no sense constitutes purposive behaviour.

Although the term 'function' is free of the connotations which may make the other expressions misleading, it would be a mistake to over-simplify its use. It does not help to claim that, for instance, to say that the function of the insect's markings is to frighten away predators is simply to say that such markings *do*; there are many things which such markings may do—e.g., interest zoologists—but which do not define their function, and while it is true that there is a relevant, more restricted sense of the verb, where it comes to 'do as of their function', to remark that this is the sense intended does not take us far towards an elucidation of 'function'. Nor will it do to say that such markings are *necessary* for frightening predators. On the one hand they may simply not be necessary—an insect can have more than one form of defence—and on the other hand there can be many things for which they are necessary but which do not *ipso facto* count as their function —the markings may be necessary for camouflage in certain surroundings, but that does not necessarily define their function.

How, then, can we know that their function is to frighten and not to camouflage? There is a sense in which, just so long as camouflage is advantageous to the insect, we may say that the markings *can* have this function—though as it were accidentally. To remove this 'accidentally' we require, not a reference to design or intention, but an appropriate causal condition. Thus, taking (A) as our guide, the sentence-form 'x has ϕ in order to g' can be translated as 'it is because ϕ leads to g (or enables x to g) that x has ψ', and I propose this latter as also a reading for 'the function of ϕ (for x) is to g'. Accordingly, to say that the function of the insect's markings is to frighten away predators is to say that it is because these markings frighten away predators that the insect has them (or that such insects have them); even though they may also serve as camouflage, that is not properly speaking their function if their existence is not to be accounted for by reference to their success in this respect. Note that when we say it is because *these markings* frighten . . ., we are referring to a *type*, even when we are speaking of a particular insect; but, equally, we are speaking of a type when we say that the function of *these markings* is to frighten . . .; in either case the statement may be true even though no predator is in fact frightened away by the markings which it sees on this particular insect—and of course we must understand the analysis loosely enough to allow for the possibility that such markings are no longer generally effective, but are still to be found in virtue of their past efficacy.

In similar fashion, 'the function (or purpose) of the heart is to circulate blood through the body' becomes 'it is because the heart circulates blood through the body that we have a heart', and so on for other instances of biological function. The qualification 'biological' is to be noted: it could be that the function of a valve was to regulate the flow of water, but only to the extent that that was what it was *designed* to do—though if the device is *totally* ineffective, we may hesitate to speak of it as having this function. When *function* connects with *design* it also connects with *designer*, but my interpretation of biological function makes it clear that speaking of the function of a bodily organ has no such implications; it could be that, knowing what a heart would do, an intelligent being had endowed us with hearts, in which case it would be true that it is because the heart circulates blood through the body that we have a heart; but the truth of this latter proposition would thereby be established in a way quite different from that in which, arguing on the basis of natural selection, we might actually expect to establish its truth. It is important to realize that the interpretation is indifferent in this way, since teleological explanations have often been rejected on the grounds that they commit us, if not to the presence of consciousness at every level of biological organization, then to the postulation of an intelligent designer, and in an effort to avoid such alternatives totally inadequate translations of teleological statements have been advanced, such as the re-phrasal in terms of necessary conditions mentioned above.

If we adopt the modification of (A) proposed we are committed to understanding *explaining the function of* ϕ in terms of *accounting for the existence of* ϕ, and vice versa, and this may sound wrong; surely the two questions are separable? However, there is a sense of the question 'why do ϕ's exist in such creatures?'—or 'why do such creatures have ϕ's?'—in which it is equivalent to 'what is the function of ϕ's in such creatures?', and I can see no real objection from this quarter. On the contrary, if someone asks, e.g., 'why do these insects have these markings?' when there is no question of assigning a function to the markings, we are inclined to reject the question by saying there is no *reason* for them. We can ask how they came about, and the questioner may have meant no more than that, but a request for a purpose or function is a more common implication of such a why-question.

Nor does it seem possible to reject the account which has been given on the grounds that teleological explanations do not conform to the pattern of acceptable explanations. In fact, it would hopelessly impede our understanding of biological phenomena if we were unable to bring together diverse phenomena under a common description which only their identity of function or purpose justified. That there is no need to prune our vocabulary of teleological terminology hardly calls for any defence at this stage, but we might consider very briefly how the argument here could run. An advocate of teleological explanations might maintain that certain activities can only be explained by reference to states which succeed them in time, the ends or goals for the sake of which the activities occur; indeed, he might hold that such a reference is involved in the very description of an activity as, e.g., 'building a nest' or 'chasing a rat'. If it is objected that the temporal order runs counter to what is required of any explanation which is to be worthy of the name, he may retort that we are concerned with an empirical matter, not a question to be settled *a priori*: there is nothing absurd in the suggestion that ϕ's leading to g (or being required for g, as some have it) should prove a sufficient condition, in certain circumstances, for the occurrence of ϕ.

In our analyses of both purposive behaviour and biological function we side with the objector to the extent that we do not require sense to be made of the claim that a goal-directed event takes place because of the future state of affairs which will result from it on this occasion; and, further, it is clear on our analysis that the truth of an ascription of function or purposive behaviour does not wait upon establishing the existence of conditions in which ϕ's turning out to have g as a consequence—or ϕ's being required for g—is a sufficient condition for the occurrence of ϕ— which is exceedingly fortunate, given the knowledge which establishing sufficiency, or even a high probability, would require. On the other hand, the form of explanation which (A) provides is in some ways interestingly different from patterns of explanation which more readily spring to mind, and there is even some doubt as to whether (A) qualifies as a form of *causal* explanation. When we say that x is ϕ-ing because ϕ-ing leads to g, what can be correctly called a 'cause' here? Not the *fact* that ϕ-ing leads to g, surely; what about *ϕ-ing's leading to g*? That too sounds inappropriate.

Still, the way in which we establish such a statement is the same as the way in which we establish a causal statement, the only difference being that the former is generally more complicated: we must first establish that ϕ-ing does lead to g, and then that

that is why x is ϕ-ing; the first may be relatively straightforward, but to follow up the second properly might involve consideration of past generations of creatures: it is because such activities have had the consequences they have had that they have been persisted in. Of course, a person who ascribes a function or purpose on a particular occasion need have no inkling of the extent to which knowledge of behaviour in the remote past might be necessary to establishing the correctness of his ascription; the evolutionary details which are relevant here represent a filling in of the support, not a part of the meaning of the ascription—though one advantage of (A) is that it makes clear the naturalness of the transition between the commonsense locutions and evolutionary theory. It is of course obvious that (A) by itself provides nothing like a complete explanation of a creature's behaviour on a given occasion; for one thing, it will be necessary to specify a cause which sets the purposive behaviour in motion on that occasion; such a specification combines with (A) to give a fuller picture, the particular cause being what prompts the animal to act, and the circumstance given by (A) being what determines how the animal will act.

Finally, it is worth mentioning a common pitfall which awaits the analysis of teleological notions. Having dispelled their doubts as to the propriety of functional analysis, some philosophers have then been prone to see the procedure as having application in a diverse range of contexts quite outside the biological sphere, in particular to 'self-regulating' systems or systems which have a 'preference' for certain end-states. Thus, an elastic band will return to its original shape after being stretched, a rod which has been made to vibrate will gradually become motionless again, and in general certain disturbances will eventually cease and there will be a reversion to the original state of equilibrium. To rule out such phenomena we might appeal to the connection of function with the furthering of conditions which are advantageous to the organism, since it does seem reasonable to say that such an implication is carried by the use of the term. However, this does not draw attention to the more important, and quite considerable, difference between the two kinds of system. It is true that in the examples given we do have a return to a single state after a variety of different disturbances have been introduced, but this does not give any support to the use of 'goal' or 'function' in such cases. The ripples which a stone produces on the surface of a pond gradually diminish and the water returns to its original untroubled state, but the gradual diminishing of the ripples cannot be said to occur *because of* the consequences which it has. The various stages in the process are to be explained in terms of the preceding states in a familiar way; there is a particular state of the system which has a special role, in that movement will eventually give way to it, but it is not because it leads to that state that the movement takes place or diminishes. I am not saying there could not be a non-biological system which did not allow of a description in such terms, but it is clear that the examples given—which are, I think, typical—are not of the right kind.

In this chapter I have tried to indicate how we can dispel some of the puzzlement which our familiar, seemingly inevitable descriptions of animal behaviour may engender. There can be many practical difficulties of verification, but these are in no way exacerbated by a need to acquire information about problematic mental states, and there would appear to be no justification for the charge that the behaviourist is forced, by a strict recognition of his own principles, to confine his accounts of animal behaviour to descriptions at the level of 'mere bodily movements'. On the other hand, there would be some justice in the observation that we have been able to cope with the notion of purposive behaviour only at the cost of an interpretation which diverges significantly from that which has a place with human beings. We understand human purposive activity in terms of *reasons* which the agent advances, reasons relating to beliefs which he has concerning the outcome of his actions. The account which (A) offers involves replacing such explanations by explanations of a radically different kind, and it may be felt that what I have provided is more in the way of a rational reconstruction of the troublesome notions, a substitute for them rather than an amplification of their meaning. To say this would, I think, be to overstate the position, but I am happy if, in so far as (A) fails to capture the sense of what it is meant to analyse, this is because it neglects only what is figurative in the animal case. The translations are perhaps rationalizations of a metaphor, specifications of what we must mean by these locutions if a description using them is to have the consequences which we take it to have without having any of the misleading connotations. In short, what is important is that (A) does furnish us with an understanding of goal-directed behaviour which renders it perfectly intelligible, if not in detail, at least in general terms.

One final point. The objections to animal behaviourism which currently receive greatest attention are those deriving from considerations of 'intentionality': we seem to discern a plan or purpose in much animal behaviour, but so to describe it requires ascribing to the animal some kind of foresight, some conception of the goal which it is aiming at. This is the objection which I have tried to answer, but there are others in similar vein. Thus, even the simplest responses by animals to environmental cues are thought by some to transcend any 'mechanistic' framework: an animal does not respond to a stimulus *tout court*, but it responds to it *under a description*, as it were. The need for introducing this curious qualification appears to be inferred from consideration of the question how we are to generalize with respect to a limited number of responses which the animal has given in a learning situation, and how we are to state what it is that it has learned. For instance, we think we have trained a rat to respond in a certain way when confronted with objects triangular in shape; further experimentation, however, reveals a persistence of the same response even when the stimulus source is not triangular. What this shows is simply that eliminative experiments are called for to determine what feature of the stimulus the animal has been conditioned to if more than one invariant to which it is sensitive was to be found in the objects used in the teaching situation. It may seem obvious to us that the shape of the object is what is effective in determining the response, but confirmation of this waits upon further tests if the shape is only one among the features which were constant. The difficulty in determining the modality which is instrumental in eliciting the rat's response, coupled with the difficulty in ascertaining what variation within the one modality is possible without loss of response, makes for a problem in arriving at a correct description of what precisely the animal has learned. But we make a needless mystery of such complications if we interpret them as requiring that the rat *judge* the object to be so-and-so rather than such-and-such, that it take it to be, categorize or conceive of it as so-and-so or in such-and-such terms as a prelude to responding. At best we might appeal to the phenomena in order to give some sort of sense to this way of speaking, but not, surely, as a hypothesis about what goes on. We can use such examples to define what 'taking to be' may be stipulated to come to when used of animals, but then that would not be to prescribe a condition for responding which we should be forced to *assume*, since it would involve no more than a re-description of the given data.

4

PERCEPTION AND BEHAVIOUR

THE problems which perception presents to the behaviourist can be usefully divided into two classes. On the one hand, perceiving—i.e., seeing, hearing, and so forth—is thought of as involving sensation, or the having of sense-data or sensory experiences; here the problem is one of how the occurrence of such phenomena can be known of, and how they can be fitted into the behaviourist framework. On the other hand, the intentionality of our everyday language descriptive of behaviour is thought to extend to perceptual concepts as well: perception cannot be thought of simply in terms of responses to the stimuli of light, sound, and other physical energies, but an account of perception must have regard to the knowledge or belief which it involves. This latter claim, which will occupy us for much of the time, is sometimes put in the form: all *seeing* is *seeing as*—to take just the case of sight. One's first impression is perhaps that this must be a needlessly extreme version of the position, too extreme to stand any chance of proving correct as it stands, since it invites the obvious objection that we frequently see something without having the faintest idea what it is. Furthermore, we can surely say of an animal that it has seen something without having to establish that it has some conception of what it sees. In either case the claim appears to over-intellectualize the sense of sight—and with other senses it sounds even less plausible; would anyone wish to hold that all *smelling* is *smelling as*?

An answer to both of these problems will eventually emerge after we have built on the basis of a broadly stimulus-response account of perception to the point where the connection of perception with knowledge has become clear. I shall deal in the main with sight since, although there are significant differences between the various senses, by and large sight presents the principal difficulties in their most acute form. I shall also continue to look at the problem as it arises for the animal world in general rather than for human beings in particular, but I want first to make a few obvious remarks about what seems a trivial question, namely, how can we tell whether a man can see?

It is only too clear how we should go about answering this question in a particular instance. We watch the person to see if he finds his way around without bumping into objects, whether he locates without groping such things as glasses and doorhandles, whether the movements of his eyes match the movements of objects around him, and so forth. And, of course, we can ask him. Not simply the question whether he sees, but, if we should doubt his word, questions about what he sees: what is the colour of my tie? what is standing on the shelf? what time does the clock say? His answers here, unlike what he may say about his sensations, can easily be confirmed by others, at least to the extent that we can ascertain that what he claims to see is in fact there to be seen. It is true that some tests would have to be treated with caution and would acquire significance only when other possibilities had been ruled out; for instance, it might be that the man's ability to avoid moving objects was due to the use of some sense other than sight. Still, provided the subject is co-operative, finding out whether or not he can see is likely to be a short business.

And yet we might wonder. Perhaps this conclusion at best follows only if we smuggle into our description of the man's actions and verbal behaviour some questionable assumptions, assumptions which we normally take for granted, but which we should be hard put to justify. After all, there does appear to be an enormous gap between seeing and the doing or saying of certain things, more than enough to make it conceivable that a person should not see the objects around him which he can locate, manipulate, and describe in detail. Perhaps he derives his information from elsewhere, from other people or by using his other senses; perhaps his behaviour could be explained by supposing a series of fantastic guesses, coincidences, and shrewd inferences on his part, so that it would be true to say only that he *apparently* saw the doorhandle and the clock on the wall. Admittedly, the hypothesis of sight is the simplest hypothesis, but can we ever do better than this, better than merely advance a hypothesis? Can our data ever be sufficient for us to be entitled to delete this 'apparently' and replace it by 'certainly'?

The case of sight in animals does not lead quite so readily to this curious scepticism. There is unfortunately nothing to be gained from asking the cat whether and what it can see, but on the other hand the concept of *pretence* has as yet no application to the cat in this connection, and its actions can accordingly be taken at their face value. And, of course, there will be no shortage of relevant data. Thus, suppose the cat's eyes move in unison with the movement of a ball of wool thrown along the floor in front of it; suppose it chases the ball, leaps at it, knocks it about with its paw and follows it further around the room. Isn't this enough for us to be able to say that the cat can see? No doubt it is, given what we know about cats, but there is a theoretical possibility which must be admitted: the cat may be guided by another sense. Perhaps it has a highly developed sense of smell which, possibly in conjunction with its other senses, sight excluded, enables it to detect the ball of wool. Still, if this is the suggestion then we can surely put it to the test by rendering the relevant sense or senses inactive and seeing whether or not the cat continues to be capable of the same range of responses. If it is not, the claim is not disproved, but if putting these other senses out of action leaves the animal's ability to follow and catch the ball unimpaired, then, it would seem, we have all we need to confirm our claim that the cat can see.

Normally, of course, that is so. But must we not concede it to be a meaningful hypothesis that the way in which the cat's movements matched those of the ball was no more than *coincidence*? If we make this hypothesis we are supposing that the cat did not move in response to (the sight of) the movements of the ball, but that any cause of its movements is to be sought elsewhere. To eliminate such an alternative we must of course show that the movements of the ball *are* instrumental in bringing about the corresponding movements of the cat, but this by itself is not good enough, since it could be that we were able to trace a causal connection between the movements of the cat and those of the ball, but that it was the *sound* of the ball moving which was operative. So, let us carry over the previous assumption that the cat's other senses were rendered inactive; this did not entail that the cat was using its remaining sense in detecting the ball, since it might not have been using any sense, but, as now suggested, its matching movements might have been no more than coincidence. However, suppose we show that a necessary condition for the cat's moving as it does is that it should have the use of its eyes, that if they are screened off or damaged then it no longer moves as before. Does the addition of this proviso yield a set of conditions which give proof of vision? To this we might reply that it depends on how the term 'eye' is being understood, If it is just its shape and general appearance that define something as an *eye* then we have not eliminated the possibility that, by using its 'eyes', the animal is enabled to respond to sounds. Admittedly, it is an easy enough matter to rule out or indeed to confirm such a possibility, but instead of having to tackle each such possibility as it is advanced it would be preferable if we had a more positive way of identifying an organ as an organ of sight.

One natural approach to such an identification is in terms of the kinds of property which are accessible to vision, and in the present context this would mean establishing a correlation between certain visual properties and the movements of the cat. However, this approach is not as straightforward as one would like. It will not do simply to speak of establishing a correlation between movements of the cat on the one hand, and on the other hand the visible movements of the ball; the visible movements are at the same time movements which can conceivably be sensed by touch or by hearing. To qualify an object of sight by 'visible' or 'visual' does not serve to convert something which can be perceived by more than one sense into an object proper to one sense and one sense only. *Colour* may appear more promising, but, among the numerous difficulties which arise here—the topic of a later chapter —there is the simple fact that the subject of our investigation may be colour-blind.

More generally applicable is the notion of *light*. Any contemporary definition of an *eye* would no doubt involve the specification of it as a *light-sensitive* organ, and without any appeal to scientific findings concerning light we can relate it directly to sight. Thus, whether or not our subject's 'eyes' are real eyes can be decided by seeing whether its performance is affected by conditions of illumination: does it appear to have greater difficulty in following the ball as the light grows darker? does it react to a flashing light? if light from a torch moves across the floor, does it follow this as it would follow the ball? does it make any difference to the creature's performance if we interpose an opaque screen between it and the ball? if we interpose a transparent screen?

Given the necessity of the 'eye' to the responses which are affected by light conditions, it would seem that we have sufficient to identify it as the organ of sight, and hence to infer that the creature can see. There is, however, some question as to whether it would be appropriate to introduce the notion of *light*, even in this unsophisticated form, into an account of our ordinary understanding of sight in such a way that it had a *causal* role, at least when what is seen is a physical object, or its movements—and not light in the sense of 'light-source'. The ball is the cause of the cat's movements, and what is required for sight to be involved is that the ball should be illuminated. Given that the ball—or its movements —is effective in determining the animal's movements, and given that it is by virtue of being illuminated that the ball can have this effect, then we can speak of sight.

Whether we regard light, thus introduced, as having a causal role depends on how broadly the notion of such a role is to be understood, and for our purposes it is not necessary to argue one way or the other. Whether, on the other hand, it is possible that light should enter into an account of our everyday concept of sight as providing a proper *object* of vision is a more substantial issue, and one which we shall tackle in Chapter 8. But for the present let us continue with our theoretical objections. I remarked above that the concept of *pretence* has as yet no application to the cat in the present connection, and that its actions can accordingly be taken at their face value. Let me expand on this. If I jab a needle into you and you let out a yell I have every reason to suppose that you felt a sharp pain. And yet, compelling though that supposition may be, we can still meaningfully reject it while conceding that the jab took place, and in support of this rejection we could propose that you were pretending to feel pain but not really feeling it. It will no doubt be held that this proposal does not stand on its own, that the ascription of pretence calls for confirmation in subsequent events. Just how much truth there is in this familiar allegation remains to be determined; not much, one would suspect, since subsequent events could hardly give *proof* of what took place at the time in question, and anything short of proof is of little interest here. More to the point, perhaps, is the necessity of explaining, as a prerequisite for pretence, how it was possible for you *not* to feel pain when jabbed in this way. Still, this could be explained— perhaps you were anaesthetized—and it is not in any case my present concern. What does interest me is the following way of describing the situation: in saying that the person was only pretending when he yelled out, we are implying that the causality of his actions was not as it seemed; he was not crying out as the result of the sensation which he experienced, but his cries are to be explained by reference to a desire to deceive us.

But now consider the yelping of an animal which has been jabbed. Once more it is possible to query the causality of the response, but not on the grounds that it stemmed, not from the painful jab, but from the creature's desire to deceive us. We can allow the possibility that the animal should display behaviour in terms of which we might give sense to the notion of pretending, but as things are this is not a notion which we have to take seriously. Still, in order to maintain the mere possibility of pretence we must suppose some condition, normally holding, which would in that event fail, and such a condition would appear to be provided by the jab's producing the yelp. So long as there is no doubt here about what caused what, there would seem to be no doubt about the painfulness of the jab, whatever this may come to. Given that it was the sharp instrument that elicited this response, there would seem to be no room for pretence, however that might be understood in the animal case.

Deceit or pretence was to be the main obstacle standing in the way of an inference to the conclusion that a person could see, in the example with which we began this section. It is very difficult to think of a plausible case in which we might say that the cat was pretending to see something; however, as in the case of pain, pretence does not provide the only possibility which might run counter to the causal sequence required for the correctness of an ascription of sight to an animal, and I shall now indicate one kind of case which would show that the creature's responses were not, despite appearances, brought about by the putative object of vision in the right way. Let us suppose that our cat does all the things which we have required of it: it chases balls around the room, follows patches of light which move across the floor, but does not do these things when screens block its view, and so forth. Can we now say with complete certainty that it can see?

By now any doubt on this matter is perhaps bordering on the insane, but a demonstration that we have here something less than vision is none the less imaginable. We have, let us suppose, a creature which looks exactly like a normal cat and which behaves in the same way as the creature just described, chasing the ball around the room when, and only when, conditions for the ball's being visible to it obtain. Then, to our amazement, it turns out that this apparent cat is a complicated dummy, a lifeless fraud subject to remote control by its offstage inventor, who has cleverly made his dummy's 'eyes' turn as if they were following the ball of wool, and has similarly made its other limbs move in exact imitation of our real cat's behaviour. Such a possibility, however fantastic—especially with a live cat—draws attention to the requirement that the cat's eyes should not be redundant in any situation in which it sees, but should play a specific role in the causal sequence involved. In a normal case the movement of the ball would be effective in inducing corresponding movements of the cat in a straightforward way. In the case imagined, the movements of the dummy—or real cat, if we had the technical skill—could, it is true, be traced back to the movements of the ball, but via the inventor who, as a result of *his* perception of the ball, was able to bring about appropriate movements in the unseeing eyes and the limbs of his mock cat.

To eliminate such circuitous paths along which the causal chain beginning with the movements of the ball could conceivably be routed, we might insist that the causal connection be mediated by an organ which is sensitive to light, that the response be brought about by stimulation of the animal's eyes by light from the object in question. However, this statement of the conditions presumes that this is in fact what we should find on closer examination of the typical, normal cases. If it were found that the everyday run of cases did involve quite unexpected causal chains, then we should simply have to allow for them in our concept of sight. It is only on the assumption, in this instance reasonable enough, that further elaboration of the causal sequence will not reveal such intermediate stages, that we reject the sequence, but what we have fundamentally is that the ball brings about responses from the cat in conditions in which exposure to the cat's eyes in a degree of illumination is necessary. How precisely the responses are brought about, indeed, that light from the object *falling on* the eye is involved, is, strictly speaking, a matter of further discovery, and not implied by the requirement that the object be present or exposed to the cat's eyes.

Given satisfaction on the questions of causality which may arise, it would seem there is no other point at which the claim that the cat has seen can be challenged; there is no call to establish the existence of inaccessible feline sense-data, or any other inner, non-physical states of the animal. We do not have simply a *hypothesis* that the cat can see; its seeing is not something which we *postulate* as a way of accounting for its behaviour, but the relevant data concerning behaviour and causal conditions define the area within which proof of vision is to be located. Note that reference to both these factors is necessary if all possible counter-examples are to be excluded. If we confine ourselves to describing the animal's behaviour in the ordinary sense of 'behaviour', i.e., without reference to the causal antecedents in terms of which this behaviour can be explained, then it is possible to deny that seeing is involved, and accordingly possible to advance the animal's ability to see as a hypothesis which would explain its behaviour—rather than as a logical consequence of such a description. It is natural and correct to restrict the term 'behaviour' in this way, but it is important to note that, so restricted, the term does not embrace all the *verifiable* data, and in particular not the crucial causal relation. There is a 'gap', if you like, between descriptions of behaviour and ascriptions of seeing, but it is a gap to be bridged by ascertaining the causal links, not by supplementing the behaviour with some accompanying mental event or experience.

The above account is still not complete, but it does look to be along promising lines. I shall fill it out little by little, but before getting on with this task it is worth pausing to mention some of the difficulties which will have to be dealt with. Thus, we may begin to have doubts about the use of the term 'cause' here when we consider how out of place it sounds with human perception. If you see me throwing and catching a ball you will have more than ample evidence on which to base a conclusion that I can see; but does the ball—or light from the ball—*cause* me to behave in the way I do? One reason why we resist this way of describing the situation stems from the fact that it is *we* who initiate action; we do not wish to relinquish this status and ascribe to something such as a ball the role of dictating what we do, but it is up to us to act as we please. If I want to catch the ball I shall position myself accordingly, but if I have lost interest in the game I may ignore

the ball altogether. In such a situation I regulate my actions on
the basis of what I see and what I learn of by means of the other
senses; the things which I perceive do not cause my actions, it
would seem, but they provide me with cues on which I may or
may not act, depending on a host of other factors.

This objection does not, I believe, present any really serious
difficulties. As has often been observed, it is to some extent an
arbitrary matter what we choose to single out as the cause of a
given event; arbitrary, in that it may depend on what factor or
factors in the situation interest us most, what we happen to be
able to manipulate or vary while the other conditions are, or are
held, constant, and what occurrence is the final addition to the set
of conditions which jointly determine the effect. In the case of the
animal we naturally think of ourselves as manipulating its movements by altering the position of the ball or dangling a piece of
string in front of it. Other conditions may be equally necessary,
and in certain circumstances sufficient, if we are to get the cat to
respond to the object, but we cannot vary these in the same way.
The case of human action is different, but not so different that we
cannot speak here of a cause, although it is true that when it is a
question of our own actions, not those of another man, we are so
conscious that our actions depend on what we want to have
happen that we do not readily see the object perceived as a cause
in the situation. However, that does not mean that, against the
background of our intentions, abilities and so forth, the ball could
not have been the causal factor which finally triggered off our
action. Just because I could have chosen to ignore the ball coming
towards me, that does not show that, in the situation in which
I found myself—hoping to catch a man out at cricket—the
approaching ball was not the cause of the various movements in
which I engaged in an effort to catch the ball. Something which is,
in the circumstances, a sufficient condition for my action is all
that I require the term 'cause' to signify.

I suspect that the complexities of the human case interfere with
the simplicity of the animal case largely because we are prone to
invoke something analogous to the notion of the 'inner man' to
apply to animals. However, be that as it may, the matter does
become genuinely complicated when we consider more carefully
a word which we naturally use in this situation, namely the word
'respond'. The examples which fit in most readily with the pro-

posed causal account are such examples as reflex actions, as when I duck at the sight of a missile heading my way, or when I start on seeing a sudden movement. When the reaction is immediate, the causal efficacy of the object is apparent, and there seems to be less inclination to postulate some fleeting intermediate state which is necessary if the object is to give rise to this behaviour and if we are to be able to speak of sight. To describe this, or any other action, as a *response*, however, threatens us with just such an intervening state, for to ask how *x* responded to the presence or the movement of the object is to speak of the latter as if they posed a problem or presented a challenge with which *x* had to cope. Actions which we should call 'responses' are generally not simple, direct reactions to a stimulus, but actions consequent upon an assessment of the situation: the creature initiates action on the basis of what it sees and how it sees it. And similarly with human beings: we have already seen when we respond.

We reach this same conclusion, that seeing may involve an event or a state which is prior to acting or responding, if we consider the familiar fact that human beings are capable of seeing something without this in any way showing in their behaviour. The bird which just now flew across my field of vision registered mentally with me, but I did not even bother to move my eyes to follow its flight. And surely with animals too we want to allow at least the possibility of sight without action. The sleepy cat briefly opens its eyes, stares straight at me and then closes them. Not the slightest movement beyond the movement of its eyelids, but you might think it at least makes sense to say that it saw me.

The causal account of perception outlined above does perhaps carry an implicit reference to the intermediate state or event in the causal chain to which the preceding objections draw attention, but if so the reference does not stand out clearly, and since this would appear to be precisely the event which we are trying to pin down, the account as formulated can hardly be reckoned satisfactory. It suggests that whether or not an animal has seen a particular object is just a question of what it does and how it comes to be doing it, and such an analysis threatens us with a reduction of seeing to some form of responding or reacting. If data on the nature and causality of an animal's responses provide us with a premise which makes the conclusion that it sees logically inescapable, it is difficult to see how we can avoid construing 'see' as descriptive of some aspect of these data. And yet, no matter how complex the animal's repertoire of responses, there seems to be no element in them to which we refer when we say that it sees, can see or has seen something. Nor would it seem appropriate to seek out this elusive element in the physiological processes which provide certain of the links in the causal chain. Our everyday notion of seeing does not connect directly enough with such processes for them to be what we identify when we speak of seeing.

As a first step towards sorting out this tangle I want to examine the question: what kinds of response give proof of vision? I shall take it for granted that the responses considered are brought about by light, not by auditory stimuli, for instance, and in general I shall assume that questions of causality are not in dispute. Even with such assumptions an objector may consider that, whatever an animal does, its responses cannot suffice to give proof of vision, but for the moment my concern is with objections which, in a given instance, argue that the responses displayed are not of a *kind* to yield such proof. Thus, we have extracted from the discussion to date the simple hypothesis that seeing can be conclusively established by ascertaining the occurrence of suitably caused responses, and the complications which called for further refinements were complications relating to the causality of the responses. I did not stop to consider whether some qualification was demanded on the side of the responses themselves, and consideration of the possible variety of these may strengthen the view that no such qualifications are to be imposed, that what counts is not the nature of the creature's behaviour, but *how* it is brought about. Certainly, there does not appear to be any response which is specific to a given visual characteristic, but to ascertain that an animal can see some particular phenomenon—movements of a certain magnitude, let us say—we look for a constancy among its responses indicating that they are made to the movements. As ever, the isolation of a cause can prove difficult, but it is here that any difficulties lie, not in the nature of what it does. However, although the question of causality seems at first sight to be all-important, the apparent simplicity in other respects of the examples which we might consider here may derive from a tacit assumption about the kinds of response which we consider relevant, and I wish to examine this possibility in terms of two conceivable situations, one involving an artificial device, the other a living organism.

First, let us suppose we have a device equipped with an artificial 'eye', a photo-receptor which reacts differently to different light stimuli. Suppose too that the changes brought about in this eye by variations in the light input are used to induce changes on a larger scale. For instance, we might have a change in the eye whenever the intensity or brightness of the light-source to which it was currently exposed varied, and this change might in turn be used to bring about a proportionate increase in the speed of a rotating disc. In such a case we have an 'organ' which is sensitive to light, and a device containing this organ which 'responds' differently to different features, definable in terms of light, in objects placed in front of it. Furthermore, if a single rotating disc does not allow of enough variation in its movements to match the numerous visually definable differences which may obtain among the objects which we place before it, we may consider the device enriched by the addition of as many other discs as we choose, so that somewhere in their movements any variation in the visual field may be reflected. There is nothing outlandish about such a piece of apparatus, but no matter how perfectly its discs correlate with subtle differences in the visual data we shall not wish to apply 'see' to it in any literal sense. Similar remarks can be made of a device which reacts in a like fashion to auditory stimuli, and indeed we are familiar enough with electronic apparatus in which the pointer on a meter gives different readings as the input through a microphone varies. Once more, however sensitive the apparatus to variations in sound, we shall surely not say that it can *hear*.

It would appear that the gap between not seeing and seeing is not to be bridged merely by increasing the sensitivity of the responding device or the number of features to which it may respond. An enrichment in another direction is called for, and one obvious capacity to add is the capacity to 'lock on' to objects; a device which seemed to fix its eye on you and follow you with it as you moved about the room would at least give you the feeling that you were being watched. Still, we may ask, is this enough? If the device with this added capacity were just our contrivance with the rotating discs I think that, despite this feeling, we should be reluctant to allow in all seriousness that the thing had *seen* us.

We can come a step closer if we suppose that the device can not only fix its 'gaze' on an object, but that it is also equipped with some sort of limbs which it brings into operation in these situations. One possibility is that it should have an arm which it can extend to grasp nearby objects and that it should do just this whenever, we shall suppose, objects of a certain vaguely specifiable shape or size pass within its reach. Another possibility is that it should have legs or some other form of locomotion which takes it towards or away from objects which its eye locks on to. Combining these possibilities we get a robot to which we might now be very reluctant to deny the power of sight. Thus, suppose that whenever an object roughly the size and shape of a cricket ball passed within the 'field of vision' of our artifact it promptly set off in pursuit of it—or so we are tempted to describe it—and seized the article, wouldn't it seem arbitrary to disallow that the robot had seen it? This description would become even more appropriate if the robot then did something with the ball—started to 'ingest' it, say. Admittedly, as so far portrayed, the responses of the device are severely limited and we have not yet detailed any other signs of sensibility, but visually it is not much, if any, worse off than a tree frog, which is capable of seeing moving flies and larger looming shapes, but which fails altogether to see a dead fly lying motionless before it. The responses of this creature are considerably restricted, but we have no hesitation in saying that it can see certain things. Why should we not treat our robot as on a par?

The gradual movement towards a case of vision which I have outlined has a feature which may appear curious: whether the device can see is surely a question about what takes place at the beginning of the various movements which start to unfold once the object to be perceived is within the device's visual field, yet we were trying to decide this matter by considering its subsequent movements, more and more removed from the time when, if it saw, it saw the object for the first time, or 'caught sight' of it. Returning to an earlier objection, we feel that our robot, R, must first see the object, O, and then set about making whatever responses it makes—which may be none at all, without prejudice to its having seen—and this in turn is like saying that R must first identify O by using its eyes. After all, in a real-life situation, the nature of the creature's responses will depend on how it identifies O since it will not, presumably, respond in the same way to everything. But now the same difficulty arises over 'identify': *R* must first see *O* in order to be able to identify it, which leaves us with the possibility that the animal should *first* see *O* and *then* identify it and only *then* engage in some kind of behaviour. With identification thus interposed, seeing becomes even further detached from behaviour.

There is no doubt that, as one pursues it, seeing tends to recede into the mental, there to vanish altogether, and we have not even begun to tackle the question what precisely it is that *see* relates to in the complex series of events which begins with *R*'s exposure to *O* and ends in its grasping *O*. In this instance it is not, we should suppose, a mental event—if this excludes its being anything more than a kind of physical event—but this negative observation does not serve to pin it down. Still, it would at least appear that, prior to identifying any particular occurrence as the robot's *seeing*, we have, with certain suppositions of a simple kind about the nature and causality of its behaviour, good enough grounds on which to base a claim that the device really can see, and the task is now to try to discover what it is about the features which we introduced into *R*'s behaviour that has made it possible to speak in these terms.

Let us return to organisms. One thing which is commonly said about the senses is that by means of them we acquire knowledge of the world. This implication is clear in such near-synonyms of 'perceive' as 'locate', 'detect', 'learn of the presence of' and 'become aware of', and it may be suggested that the reason why such responses as grasping and moving towards an object brought us nearer, if not actually to a case of seeing, was that these responses are intimately connected with the knowledge acquired through use of the eyes. This suggestion is strengthened by consideration of the following kind of possibility. Let us suppose that a certain animal, which we shall call 'Fred', always breaks out into a rash whenever a snake is placed before him. Suppose too that by eliminative experiments we establish that Fred's 'eyes' must be open and directed at the snake for this to occur. (I use quotes here, not wishing to beg any questions, but I assume that the organs described as 'eyes' have at least been found to be light-sensitive.) If this rash occurs when and only when Fred is in such a situation, we shall have what may be described as a 'differential response' to the snake. Should we be prepared to ascribe sight to

Fred on the strength of such a response, perhaps frequently repeated?

Taking such responses in isolation, and with no further knowledge of Fred's behaviour, it would seem to me that we have at best a borderline case of seeing. If we have already established that Fred can see then we should no doubt suppose that the rash is some sort of nervous response brought about by the sight of the snake, or something along these lines, but without such additional knowledge we should be reluctant to offer this type of occurrence as conclusive proof that Fred can see. Even if we are sure that the rash is the result of the action of light reflected from the snake on to Fred's 'eyes', it cannot be described without further ado as anything more than 'merely an effect on the animal' brought about by the light-stimulus. We may trace a causal chain from the snake through Fred's eyes to the rash on Fred, but for the response to be relevant to seeing we do not want the causal chain always to terminate there. Roughly speaking, if Fred is to have seen the snake we want his behaviour to be in some way directed to what he saw; whatever the sequence of events, if their upshot is never more than a change or an effect in the animal we have something less than perception.

The example of Fred is intended as a difficult rather than a realistic case, a case which comes close to one of sight without being clearly acceptable. Like a sunflower, Fred provides us with an example of light-sensitivity which falls short of actual sight. Thus a sunflower may move as the sun moves, and indeed move as a direct result of the light from the sun falling on it (at a certain angle). It responds to a light source, but its 'discriminatory behaviour' is lacking both in range and quality. It reacts to the strong light of the sun by moving, a reaction which is more relevant to sight than, say, becoming bleached, but it is indifferent to any other feature definable in terms of light—shape, colour, and so forth; it cannot pick out a mouse from an elephant among the surrounding objects. Fred is, like the sunflower, severely limited in his responses, but he does have the ability to discriminate one particular form, and one which may present itself in a variety of ways; it is just that his response to this form is not of the right kind for us to say without considerable reservations that he sees it. If the rest of his behaviour gave evidence of vision we could reasonably say that it was a question of sight here too, but given that the response occurs in isolation we can at best speak here of a borderline case.

The upshot of our discussion of the artificial device and the organism is roughly as follows. Mere complexity of response matching changes in the visual field does not suffice to give proof, of a logical or a non-logical kind, of sight. We could, after all, take an eye away from its body, preserve its efferent nerves and so maintain it that, as before, the nerve cells in the retina would continue to fire when subjected to light-stimuli, but there would as yet be no question of seeing. For this we require that the eye be incorporated in a device that *does* something; more precisely, we look for externally directed behaviour, behaviour directed to the source of the stimulus, the object from which light is reflected or emitted. As examples of such behaviour we might cite moving towards an object, seizing and manipulating it, alighting on a branch, taking flight at the approach of an aggressor and skirting an obstacle—all actions which, we may note, can be seen as in some sense manifesting *knowledge,* whether it be knowledge of the location of something, or, in addition, knowledge of an identificatory or recognitional kind. What we should not count would be, for instance, some sort of scratching which the animal engaged in as a result of a disturbance brought about in some part of its body by the action of light, even if the light was channelled through a photo-receptor.

When we say that, for it to be the case that it actually sees, the device or animal possessing the eye must *do* something, or at least be capable of doing something as a result of stimulation by light, we could put this *figuratively* by saying that it must act on the information which it gets through using its eyes; its responses should be such that we can see the informational value of the stimulus as operative, and not merely its stimulus value: the response is to be not merely a change or a movement triggered off by the stimulus, but it is to show that the visual characteristics of the object perceived are being treated as indices of the nature of the object—as something to be pursued or avoided, for instance. The appreciation of the nature of the object seen is shown by the *appropriateness* of the response: it is somehow geared to the characteristics of the object perceived taken in conjunction with the creature's wants and needs. Thus we say that the animal can tell (by using its eyes) that its mate or a predator is there before it on the basis of the aptness or fittingness of the action which their presence brings about.

I say that talk here of acting on information is figurative: there is no question of the animal being told something and acting on the basis of what it has thereby learned. Without further elucidation, the notion of behaviour which is appropriate or which manifests knowledge is perhaps not much more perspicuous, but it is at least fairly clear in outline what is involved. There is no call to understand knowledge in terms of the creature's having thoughts, but the appropriateness of the behaviour which is taken to manifest knowledge is to be understood in terms of the relevance of the behaviour to the attainment of a goal or a condition which is advantageous to the agent. Thus, to take up the earlier example, a dog which is making for its food embarks upon a course which it modifies to cope with the obstacles which it meets in its way. The mere fact that the obstacles encountered have some effect on the dog is not of itself sufficient to establish the creature's awareness of them, but the specific activity of avoiding these obstacles is of a kind which shows knowledge of their presence, awareness of them as located at a distance from the dog.

If I am right, we might conceivably change our minds about the inappropriateness of a piece of animal behaviour and come to see its fittingness under the assumption that the animal wanted such-and-such or was directing its actions at bringing about such-and-such, and in this way we could come to regard what seemed a 'meaningless' response as in fact manifesting knowledge. Thus, if the rash which broke out on our organism Fred when confronted with a snake actually had the function of frightening off the snake we should be more inclined, I imagine, to take it as showing that Fred saw the snake.

I have suggested that we view certain behaviour as appropriate, and hence as manifesting knowledge, under the assumption that the animal has certain wants or goals, but it may be suggested that the true order can be a reversal of this: we might infer the creature's wants from its behaviour, under the assumption that this behaviour is a manifestation of knowledge. I do not wish to reject this possibility, but all I require is that it be possible to establish that x is what the animal wants independently of any assumptions about what it knows—though what establishes the want may be what establishes the knowledge. That this is possible is clear if the want is made evident by the creature's distressed state and the efficacy of the means adopted to alleviate it; here the want is identifiable without any assumptions concerning knowledge. The interesting case is where there is no question of distress but the wanting is to be understood just in terms of the goal-directedness of the behaviour. Thus, suppose we have an insect which flies straight into a wall. One man says that it obviously wanted to do or aimed at doing this, since it knew that the wall was there. Another man says that the insect did not want to fly into the wall, hence it cannot have known it was there. How do we choose between these two accounts?

Given just this isolated incident, there is perhaps not much we can say. However, a repetition of this pattern of behaviour will lead us to surmise that we have here an instance of purposive behaviour, that the insect is flying into the wall for the sake of the consequences thereof, and if we do succeed in establishing this we shall *ipso facto* establish the insect's knowledge of the location of the wall on those occasions. What I have been arguing is quite consistent with the possibility that both the purposiveness and the knowledge be established by the same events, since all I require is that no assumption as to knowledge need underlie our identification of a creature's want or goal.

It is of course not the case that the only kind of appropriate behaviour is behaviour which is adapted to the attainment of a goal. There may be no purpose to the dog's barking, just excitement at his master's return, and yet it is not stretching the term 'appropriate' too much to use it in this context. (This barking may, as in our earlier use of the example, connect with knowledge in another way, in that the response may occur when the dog has no more than evidence of his master and where accordingly a transferred use of 'infer' can get a grip.) However, I do not think that a creature's responses could be confined to this type if we are to see in them proof of perception, for we should then have just a more complicated version of the illustration with Fred.

Another example, different again, is provided by imitative behaviour: a baby copies the movements of its mother's lips, let us suppose. Here we might mention a very natural statement of the grounds for saying that the child could see the movements of its mother's lips, namely: how otherwise could it have done what it did? We might have introduced the same consideration when speaking of the animal's rash: a variety of causes could give rise to a rash on Fred's skin, but it could hardly jump on to the top of a fence and walk along it if it could not see. However, this reply needs further elaboration before it is satisfactory. In the circumstances, after all, it simply might have been impossible that Fred should have broken out in a rash except as a result of exposure to this particular visual stimulus. What is required is that we distinguish breaking out in a rash and jumping on to a fence on the grounds of their being different things *done*. Or, if you like, while the latter is something which the creature does, the former is not, or not in the same sense. And, clearly, deciding what does and what does not count as something which the creature does, in the relevant sense, just brings us back to the question of characterizing purposive behaviour.

I have been concerned in this last section to show that only certain responses can be held to give proof of vision, but it might be wondered whether there really is any need to bother with this search for the appropriate qualifications. The counter-argument might run as follows. The senses of animals and men are, we may assume, the outcome of evolutionary developments over many thousands of years. Possession of these senses makes possible various responses to aspects of the environment, and it so happens that conditions have favoured the persistence of some responses rather than others. In particular, responses which lead to the prolongation of the species are likely to persist, and so we find the connection of the senses with location and locomotion, with the movements of flight and pursuit, and actions generally which favour survival. Given that it is behaviour that is adapted to the environment that is likely to persist, it is not surprising that we think of such examples when looking for actions which give proof of vision. We might still wonder, however, whether our concept of sight is such that only certain kinds of response give the proof we seek, or whether, as far as the sense of 'see' is concerned, the nature of the response might not be accidental. The position presented has ruled out this latter possibility, but we could be accused of reading into the situation features which are inevitable in evolutionary terms but which do not have logically the same significance.

Thus, suppose we come across a piece of behaviour which, although elicited by reflected light, is in no way appropriate to the nature of the stimulus source, but is what we should be inclined to call 'meaningless' behaviour; e.g., we come across insects which invariably fly in small circles when confronted with an object of a certain colour. Might we not be more willing to say that they could see than to say that there was something appropriate about such behaviour, something which, figuratively speaking, showed an appreciation of the character of objects so coloured? Certainly, if we have more straightforward evidence that they can see we shall no doubt say that they can see on these occasions as well, but the suggestion is that all their behaviour could be of this sort, as far as responses to light are concerned, and yet that we should still speak of them as 'seeing'. For one who wishes to speak of seeing in this instance without forgoing the condition of appropriateness it is reasonable to suggest that the pattern of behaviour developed in circumstances in which it was appropriate, and only lost its point when these conditions ceased to obtain. Think of a moth flying to its death in a burning flame. This rejoinder does succeed in finding some place for the notion of appropriateness, but if it takes no more than the correctness of such a hypothesis about past members of the species to make the necessary difference on the question whether this present response gives proof of vision, we might well conclude that the qualification of appropriateness is of little account. Furthermore, at least with most movements it is almost always going to be possible to make out a case for a connection with behaviour of an appropriate type, since practically any movement (of the whole animal) is going to qualify as one of flight or pursuit; so, provided it is suitably caused, there will in practice be an overwhelming presumption that such a movement gives proof of vision.

The requirement of appropriateness is threatening to become so readily satisfiable as to be of no great consequence, but I still wish to hold that our understanding of 'see' is such that we do require some sort of connection with appropriateness, some place for the notion of acquiring knowledge, for the term to be in place. After all, light can have a variety of effects on an organism, some of which—effects on the skin—have nothing to do with vision. Certainly, responses which come about as a result of light falling on an organ resembling an eye are likely to be of a kind which entitles us to speak of seeing, but I do not think that all responses so produced need be relevant. After all, some could conceivably be the same as changes which come about when the skin is exposed to light, changes in the animal's state of health, for instance. What is true is that practically anything which we are inclined to call 'behaviour', as opposed to a mere change in the creature—as a change in colour—is likely to satisfy to some extent the condition of appropriateness, usually, though not invariably, because of movement involved either towards or away from the source of the light.

I have barely touched on many of the interesting questions which abound in this area, but I hope I have said enough in this chapter to indicate the plausibility of an analysis of animal perception which will find favour with the behaviourist. We are still not done with our analysis, but we already have good grounds for the contention that, given certain behavioural and causal conditions, we can assert that x can see y, not just as a hypothesis, but as a logical consequence of these conditions; or, if anything stands in the way of this inference, it can relate only to imprecision of statement, not to omission of data which are neither causal nor behavioural. There can be something of a problem in deciding which responses are characterizable as manifestations of knowledge, but those which are remain purely behavioural just as much as those which are not. To be such a manifestation is to be oriented or adapted in a certain way; it is not to be the outward effect of some inner mental state, a state whose existence might be conjectured but not proved by the creature's actions.

5

PERCEPTION AND KNOWLEDGE

THE verbs 'know' and 'want' do not have a simple connection with behaviour comparable with that of, say, the verbs 'spit' and 'squeal', but if the account proposed for them is correct we have here a complication which provides only a passing embarrassment for the behaviourist. With the verb 'see' we are also hard put to isolate the event which it designates from among the various happenings which lead us to say that an animal sees, and this difficulty remains undiminished even granting that responses of a certain specific kind, suitably caused, somehow add up to a logically sufficient condition for the truth of the ascription of sight based upon them. And, moreover, whether such a condition is in fact to be found in behaviour is perhaps not beyond all doubt even now; difficulties were mentioned when the position was advanced, and other objections are readily developed. For instance, we are inclined to say such things as 'on seeing his master the dog ran towards him', or 'at the sight of his master the dog broke into a run', in which the response providing the evidence for seeing is explicitly set apart from the seeing, and this separation of seeing and responding makes it hard to understand the *logical* connection alleged to hold. We could, it would seem, draw some sort of line between the time of seeing and the time of acting, and we could even suppose that no action whatever was consequent upon the seeing. If seeing can be thus independent of acting, it would seem that it could occur without our being able to have any knowledge of the fact. This does not constitute a problem for the realist; it is, he will maintain, just a fact about the limitations of our knowledge which must be faced. For the anti-realist, on the other hand, there could be no recognition of such a 'fact', and so, it might seem, no acknowledgement of sight which is not manifested in behaviour.

So far we have tried to pin down *seeing* by considering how attributions of sight may be verified. To have a clearer idea of what it is we are trying thus to circumscribe it is helpful to examine the 'grammar' of the verb more closely, but before taking up this topic we might consider how we should have fared had we sought to elucidate 'sees' by proceeding directly to other locutions with which it is more or less synonymous. There are a number of expressions, e.g., 'locate', 'differentiate', 'discriminate', 'learn of', 'detect' and 'become aware', which, if coupled with 'visually' or 'by using the eyes', give, singly or in disjunction, reasonably accurate paraphrases of the verb. However, as far as I can tell there is no way of avoiding the questions which we have raised, since, leaving aside the difficulties posed by such a qualification as 'visually', in their application to animals verbs such as 'locate' pose the very problems which engaged us when considering the kind of responses which give proof of vision. Why, for instance, does walking up to and handling an object give us better grounds for saying that the creature had *located* it than if it had simply quivered when confronted by the object? All the same, it is worth giving some of these phrases more attention, and I shall begin with a few observations on the phrase 'differentiate visually'.

This phrase has two relevant interpretations: (1) we may have in mind the differentiation of an object or a feature of some object from its background, or (2) we may mean (in addition) the ability to respond differently accordingly as the object or feature is or is not present. Let me explain what I mean by this distinction. In many cases seeing does seem to be a matter of differentiating or discriminating an object from its background, but, rather obviously, this does not apply when what is seen is the whole of the scene in view or some all-pervading aspect of the scene. For instance, we may be made aware of a bright flash not by observing a boundary separating the flash from adjacent areas in the field of vision— though this is of course a possibility—but in virtue of the contrast with the scene before the flash. In short, the differentiation may be between temporally as well as between spatially separated phenomena. The necessity for allowing both forms of differentiation is particularly evident in the analogous example of hearing sounds. When I hear a sound I may pick it out against a background of other sounds, but I may equally —stretching language somewhat —differentiate it from no sound at all. This latter possibility compares with the case where our eyes are shut one moment and open the next: suddenly seeing what is before us after not seeing anything is like hearing the sound after a period of silence. (2) is a stronger candidate than (1), then, though I doubt that the term 'differentiate' is really appropriate to the temporal case, and in any event it does not seem that the definition will do more than confirm, after elaboration, the rough analysis of 'see' which has so far emerged, for a little reflection indicates that, in its application to creatures other than men, an analysis of 'differentiate' will require us to define the subclass of responses which has been the focus of our attention.

A verb which in many contexts comes close to 'see' is 'detect', suitably qualified by such a phrase as 'by means of the eyes', but it is appropriate to more restricted circumstances, namely when the object seen is partially obscured, or very small, or hidden away among other things which make it difficult to pick out; it does not fit happily into such a context as 'I saw the plains stretching out before me'. A similar narrowness may affect 'locate' (by use of the eyes), which often suggests the successful termination of a search and the discovery of the whereabouts of an object, implications which make it unsuited to such a context as 'I saw the blue sky above'. It becomes more generally applicable if we play down the suggestion that one who locates something is aware of its specific location, as being to his left or right, above or below him. Thus a shellfish which withdraws into its shell at the sight of an approaching fish may not show awareness of the fish as situated at one place rather than another, but it locates it in the more general sense that it becomes aware of its presence, or the (presence of the) fish in some way 'registers' with it. *Location* in this general sense surely is central to *seeing*, even if there still is the question of specifying the kinds of response which are relevant here.

Talk of *awareness* in the context of perception is certainly apposite, as well as traditional, and I shall have more to say about this notion later. The notion of *registering* is less commonly invoked, but it perhaps accords better with our intuitions than the more specific 'differentiate'. In order for it to be true that a creature should see an object it surely must be the case that seeing should make *some* difference, that the object should have *some* effect on the creature. There are many objects which it is in a position to see, but despite the fact that they are there in plain view before the creature, it may still fail to see them; that they should in some sense register with it seems to be the minimal requirement which talk of *seeing* demands,|though once more precisely how it is to be interpreted is what defines our problem.

If Ryle's well-known characterization of 'see' as an 'achievement' verb is accepted, merely to begin trying to relate seeing to responding, as our account would have us do, is to run the risk of confusing two quite distinct categories of verb; on this view there is no such phenomenon as seeing, in a sense which would allow the identification of it with an activity to be even grammatical. To quote Ryle:

> 'To begin with, seeing and hearing are not processes. Aristotle points out, quite correctly (*Met.* IX, vi. 7–10) that I can say "I have seen it" as soon as I can say "I see it". To generalize the point that I think he is making, there are many verbs part of the business of which is to declare a terminus. To find something puts "Finis" to searching for it; to win a race brings the race to an end' (*Dilemmas*, p. 102).

Elsewhere Ryle writes that ' "see", "descry" and "find" are not process words, experience words or activity words. They do not stand for perplexingly undetectable actions or reactions, any more than "win" stands for a perplexingly undetectable bit of running, or "unlock" for an unreported bit of key-turning' (*The Concept of Mind*, p. 152). The 'achievement' which Ryle claims 'sees' signifies can be assigned a moment in time, but nothing which takes time or extends over a period of time, and so not an experience process or activity, however brief.

This account fits in well with those cases where we see something as the result of looking for it, for in such cases we can regard seeing as the successful termination of the task of looking for that thing— 'task' being for Ryle the correlative of 'achievement'. Curiously enough, Ryle writes as if seeing always arose in such a context, i.e., as the upshot of looking for something, but, as has often since been pointed out, as well as looking *for* there is also the case of looking *at*. While looking at the wall I see a fly; it is not something I am looking for and which I successfully locate; it just happens to be within my field of vision and I somehow come to see it. And, of course, seeing does not mark the cessation of looking at or its successful termination; we often keep looking at what we have seen. Further, looking *at* is not the only alternative to looking *for*. Suppose I am gazing vacantly into space, wrapped in thought and not registering anything of the scene before me, when the movement of a bird coming into my field of vision catches my attention and I see it. Until the moment when I saw the bird I had not been looking at anything.

I can be looking at *x* and fail to see it or something which is on it; so by contrast with the possible failure there is perhaps room to speak of seeing as an 'achievement' in such cases. However, it is questionable whether Ryle's category of 'task' goes happily with 'looking at', and in any case there appears to be nothing resembling a task of which seeing is the successful terminus if I am merely gazing into space, not looking at anything, when I suddenly catch sight of a bird. If we try to generalize, it seems we are left with no more than the contrast between seeing and the preceding condition of not-having-seen, since nothing more specific than this, in the way of tasks or otherwise, can be said to apply generally. None the less, this apparent weakening of the position does not affect the essential point in Ryle's conception of 'see' as an achievement verb, though it may show the term 'achievement' to be misleading. The distinctive feature of 'see' *vis-à-vis* the question whether it signifies a process, experience, activity, or what, does not, in my opinion, concern the availability of a relevant task and the consequent appropriateness of the term 'achievement', but it concerns questions of time and duration: does seeing last a certain time, however short, or can we only say that it occurs at an instant? (An account of achievement verbs which places emphasis on this temporal qualification is given by Zeno Vendler in his 'Verbs and Times', *The Philosophical Review*, 1957. Just what Ryle takes to be important for the definition of the achievement category is complicated by his recognition of 'protracted' achievements (*The Concept of Mind*, p. 149). The ambiguity thus introduced, along with other difficulties, is well exposed by F. N. Sibley in 'Seeking, Scrutinizing and Seeing', *Mind*, 1955.)

If an occurrence can occur only *at* an instant and not *for* a time, then it logically requires an extended process, state, or whatever, of which it is the end-point. To reach a place is to terminate some activity in a particular way, and, correspondingly, the moment of reaching the place is the limit of the period of time correlated with the activity, and not just a very short interval of time. As an instant, a point without duration, it logically requires a longer stretch of time which it can terminate, just as a surface—'where a body ends', we might say—is a feature inconceivable apart from the extended body whose boundary it is. However, the logical requirement is equally satisfied if the instantaneous occurrence is at the end or at the beginning of a state or process: the dimensionless moment at which an object which I let go starts to fall is at the end of its period of rest and at the beginning of the period of time throughout which it falls. Looked at in relation to what happens subsequently, 'started to fall' does not signify a successful termination in this sense, but the inappropriateness of 'achievement' here is surely of little consequence. Ryle was apparently of the same view, since in *Dilemmas* he cites 'verbs of starting' among analogies for 'see' (p. 103) and he no longer speaks here of 'achievements' but of 'terminus-verbs' (p. 105). I shall adopt this latter description with the understanding that the terminus can be either a beginning or an end, not exclusively the latter.

If we cease to lay emphasis on the appropriateness of 'achievement' we shall have no special call to retain 'task' as signifying that which an achievement terminates; whether it be a state, process, activity or performance, as long as it has a temporal extension it will be such as to allow of termination by an instantaneous occurrence. And, as just indicated, 'see' may not only signify the termination of a preceding state or process; it may at the same time mark the beginning of another state or process. Indeed, if 'state' is construed widely enough this is bound to be so. No one will dispute that 'see' can mark the successful termination of looking for, but in other cases, as when we simply see something on opening our eyes but without first looking for or at something, we appear to have nothing which 'see' can connect with in the same way. The state of not-having-seen is of course terminated by seeing, but 'see' must also mark the end-point of some more substantial state, process, or activity as well, and given that nothing appropriate precedes seeing we are forced to construe it as *initiating* a succeeding state. Compare the verb 'hear'. This can indicate the successful termination of *listening for*, but suppose there is absolute silence and I am neither listening for nor listening to anything. If, then, I hear something, this hearing marks the end of the state of not hearing anything, but, more importantly—for it cannot *just* do that—it marks the beginning of a new state.

What we have said so far about achievement verbs has been fairly general; we certainly have not shown that 'see' in particular always belongs to this class, or to the wider class which I have taken to constitute Ryle's main concern, the class of terminus-verbs. Part of the difficulty in deciding on the status of particular verbs lies in knowing just which of the marks which we should intuitively associate with achievement or terminus status are to be treated as providing a sufficient condition for this status. Thus, Ryle mentions with approval Aristotle's observation that we can say 'I have seen it' as soon as we can say 'I see it', but we can also say 'I have whistled' as soon as we can say 'I am whistling', so it is not clear that this test is of much use. The most direct test in terms of the temporal characterization of terminus-verbs is simply whether or not one can speak of ϕ-ing *at* a time but not *for* a time. It will no doubt prove necessary to refine this criterion if we are to be sure that it catches just those verbs which qualify intuitively, but it seems to be the best test so far proposed. Now, however, it would appear that 'see' is not invariably a terminus-verb, since we can ask such questions as 'how long did you see the comet for?' and give such answers as 'I saw it for a full ten minutes'—cf. the articles by Sibley and Vendler. Are we accordingly to abandon the claim that 'see' is a terminus-verb, introduce qualifications, or reject the test proposed? If we take this latter step it will perhaps no longer be clear what it is we are saying when we say that 'see' is or is not a terminus-verb, and the most reasonable move would appear to be simply to recognize that the verb has two uses. But now, even granting that 'see' can be a terminus-verb, the problem immediately shifts to the question of what it is of which 'see' marks the terminus or defines the limit. Recognition of its terminus status will prevent us from raising seemingly unanswerable questions about the sort of process, say, which the verb might be taken to signify, but to have any more adequate understanding of what is involved we must surely get clearer on the nature of the state, process, or whatever, of which 'see' marks the beginning or end.

Since, then, the negative condition of not-having-seen may be all we have to go on among conditions prior to seeing—and similarly for hearing, tasting, smelling and feeling—there is more to be hoped for from a consideration of conditions subsequent to the moment of perception, and with this and our earlier discussion in mind it is natural to try to connect 'see' with the initiation of a response. So, let us look at a case in which a visual stimulus triggers off an

immediate observable response, the sort of case which was originally advanced as giving proof of vision. For instance, I wave my
hand at a fly and it immediately takes itself off. (As ever, we suppose
that it is the visual stimulus that is operative here and not the
movement of the air, for instance, that gives rise to the movement of
the fly.) Here we might well assign the same time both to the
moment at which the fly saw the movement and the moment at
which it started to respond, the moment at which the visual
stimulus started to take effect or become operative, and this
suggests that we might actually define 'x saw y' as 'by virtue of
being illuminated and exposed to x's eyes, y brought about a
response from x'.

It is at least reasonable to claim that two such propositions will
frequently be true together, but can the second be held to define
the first? Is it not possible to raise yet again the difficulties which
have dogged the behaviourist? In the first place there may be some
doubt as to whether the time of seeing and the time at which the
response begins *must* coincide. We can safely say that the latter
will not precede the former, and that the two, however they are to
be pinpointed, are generally sure to be close together, but so far
we have no argument compelling us to see them as coinciding.
On the contrary, if we had to generalize, it would be safer to allow
a time-lag between the moment of seeing and the point of time
at which the creature started to move. More interestingly, and to
revert to the objection in its original form, can we even rule out
the possibility that the fly should see the movement but give no
sign of having done so? Not simply that there should be a delay
between seeing and responding, but that the fly should never
respond at all. Isn't it possible that I should wave my hand in
vain at the fly, that it should see the movement, but not, as we
might put it, 'consider it a threat'? In the second place, however
close their respective temporal co-ordinates, would it not be rash
to identify the two occurrences, the seeing and the inception of
the response? To equate these seems to be as absurd—if it is not
the very same thing—as the identification of the seeing with the
response itself, yet it would appear that one implication of the
definition is that 'x saw y' may in suitable circumstances describe
exactly the same occurence as 'x began to fly away'. And this
surely will not do.

Let us concentrate on the difficulty of trying to make sense of seeing in the absence of behaviour. So, imagine an animal staring at you, quite motionless. If you now move and its eyes follow you around you will at least have a sign that it has seen you; but consider the time just prior to your moving, when both of you were motionless but, you conjecture, the animal had seen you. Something must have happened to the creature for there to be a difference between seeing and not seeing, but what? The first inclination, to say that a mental event has occurred, would seem to lead nowhere, and by hypothesis nothing is to be gained from an appeal to what the animal can be observed to do. So what are we left with? Most obviously, no doubt, the possibility of some relevant physiological change in the animal, a change in its eye and/or that part of the brain associated therewith. And this does seem a possibility worth considering. Thus, I said above that we might well propose to identify the moment of seeing with the moment at which the visual stimulus starts to take effect, and this I took to be the moment at which the creature starts to respond. In many cases it may be that to all appearances these two moments coincide, but it must be allowed that the stimulus may take effect without actually giving rise to a behavioural response, since, without actually going so far as to initiate action, the stimulus may none the less affect or activate the creature's sense. And this, the organ's being activated, we might propose to equate with the creature's seeing.

Admittedly, it is only conjecture that the animal's eyes have been thus affected; but then it is only conjecture that the animal has seen, so there seems to be no likelihood of refutation on that score. Of course, although the object or feature which is sensed must have some effect on the organ, not just any effect will do. To take a different example, let us suppose we have a dog which is going around sniffing at things the way dogs do. That the dog is sniffing is apparent from casual observation, but that he has smelled something is likely to be no more than conjecture if no appropriate change can be noted in his behaviour. What, then, are we surmising has happened when we suppose the dog to have smelled something? The animal is not deviating from his course or otherwise altering the pattern of behaviour which he has been engaged upon since before the time at which, we wish to suggest, he smelled something. Since any evidence from this direction is ruled out the only hypothesis left would appear to be that the dog's olfactory organ has been stimulated by whatever it is he is supposed to have smelled. Once more, in order to speak of sensing it is not sufficient simply that the organ should have undergone *some* change; it must have been stimulated in such a way as to make certain kinds of discriminatory behaviour possible—those connected with location and identification, and, more generally, knowledge, in the way suggested in the last chapter. On this account it becomes possible, at least in principle, to isolate a condition of the organ which, in conjunction with factors which obtain on other occasions, leads to action of the appropriate kind, and such a condition could be identified on a particular occasion when no behaviour was forthcoming. The reason why the animal did nothing of the requisite kind on such an occasion would be, it is implied, not because its sense had not been activated, but the missing causal factors would have to do with something other than a deficiency at that point.

The attraction of the above account is twofold. It accommodates the difficult cases of perception without behaviour, and it paves the way for physicalism, making it a simple matter to pass from the ordinary conception of seeing to its scientific elaboration in terms of physiological states of the organism. The physicalist is not obliged to start by merely *correlating* with sight the physiological processes involved in it, but from the outset it is clear that it is sight itself he is investigating. It is, then, something of a pity that there is another account which is to be preferred, but that is the conclusion which, I believe, we are compelled to accept. In establishing that *x* saw *y* in those cases in which there was a behavioural response from *x*, the central condition was that the responses should have been brought about by *y*. To ensure that it really was a question of sight, and not the exercise of some other sense, we required that the animal use its eyes, but what was perhaps more fundamental was the requirement that a certain condition pertain to *y*, that it be in virtue of being illuminated that *y* bring about the response from *x*. This appeared to be more fundamental in that the very identification of an organ as an *eye* was dependent on ascertaining a response in conditions thus characterized, and it might even be suggested that seeing is conceivable without requiring that an organ of sight be involved; it is sufficient that we have the right responses in the right conditions, and perhaps the right conditions can be construed sufficiently generally so as not to make any essential reference to an eye.

Admittedly, it might in this event prove difficult to understand how y might elicit a response from x, but to grant that is not to grant that the necessity of an eye for sight be logical necessity.

It is not clear that we should, or that we should not allow the possibility of eyeless sight, in the event that circumstances should arise which called for a decision from us, but I do not believe that this is a particularly important matter to decide. What is important, and tells us far more about seeing, is the consideration that, supposing reference to an eye to be essential, there is none the less no requirement that the eye be affected or undergo any change whatsoever, where any such changes are to be understood in terms of what inspection of the eye might reveal to us. This is not to deny that the eye must be affected for sight to take place—or the brain; the organ of sight is to be construed here very broadly— but the *must* is not a logical *must*; our ordinary understanding of 'see' is such that the truth of 'x saw y' is not logically inconsistent with the finding that no change had taken place in the organism's eye. We are allowing that possession of an organ of sight is a logically necessary precondition for exercise of the sense of sight, but proof that the sense has been exercised does not in the first instance rest on discovery of some sort of physical change within the organ. I say 'in the first instance', since clearly such a change could come to serve as an index of the occurrence of perception, given that it had been found to co-occur with actual perception; it is just that it is not in terms of such changes that seeing is to be initially understood. More generally, even if we do not logically require an eye for sight, we should not regard changes at the physiological level as giving anything more than indirect proof of vision.

But now, if it is not in the mind, in behaviour, or in physiology that the creature's seeing is to be located, where is it to be found? We seem to have disallowed ourselves the use of any of the conceivable solutions, and to have reached a point where we are forced to say that 'see' simply does not signify any event at all—a position which, we shall see, Ryle approaches at times. However, the situation is not that black. What, primarily, the stimulus gives rise to is not an act or an occurrence, whether mental, behavioural or physiological, but a state, a state definable as an ability to do certain things; this, I suggest, is the key to the difficulties we have had to grapple with. The view just rejected chose as the appropriate effect of the visual stimulus certain physiological changes in the organism which could become instrumental in determining its responses; such changes certainly do take place, but all that our understanding of 'see' requires is a change in the organism's abilities: by virtue of the illumination of y, x has now become able to perform certain goal-directed actions with respect to y—those of the kind which we were at pains to characterize in the last chapter.

Confirmation of this solution can be found in a number of considerations. Most important, perhaps, is the recognition that any state lacking certain of the logical characteristics of an ability or capacity is disqualified from functioning as a state whose inception 'see' marks. Thus, to hold that suitably caused behaviour provides a logically adequate basis for an ascription of sight is to acknowledge that certain constraints are imposed upon the definition of any state which we might hope to introduce into an analysis of seeing. Any state which is required for the truth of 'x sees y' will have to be (i) capable of existing in the absence of behavioural responses, and (ii) logically implicit in any statement of conditions sufficient for the truth of 'x sees y'. Hence, if our description of suitably caused responses does not explicitly refer to a state, the notion of state which we come up with will have to be of a logical or grammatical kind, got, for instance, by rewriting the description in some way; not, certainly, by discovering or postulating an intervening physical or mental state of x which y gives rise to and which is causally related to seeing. It is clear that an ability satisfies this condition, since its existence is established by the occurrence of the appropriate responses, while if x does not respond that is no proof that it cannot see y, so long as y is still effective in bringing about the unexercised ability of x to act in a certain purposive way.

That a creature has an ability which has not yet been exercised is a matter which, if circumstances are favourable, can be put to the test, but that it had an unexercised ability at an earlier time is more difficult to establish. Given advance warning, we could conceivably have manipulated events so as to make the ability show itself at any given time, and this consideration might be taken as indicating that verification is only accidentally precluded—as in the earlier example of the ape and the bananas—but this observation does not make clear how we might tell or how we might have told when the ability was first acquired. To establish this it would seem that we must be able to make use of a correlation between cases where the ability actually has been exercised and some other condition which has been found to hold on such occasions. If, then, that condition is found to obtain it may be reasonable to assert that the ability is there, even if it is not currently exercised. This is where physiological conditions could have a part to play: we ascertain that x's eye and brain are in state S when it sees y, its seeing being proved by what it does, and, noting S on a later occasion, we make use of this correlation to affirm that x has seen y, even though now it does nothing. There is more to be added to this account, but it is an indirect connection of this type which shows the kind of relevance which the physiological data can have.

There are two reasons why I have made this use of the notion of an *ability:* by means of this we can make clear the logical character of the state signified by 'sees', and it readily applies to the form which an animal's knowledge takes. However, it is only because it has this latter connection that the notion has a place in the analysis of perception; first and foremost is the conception of seeing as involving the acquisition of *knowledge*. That this is so was indicated by the earlier argument that the kinds of response which give proof of vision are those which can be said to manifest knowledge, and it is no great leap from this to regarding 'see' as signifying the acquisition of such knowledge. With an animal this knowledge is to be conceived of in practical terms, as manifested only in behaviour, never receiving verbal expression, and this makes an accurate characterization of the knowledge particularly important. Thus, a given object of perception will be specifiable in a variety of ways: my grandfather's clock, his priceless heirloom, this antique, our largest item of furniture. We can readily speak of the cat as having seen my grandfather's clock, or indeed use any of the other descriptions which might be given of the clock without bringing about a change of truth-value. Here at least the context 'x sees y' is extensional. I claim, however, that this sentence-form can be rewritten in terms of *knowing*, and a natural enough way of expressing this part of the analysis is as 'x knows (by using its eyes) that y is there'—or, 'by using its eyes x has learned that y is there'. But, now, it might be argued that the use of a precise term for 'y' in such a context has implications of knowledge beyond what is involved in mere seeing, as is evidenced by the intentionality of the context 'x knows that y is there'; even if y and z are the same we cannot infer from this proposition that x knows that z is there.

However, this is not the formulation which I need give to the knowledge implied by a perceptual judgement, but what I wish to claim is that if x sees y then x knows of the presence of y, and this latter context is extensional. We can say indifferently that the cat knows of the presence of this clock or of this antique; in neither case need anything more than accuracy of reference concern us. It is perhaps elevating a mere suggestion into a logical implication to affirm the intentionality of 'x knows that y is there', but to the extent that this is likened to 'x knows that it is y that is there' or, still more explicitly, 'x knows that what is there is y', it is quite inappropriate for my purposes. That is not to say that it may not be true: the dog may know of the presence of his master, in this minimal way involved in his seeing his master, but he can also know that his master is there, in the sense of knowing that it is his master that is there. But this latter knowledge goes beyond what is required for the truth of the perceptual judgement.

The sentence-forms 'x knows that p' and 'x believes that p' are intimately connected with linguistic contexts; they are, after all, instances of the indirect speech construction, a construction which has its origins in direct speech, and it is not surprising to find that they allow only of an extended use in application to animals. I have shown that 'knows that' is not generally appropriate to present purposes, and it is worth mentioning how 'believes that' may be similarly out of place. Perception is commonly taken to involve belief, and it might be urged that it is this weaker notion that is to be invoked in any general account of perception. Thus, by using my eyes I acquire the belief that a cat is here in the room; this belief may not in fact amount to knowledge, since it could be that I was mistaken in taking what I saw to be a cat; but such knowledge is surely not necessary for perception.

In answer to this I wish to insist that it is only in so far as the erroneous belief points to or embodies knowledge that it can be taken to establish perception. To repeat, what is required on the part of the perceiver is knowledge, acquired in a certain way, of the presence of the object perceived. A man may know of the presence of the cat even if he does not know what it is, or even if he identifies it wrongly, and it is this notion, 'knowing of the presence of x', where choice of description in place of the variable has no bearing on truth-value, that I hold to be primary. Once more, we can make sense of the suggestion that an animal believes that a chair is there, but the analysis of perception does not require us to show how this locution can be extended to apply to animals.

With these clarifications one of our original questions, 'does seeing involve seeing *as*?', can be found to be answered. An affirmative reply requires us to make sense of the suggestion that an animal has some conception of what it sees, so that while it in fact saw y as a so-and-so, it might conceivably have seen it as a such-and-such. Our account of perception does not rule out this possibility altogether, but there is perhaps a weak sense in which the behaviour which gives proof of vision at the same time justifies a particular description of how the object was seen; if it is a matter of the creature walking around the object then this was seen by it as something in its way, it might be argued. This interpretation involves somewhat stretching the notion of *seeing as*, but any stronger claim stands no chance of being correct. There is no question of x's seeing a ϕ entailing x's seeing what it sees as a ϕ, and any position which requires an analysis of perception in terms of knowledge or belief, where the verbs 'know' and 'believe' govern intentional contexts, has to be rejected.

It is only too easy to read into an animal's or a baby's behaviour all manner of mentalistic suppositions whose sense is far from clear when they are dissociated from the adult human case. In particular, it is difficult to avoid doing just this when trying to make sense of perception in the absence of a behavioural response. As a check, then, on the kind of analysis which has been offered, we might consider how we should deal with a new or unfamiliar sense, and to this end I propose to consider very briefly the 'electric' sense, a faculty which is totally lacking in human beings and absent from all but a small number of other species.

There are certain fish which, by generating an electric field in the water around them, are enabled to detect prey, predators, and other objects which come into this field. Indeed, the slightest differences in the sizes of things may be discriminated by these creatures as a result of the distortions which the presence of an intruder induces in their electric field. (On the topic in general see H. W. Lissman,

'Electric Location by Fishes', *Scientific American*, Vol. 208, No. 3 (March 1963).) Corresponding to the verbs 'see' and 'hear' let us introduce the word 'electrocate' to indicate the exercise of this sense. Although we are quite without any personal experience of electrocation, this does not stand in the way of our laying down conditions under which we might speak of a fish as 'electrocating' something, but the real difficulties will be just like those which we encountered with 'see': we know in general terms what sort of behaviour is to give good evidence that the fish has electrocated an object in its vicinity; we know that to give proof of electrocation the fish's responses must be due to the object's effect on the fish's electric sense; what is difficult is the task of specifying precisely what occurrence is to be signified by 'electrocate'.

Once more we shall have to cope with (a) cases in which the fish responds immediately an object is placed within its electric field, and (b) cases in which the response comes, if at all, only after a period of time, even though there is no doubt that the object is within the range of the sense. (a) suggests relating 'electrocate' to the moment at which a behavioural response is elicited; we shall certainly want to say 'it has electrocated the squid' the moment we see it set off in pursuit of a squid which has strayed into its field— given that its ability to pursue is not due to the exercise of another sense. On the other hand, if, as in (b), the response is delayed, or if we wish to speak of electrocation in the total absence of a response, then we shall take the appropriate moment to be that at which the fish knows or learns of the presence of the intruder. This moment will no doubt be the same as that at which the fish's organ is initially affected, in such a way as to enable it to act in a certain fashion, but once more it is the state of knowledge or awareness rather than the physiological state of the organ that is to be introduced into the meaning of 'electrocate' if we are to take this to be on a par with 'see' and kindred perceptual verbs.

The account of perception which has gradually emerged can be considered a causal theory of perception. Not in any scientific sense: I have not been concerned to specify physical details of the causal processes which are the subject of the scientific study of perception; nor is the theory a causal theory in the sense that it traces a connection between the object perceived and a 'sense-datum' occurring at the end of the physical processes which the object is effective in producing. I have aimed at making explicit a certain assumption, causal in nature, which is implicit when we speak of an animal as perceiving something. What this assumption is can be indicated in two stages. First, I argued that the object perceived must be instrumental in bringing about the responses in which we are to find proof of vision. Such an account harmonizes with the stimulus-response framework in terms of which behaviourism is customarily understood, but from the outset a certain awkwardness was evident in this simple picture. The objection first mentioned was based on our own experience of perception, where it would seem that *we* rather than the object perceived had the role of initiating any response to the object; there is an unaccustomed shift of emphasis involved in elevating the object, usually conceived of so 'passively', to the status of cause, and not merely a condition which, given the other circumstances, was sufficient for the response. However, it seems that no more than a shift of emphasis is involved, and more important was the objection that any behavioural responses which the object might elicit seem to *follow* on sight; we come in on the phenomenon of seeing at too late a point if we pass straight from the object to the response which it induces. We do thereby, it is true, avoid coming to grief on any intermediate states, states which intervene between the time at which seeing first occurs and the time of any subsequent responses, but this very success means a failure to characterize what we are bent on isolating. This point is further reinforced by the possibility of sight without responses; that we can see without doing anything, without any behaviour which might show others that we see something, is only too familiar, and it would be rash to accept a theory which ruled out such a possibility from the outset, even if it is aimed at animals rather than men.

Accordingly, we were led to seek something which the creature's responses can be taken to establish, but which may come about at a time prior to the occurrence of the responses, and this we found in the state of knowledge or ability to act which exposure to the object brought about. Thus, although we can regard objects perceived as causal factors determining the animal's behaviour, certain other such factors are contributed by the creature itself. The animal is not, as it were, entirely at the mercy of the stimuli which impinge upon it, but it may have the ability to act or to refrain from acting when an object is presented to its senses. It may not act at the time, and we may surmise that it has not seen the object, y, but if its actions at a later point of time apparently manifest knowledge of y, and if these actions are traceable back to the original situation in which y was presented to it, then we may deem that it did see y on this earlier occasion when it did nothing. And, of course, if this can happen, if there can be any delay at all between seeing and responding, then it is conceivable that we should have sight without any subsequent response, since the animal could be prevented from exercising the ability which it has acquired, or not provided with an occasion on which it might manifest this knowledge.

When I speak of knowledge I do not have in mind some underlying hypothetical state which might bear a causal relation to the behaviour which is said to manifest it; this is clear from the consideration that I regard the attribution of knowledge as *entailed* by the characterization of the behaviour as 'appropriate', in the way explained—and given satisfaction of the other conditions mentioned. On the other hand, we can take the object perceived and the creature's knowledge of its presence to be causally related, and this is how, finally, I wish the causal relation to be understood: the object perceived is operative in bringing about the animal's knowledge of its presence. This gives a new twist to the causal relation, hitherto thought of primarily in terms of the object perceived and the responses which it occasioned, since it is now a matter of the object perceived bringing about a state rather than an episode. Clearly, however, the general account of perception which covers delayed as well as immediate responses, not to mention the absence of any response, favours a relation between object and knowledge as primary.

It is useful to set this account alongside another causal theory of perception, namely that of H. P. Grice in 'The Causal Theory of Perception' (*Proceedings of the Aristotelian Society*, Supp. Vol. 35 (1961)). Grice contends that if it looks to someone as if there is a so-and-so or if it seems to him that he perceives something, y, then provided this looking or seeming is causally dependent (in a way to be indicated by example) on some state of affairs involving y, we can infer deductively that he does in fact perceive y. One of the more obvious objections to this theory is one which shows, by contrast, the greater plausibility of the account in terms of knowledge. It is difficult to see how reference to the acquisition of knowledge could be omitted, but there is not at all the same need to speak of the production of sense-impressions. On the contrary, a man can surely see something without its seeming to him that he sees it or without its looking to him as if the thing is there, and when we turn to animal perception this point can be made even more emphatically. (It may seem to *us* that the man or the animal sees, but that is another matter.)

The interest of Grice's account lies in its specification of the kind of addition allegedly required to convert seeming to see into actual seeing, and although its presupposition of a situation in which it seems to the subject that it sees reduces its scope, if it is correct that the causal condition is all that is required in such a context, then it is a theory of considerable significance. After all, it would appear that *seeming to see* can be understood in terms which make no reference to sensations or sense-data as traditionally understood—perhaps in terms of an inclination to judge—and if it is in fact sufficient that it be understood in non-sensational terms, and that all that is required in addition is the appropriate causal condition, this obviously simplifies our picture of human perception. (Grice actually starts from the position according to which statements about sense-data are to be understood in this apparently less demanding sense. It is more interesting to refrain from making this equation at the outset and to start with the weaker sense, showing that it is sufficient and hence concluding that our understanding of *sense-data* must be expressible in terms which do not go beyond the 'seeming' locution.) However, even when an initial seeming is granted, the condition still lacking is not, I believe, causal in nature, but it is essentially the judgements of others that a man requires to support his own impression. If I am right, not only must Grice's account be rejected, but there can be no question of simply extending to human beings a version of the theory which we have advanced for animals. As will become apparent when the topic is eventually revisited, at several crucial points in the development of that theory totally different considerations would have had to be taken into account had we been concerned with human beings.

A rather different approach to *sense-data* will be implicit in the argument of chapter 8 and we shall also have more to say on the role of *seeming*. For the present, let us conclude discussion of the general topic with some observations on those causal theories, directed principally at human vision, which are inspired by the scientific account of perception. If charitably interpreted, there may be little to dispute in the claim that perception is a matter of certain physical and physiological processes resulting in the production of a sense-datum, but the facts which are held to be puzzling and the analogies which are customarily invoked in an attempt at clarification suggest that charity here is a misplaced virtue. For instance, there is surely nothing remarkable in the fact that inspection of the brain does not show nerve impulses from the eye to be at some stage unscrambled and converted into a pictorial likeness of the initial scene, and the flaws in the usual analogies—that of the telephone switchboard operator receiving messages from the outside world, or the analogy of the man watching the picture on his television set—have been exposed often enough: if we are puzzled about the notion of someone seeing what is before him, then we should be equally puzzled about how an inner man perceives the picture which his nervous system somehow places before his inner gaze.

It is tempting to dismiss the alleged problem as *totally* misconceived, and this is the step taken by Ryle in chapter 7 of *Dilemmas*, where he hopes to show that 'there is something which is drastically wrong with the whole programme of trying to schedule my seeing a tree either as a physiological or as a psychological end-stage of processes' (p. 101). 'It is not', he goes on, 'a question of my seeing the tree evading observation and experiment, but of its not being the sort of thing that can be found *or* missed in either the one place or the other.' The reason why Ryle's seeing a tree cannot be scheduled as a physiological or as a psychological end-stage of processes is simply that 'it is not a state or process at all'. It is, as we now know, an achievement, the 'scoring of an investigational success'.

I shall restrict myself to the following comments on this manœuvre. Ryle appears to assume that if 'see' is an achievement verb, or a terminus-verb, as he here describes it, there is no detectable (or undetectable) event which it signifies: seeing does not, he claims, constitute a phenomenon, and I take it that 'phenomenon' is to cover at least events, episodes, states and processes. Now we have seen that 'see' can be taken to mark the end of one state or the beginning of another, and it is appropriately styled a 'terminus-verb' when so used; we have also seen that it can be used with reference to an extended state, but we need not rely on this more devastating objection to Ryle's position. Considering it only as a terminus-verb, it is surely clear that this function is not incompatible with the verb's signifying an event or an occurrence; it does not in any way imply that seeing 'is not a phenomenon at all'. States and processes are not the only phenomena to which psychological verbs can refer, but as far as the status of 'see' as a terminus-verb is concerned, it would seem to be admirably suited to indicating a physiological or psychological end-stage of processes. It is surprising that Ryle should have held that such a status debarred it from this function; I can only suppose he assumed that the end-stage of a process was itself a state or process extended over time, i.e., that it correlated with a task rather than with an achievement verb. Of course, if the relevant end-stage is thought of as an instantaneous occurrence, then we have still to tackle the question whether 'see' marks the terminus of a physiological state, a psychological state, or what. But then that is just one way of formulating part of the problem which is our present concern. There is no question of its having somehow been spirited away by the recognition of special features of the verb 'see'. To repeat the earlier point: it is important to note that 'see' may be a terminus-verb, but this merely shifts interest to the question of the nature of the state whose terminus it signifies.

How then are the physiological facts to be accommodated in our understanding of perception? I shall not argue in detail for the position which I think should be put forward as a corrective to the misinterpretations of the physical data, but the main points to be made are these: in so far as there is room to speak of anything *mental* in perception, it is not to be thought of as an item which we might encounter on tracing the physiological happenings back far enough, and hence as something whose existence is disproved if it is not revealed by an inspection of the man's nervous system. Conversely, the causal chain which can be discovered in this way is not thereby shown to be incomplete; we do not have to suppose that at some point the sequence of causes passes into the unknown, into a realm of mental causes and effects whose existence defies detection and which bear problematic spatio-temporal connections with the physical. To satisfy this condition some kind of identity between seeing and certain physical events is required, and it is interesting to see how the

anti-realist, with his refusal to rest content with merely hypothetical causes, here comes close to the physicalist, with his
refusal to allow anything other than physical causes. In the sequel
we shall take some steps towards establishing their common
position on this question.

6

SENSATION AND BEHAVIOUR

So far we have concentrated almost exclusively on animal
perception, paying little attention to human perception and
disregarding both animal and human sensation. In this chapter
I shall set about making good this neglect, beginning with the
question whether animals can have—and be known to have—
sensations or feelings. We may introduce this topic by picking up
a theme of the preceding chapters concerning the significance of
the different kinds of response of which an animal is capable. It
would generally be rash to regard a single response as giving proof
of perception, even supposing there are no doubts about the way
it was caused, but for the more central cases we must look to
behaviour comprising sequences of movements, such as those of
an animal manipulating something, climbing a tree, alighting on a
fence, burying nuts, pursuing its prey, and so forth; activities in
which the animal modifies its behaviour to cope with the various
things which it encounters and which take place about it, activities
in which feedback has an important role and where there is a
question of the creature keeping something in view or otherwise
perceiving it over a period of time. A single response to a stimulus,
such as a sudden jump, in many cases goes better with sensation
than perception; at any event, it is clear from the earlier analysis
that the connection with perception could often be questioned:
such isolated responses as recoil movements and startled reactions
are not generally such that the notion of *manifesting knowledge*
finds a ready application to them, though there can be many
borderline cases. An animal starts at a noise. We say that it hears the
noise and we take hearing to be a form of perceiving, a way of
acquiring knowledge. On the other hand, if such responses were
the only responses which a given species made to sounds then we
should come to think of their relevant organ somewhat differently;
it would not contribute to knowledge of the animal's surroundings
in the way it does at present, and so could not be considered an

organ of sense perception. (Recall the remarks on such a response as barking. Given the dog's capacities, we can consider its bark as proving that it has detected something, but if that were the only kind of response which the relevant 'sense' enabled it to make we should hardly regard it as manifesting knowledge.)

If the behaviour prompted by a stimulus is merely a reaction away from the stimulus, as a withdrawal on contact with a sharp object, it is natural enough to speak of sensation. Natural enough, but if that is to imply the adequacy of a behaviourist account of animal sensation, opposition is only to be expected, and I propose now to set forth some of the arguments on either side of this question. One fruitful objection against the possibility of the behaviourist's enterprise can be developed by going back to the topic of perception and considering how we might have introduced the notion of *awareness* into our analysis. A preoccupation with human awareness has doubtless been the source of the belief that the notion will prove resistant to any form of analysis congenial to the behaviourist, but this presumption begins to look far less plausible when we confront it with the sort of example in which we unhesitatingly attribute awareness to an animal on the basis of what we observe it to do. For instance, it is clear enough what we go on when we say that the cat is aware of the piece of string which I am dangling in front of it: the cat follows the string with its eyes and is otherwise responsive to its movements, chasing it about, grabbing at it, and so forth. Awareness is not, of course, connected merely with sight, but when suitably qualified to indicate the relevant sense the notion can be used to provide a close definition of various of the perceptual verbs; 'become aware' signifies the initiation of a state, and corresponds to the terminus use of 'see', 'hear' and 'feel'; 'be aware' signifies being in the state thus initiated, and goes with the use of such verbs with respect to a state which can endure over a period of time: 'x saw y at six o'clock'—'x became aware of y at six o'clock'; 'x saw y for ten minutes'—'x was aware of y for ten minutes'.

In support of the claim that it is a decidable and frequently straightforward question whether an animal is aware of something, we might appeal to instances of awareness in human beings where attribution of the state equally presupposes little that cannot be readily ascertained. Thus, the cases in which we speak of a person as being aware of something fall into two classes. On the one hand, there are those occasions when we give our full attention to an object, sound, smell, or other sensible phenomenon, taking note of its features, examining it closely, all the while with our minds on what we are doing. Such cases, which often merge into instances of self-awareness—we think not merely of the phenomenon but of ourselves as experiencing it—tend to be favoured by philosophers, and of course they are real enough. But they do not represent the only possibility. Suppose, for instance, I am walking up a familiar flight of stairs. I do not stumble, I keep to the middle of the stair-case and generally regulate my movements as one who can see the stairs perfectly clearly. In one sense, we are inclined to say, I may be quite unaware of the stairs; certainly, with my thoughts elsewhere I do not notice features of my surroundings which my movements show me to have taken into account, and I should not report that I had been aware of these features. However, it may also be true that my eyes were instrumental in guiding me, in allowing me to ascertain height, distance, direction, position, and so on and, this being so, we wish to say that there is a sense in which I was aware of the stairs, and therewith a sense in which I could be said to have seen them.

There are complexities here—what is to be put down to memory, what to perception?—but it appears there are many instances where we show by our behaviour that we are aware of something, where the sense of 'aware' is such that the behaviour gives *proof* of awareness, not merely evidence on the strength of which it might be conjectured to occur; we may be quite absorbed in other matters and totally oblivious of the responses which we are making and which, despite perhaps our subsequent denials, another person rightly regards as establishing our aware-ness. The more reflective form of awareness appears to be bound up with thought and language, so cannot be attributed to animals, but the awareness which is shown in appropriate behavioural responses is certainly not confined to human beings, but is commonplace among lesser creatures as well. (The two forms are interestingly discussed, with particular reference to associated physiological phenomena, by D. C. Dennett in his *Content and Consciousness* (1969).)

We have, then, two forms of awareness which have application to human beings, either of which can be sufficient to justify an ascription of sight or the exercise of some other sense, and one of which can be extended to animals as well. However, can we claim that the situation is similar when we turn to sensation? Is it possible to specify logically adequate behavioural grounds for the attribution of a sensation to an animal? In this instance the behavioural form of awareness may seem just not to the point, and, accordingly, the account which would most obviously satisfy the anti-realist appears unavailable. Let us elaborate on this difficulty.

It is possible to think of instances of apparent sensation which bear some analogy to the example of perception without full awareness. For instance, we notice a man scratching himself, and we can perhaps detect the source of irritation—an insect-bite, a rough edge to his cuff—so we assume that he feels an itch. However, even if it proves warranted, this *is* an assumption. The man could have all his attention on some other matter and be quite unaware of any sensation in the relevant area, or even that he is scratching himself. There is an analogy here with the perceptual example, but whereas there we could regard the behaviour as establishing perception, it appears that we have no use of 'feeling an itch' which can be justified solely on the basis of behaviour (together with causal assumptions). There may be nothing lacking in this respect, but the relevant difference would appear to be an 'internal' difference; the subject suddenly becomes aware of the itch, but this change is not one which others can necessarily or indeed ever with certainty detect in his behaviour. A person can of course tell us of the sensations which he has and of which we are otherwise ignorant, but doesn't that suggest that animals too could tell us of sensations they have and which never show themselves in behaviour, if only they had the words to communicate them to us?

The argument is not developing in a way which can give much solace to the anti-realist, so we might retrace our steps a little and consider whether it really is impossible to make sense of the suggestion that a person might have a sensation without being aware that he has it. For instance, could it not be true to say that my headache persists even if for a time I become unaware of it? It is true that the notion of persisting unfelt goes ill with anything describable as a 'feeling', but certain common experiences do favour the picture of inattention to a continuing phenomenon—e.g., occasions when we are momentarily distracted—so it might be contended that we have a choice as to how to describe the phenomenon: either we say that the headache stopped for a time and then started anew, thus making its being felt a necessary condition for its existence, or we allow that it can persist even when we have no awareness of it.

Supposing we do allow this choice, the interesting question which arises is that of determining the sense of 'persisting without our being aware of it'. There is a curious tendency to think of unconscious thoughts, desires, and so forth, as like their conscious counterparts but for this one fact, the fact that the subject is unaware of them; as though there were something with a clear identity which occurred in either guise, with awareness or un-awareness marking an inessential difference. We need not go along with this misconception, but then it is not immediately obvious how we are to understand the suggestion that a headache might persist for a time during which one was unaware of it, if this is to mean something other than that it was there until a certain point of time and was there again when you had ceased to be distracted by other things which claimed your attention. To make something more of the assertion, should we link continuation of the headache to continuation of an associated physical state? Only to the extent, it would seem, that we could regard the presence of the state as supporting a conditional of the form 'if the subject had not been distracted, then he would have continued to feel his headache'. (Compare our treatment of the physiological data on the issue of sight in the absence of behaviour.) After all, it is not imagined that there was a headache there to be experienced, like a sound to be heard, and it would involve a radical change in the sense of 'ache' to somehow equate it with any physiological occurrences or states, to allow that we might, by opening up a man's head, be able to identify something located there as an 'unexperienced ache'.

In view of these considerations it is surely more appropriate to take the conditional, or some more general version along the same lines, as giving the sense of the original statement, a statement for which physiological data might provide evidence. In this way we do not do the same violence to our ordinary notion of an *ache*. But, once more, there is little here to encourage the anti-realist. Thus, the aim of this discussion has been to examine the possi-bility of speaking of sensation in the absence of awareness that one was experiencing the sensation, and so to find a model on which our understanding of animal sensation might be based. However, we have not found a way of speaking which does have application to the animal case, as might come about if talk of sensations could on occasions reduce to talk of physiological states, but in so far as we have any use for the notion of an unfelt sensation it would appear to be best construed in terms of what one would have experienced had the conditions been otherwise: if there is no independent physiological (or other) identification of an ache, the only alternative is that the assertion of an unfelt ache should relate to conditions in which it would have come into existence, rather than conditions in which it, an already existing phenomenon, would have been experienced. Given that, even in the most favourable case, no such interpretation is appropriate, there would seem to be little hope of making sense of sensation terms as applied to animals in anything like the straightforward way which was possible with perception.

The above doubts are reinforced by the circumstance that even the non-philosopher is frequently puzzled about whether certain creatures can be said to have feelings, whether insects feel pain, for instance, and the conclusion which appears to draw ever nearer is that they may or they may not, but we cannot ever really tell. However, there is another side to the question. First, I think it is more accurate to represent the non-philosopher's puzzlement as arising within the animal realm, rather than as marking off animals from men. It is surely not a general bewilderment which affects all our judgements concerning animals (and infants), but there are occasions a-plenty when there is no question of any real doubt, however difficult it may be to provide our confidence with a rational backing. No one will contest that babies suffer from teething troubles, that they feel it when you pinch them, that they get thirsty, hungry, sore, chafed, too hot, too cold, and so on; if anything, we might suppose them more sensitive than we to such afflictions. Again, if the cat lets out a shriek and speeds away when I jab it with a needle or pour boiling water over it, there is no doubt about the propriety of saying that it *felt* the jab or the boiling water. As ever, mistake is possible: the cat could in fact be anaesthetized but fitted with a device in its brain which someone might activate to call forth the relevant behaviour at the appropriate time. However, as with seeing, the counter-examples which can be devised seem only to call for a more careful specification of the causal conditions, and with that problem settled there seems to be no room for doubt, no need to postulate an undetectable feeling in order to vindicate one's description.

But we cannot leave the matter there. In the first place, to the example of the cat it will be objected that the feeling involved need not be an extended state, and so comparable with sensation, but feeling in a terminus sense, signifying an unextended episode, the detecting of the needle or the water. There is no call for scepticism about the cat's sensitivity in this regard, but have we any need of the hypothesis of an 'extended' sensation? In time, presumably, we shall be able to trace out the causal connections which lead from the jab to the cat's rapid departure; such an account will allow us to introduce talk of detection— as a redescription, not as a hypothesis—but reference in addition to a sensation felt would seem to contribute nothing: against the full physiological account which can be supposed to be available one day, any sensation we might postulate would appear to be superfluous. Again, although it must be granted that a baby or animal can be said to *be* hungry or hot, it may be questioned whether they can be said to *feel* hungry or hot. Perhaps there is simply not the appropriate form of consciousness for us to be able to speak in any literal sense of feelings or sensations when we consider the animal world.

The anti-realist will go along with these observations at least to the extent of agreeing that feelings cannot be held to be irremediably hypothetical, whether as temporally extended states or as unextended occurrences. This much we know from his general position. If it can actually be maintained that we have no occasion to speak of *feelings* here at all, or at least not in any problematic sense, then this too is a possibility which he can readily accept. However, this latter claim is not obviously correct. It is true that we often do have a preference for speaking in terms of *being* rather than *feeling*, and one reason for this preference becomes apparent when we consider the distinction which is associated with the use of one rather than the other in the human case. The extent to which a person can be said to merely feel so-and-so, e.g. tired, as opposed to actually being so-and-so, may depend on what he says rather than—indeed, in the face of—what he does or the physical condition he is in. The possibility of a difference between a man's condition as revealed to our observation and as reported by him enables us to suppose that a man not only feels, but really is tired, whereas with an animal it would appear that the second possibility is all we have; at any event, that 'feels' adds nothing to what is asserted by 'is'.

There is much to this account, and much of importance, but not enough, unfortunately, to allow us to dismiss the problem. First, I do not think it is true that we have no room for the distinction as applied to animals; it is just that in this instance the appropriate interpretation is not so obvious. Second, the account given bears primarily on the use of 'feels' coupled with an adjective; its use with a following noun, or the use of 'feeling' as a noun, presents different issues. (There is, we may note, the consideration that 'feeling a pain' goes better with short-lived pains than does 'being in pain'.) Finally, and most importantly, there is the fact that we certainly do make use of various locutions, such as 'to be in pain', which present a problem for the anti-realist even if it is a mistake to suppose that other phrases present him with the same problem.

A point which I think is valid and which bears on the interpretation of the language of sensations as applied to animals is the following. We are inclined to judge the problem facing the anti-realist as insurmountable because an uncritical anthropomorphism leads us to read into the notion of pain a possibility which makes sense only with respect to creatures endowed with language. In the human case this possibility does not give rise to the same difficulty, since in explicitly recognizing the power of speech in men we thereby provide not only the problem but the materials for its solution: it is ultimately because men have language that we can attach a sense to their having states of consciousness of which we can learn other than by considering their behaviour. With animals, however, we implicitly incorporate that much of what goes with language to make for the problem while denying their actual possession of language, and so denying what makes for the solution. This claim will become clearer when we are in a position to draw the appropriate contrasts between men and animals in greater detail. For the present I shall content myself with arguments, pointing in the same direction, which prepare the way by attacking the analogy in terms of which it was proposed to elucidate animal awareness.

The example of a man successfully manoeuvring obstacles in a way which required the use of his senses, but with his mind far removed from his surroundings, seemed to provide us with an appropriate analogy for animal perception. And, with regard to an animal which is ostensibly scratching an itch there is, we might say, only as much of a sensation as there is when a man is observed to scratch himself while his mind is wholly directed elsewhere; he was aware of an itch at a previous time and will perhaps feel it again, but for the moment he is so engrossed in what he is doing or witnessing that he feels nothing.

These are not the models on which animal perception and sensation are to be understood. What happens when we consider this question is, I suspect, that we put ourselves in the position of the animal and specify conditions which for us, beings capable of thought, constitute sight or feeling without the full degree of awareness of which we are capable. Not only that, but we may even imagine ourselves as trying and failing to become aware— and what kind of a sensation could it be that allowed of such a failure? A much better picture is to imagine ourselves as totally immersed in the experience, mesmerized by an object, say, or our whole body tensing from a severe pain but with no recollection of the experience, however close to the time we have it. No recollection means, as we make the time interval ever shorter, no thoughts at all, but that does not mean thoughts elsewhere. Our attention is completely taken up by the object or the pain.

We are inclined to contrast the animal phenomena with human instances which typically, if not invariably, involve a capacity for thought: we think of the consciousness which we have but which animals lack as one involving attention, absorption, concentration, and the like, understood as peculiarly human states. The contrast should really be *within* such categories as these, between uses of 'attention', say, as it applies to men and its use of animals; not between its use of men and its total non-use of animals. It is not that we can attend to something there before us while the dog cannot. We both attend, but this may not involve the same for the dog as it does for the man. However, this does not mean that the dog does not give the object his *full* attention. He may be totally absorbed in the object in view or in the sound of approaching footsteps, totally 'single-minded' in his concentration on the movements of the creature which he is stalking. The 'mindless' animal is not to be thought of on the model of a 'minded' being with its mind elsewhere: it is only a distracted animal that is like a distracted man. Or, to the extent that we can say that the animal has a mind, to that extent we are going to have to say that it has its mind on what it sees or feels, and for this we shall want a contrast where the dog is, like a man, distracted from his sensation or from his concentration on something he sees. And this too makes sense. We can divert a baby or an animal from its suffering or discomfort, and we can imagine cases where, just as we say that the soldier may not feel the pain from his injuries in the heat of battle, so the dog may be so excited that he forgets the pain which has been disturbing him.

Again, the appropriate analogy is not with a man who is asleep or semi-conscious. Such a person—e.g., a sleepwalker—may be able to see and to respond to other features of his environment, and it need not be true to say that his mind is elsewhere, since he may have no thoughts at all. But although this comparison does not involve the previous disanalogy, it fails to do justice to the (assumed) fact that the dog is alert, responsive, and in full possession of his faculties.

Destruction of these false analogies removes one obstacle to an understanding of what is involved in attributing sensations to animals, to the extent that we have occasion to do so, and leads to a rejection of the claim that thought and language are necessary to sensation. This is in harmony with our unreflective views—we surely suppose that children feel pain from the beginning, not just when they acquire language—but it still does not give us an answer to our most vexing question, namely: just what is pain if its ascription can be said to have a logically adequate basis in behavioural, physiological, or other verifiable data? We can say that a dog has received a painful blow if as a result of being struck he whines and howls with some persistence and keeps clear of the person or thing which caused the injury. But where is the pain in all this? One thing is clear. We do not arrive at an attribution of pain, whether to man or beast, by identifying something as a sensation; there is nothing we can point to as *the pain*, nothing to be located in the creature's physiological states or in its behaviour. I said above that there was no need to postulate an undetectable feeling to vindicate one's description of the cat as feeling a jab or the boiling water, but the absence of such a need is not due to the feeling's being *detectable*. Whether the feeling be an instantaneous occurrence or extended over time, it could never be that our justification in speaking of its existence lay in our having seen, touched, or otherwise observed it. On the other hand, this is surely no bar to finding out that the dog is in pain, even, perhaps, that it has a pain in this particular part of his body. We can point to the place where the pain is, even if we cannot point to the pain.

In order to speak of an animal as being in pain, then, I claim there is no need to identify pains either with observable or with un-observable states of the animal, and this holds even if the state of the animal which entitles us to say that it is in pain is construed sufficiently widely to embrace all the underlying nervous activity, the firing of C-fibres, the excitation of nerves which lead to convulsive or recoil movements, or anything else detectable that might be deemed relevant. If you wish to identify the creature's pain with some state of its nervous system, then that is another step you are taking beyond the position here outlined. Thus the physicalist might maintain that pains are essentially physiological phenomena, possibly presenting a different aspect to the creature which experiences them from that aspect which we can detect, but not in such a sense that they could not be identified with certain processes of a physical kind taking place within the animal—and that is why a pain is no more than such a process, even though the identity is not to be disclosed to us by consideration of the sense of the word 'pain'.

I am not so much concerned at the moment to refute this variety of physicalism, but what I am claiming is that there is no necessity to extract the word 'pain' from 'being in pain' or 'having a pain' and to assign some state or process to it as its reference. (Compare the repudiation of the misguided behaviourist's attempt to identify wanting and knowing with items of animal behaviour.) *A fortiori*, it need be no part of my position that 'pain' be construed as signify-ing some form of nervous activity which presents one side to us, another side to the animal in whose body it occurs. Even if such an identification is in some sense possible, it plays no part in our characterization of a creature as being in pain or as having a pain. To be in pain is to be in a certain state, and to say accurately *what* that state is—i.e., what must be true of the creature for it to be in pain—is no easy matter. However, it is not a condition of a correct analysis that it find room for a conception of pain as an object of both inner and outer perception, the former going with

its immaterial aspect, the latter with its character as a physiological state of the animal.

Any account of animal sensations which would require them to
be possible objects of observation by us is clearly untenable. On
the other hand, it would be equally mistaken to see in this fact
a basis for a distinction here between what can be and what we can
come to know. It would be wrong, that is, to allege that observation of the pain would be the only way we might come to know of
its occurrence, and, since such observation is denied us, to allege
that we just cannot find out for sure that a creature is in pain.
We could accept the possibility of facts here which consideration
of the animal's behaviour and physiology might fail to put us into
a position to appreciate if we could allow that there was something
which at least the animal knew. However, the difference between
being the subject of a sensation and being a mere observer of that
subject is not a difference which brings such a possibility with it.
The difference between being the one whose body is in a certain
state and one who observes a body in that state is a relevant
difference if we are speaking only of human beings, since the former
condition may then not be separable from the knowledge that one
is in the state in question. If the subject is an animal, on the other
hand, we surely cannot introduce such a contrast. I verify the
occurrence of various states of the animal, but without my body
being in any way similarly affected; we may say that the suffering
animal has something which I do not have, but that does not mean
that there is a fact of which, since it is not my body that is afflicted,
I must remain for ever ignorant: it is only if it brings with it
unsharable knowledge that the animal's condition, or the distinction between being subject and being observer, can give any
support to the possibility of scepticism.

The prospects for a satisfactory anti-realist account of animal
sensation did not appear promising at the outset, and even now
the account sketched is perhaps counter-intuitive, for it seems to
be a common enough belief that, in the last analysis, we have no
more than an argument by analogy upon which to base our ascriptions of pain to an animal, the analogy entering at the level of *proof*
rather than, as here, description of the state of being in pain.
With this view goes the objection, plausible on other grounds as
well, that the account given can find no room for pains and other

sensations as *causes*. I claim that behaviour and observable conditions generally can be definitive of being in pain in the animal case, but this runs counter to the natural conception of the relevant behaviour as the *effect* of the painful sensation, since if pains are to have such a role they must of course be distinct from whatever it is they cause.

In answering this objection we may note that there can be some doubt about many examples which seem at first sight to support it. If I ask why the dog is writhing the reply might be 'because he is in pain', but this form of words need imply nothing more than the equally natural 'he is in pain'. To answer either way is to attempt to explain the creature's behaviour by giving a more general description under which it falls, just as, if asked why a man is behaving in a certain way, I may say 'he is in love', explaining his action by citing the more complex pattern of which it is a part. In neither case, given the way in which the behaviour is partially constitutive of the state, is it possible to see the explanation as causal. On the other hand, if the behaviour is not to be viewed in this way, then, to the extent that we have occasion to offer a causal explanation of the behaviour in terms referring to the creature's pain, it can be provided for on the account given: there appears to be nothing which the animal's distressed state, say, will not explain but which its pain will. What is more difficult is finding a plausible instance of this alternative, for if we say that a man acted in a certain way because he was in pain it is generally a matter of his being in pain giving him a *reason* for acting, and this notion has no ready application to animals. (As another example of the contrast we may take the explanation '(because) I am tired' offered in answer to the questions 'why are you yawning?' and 'why are you going to bed?'. Being tired does not give one a reason for yawning; on the other hand, going to bed is in no sense constitutive of being tired. I do not wish to say that it is only the constitutive case that has application to animals, but this is generally so, and where it is not the account which construes the behaviour as cause seems to me to be adequate.)

However, it may still be felt that I have not really got to grips with 'the pain caused the behaviour'. Surely it can be said that the creature's pain caused it to recoil? Haven't we just been avoiding such a case? Let us approach this via the human analogue. Suppose I touch something very hot and immediately withdraw my hand.

You ask me why I did this and I say 'because of the pain which I felt'. Now we could make sense of the suggestion that I felt a pain and decided accordingly to remove my hand from what was causing it. This would be an example of the pain's giving me a reason for acting, but if the withdrawal takes place almost as soon as I touch the hot object this is hardly likely to be the correct account. The pain did not cause me to withdraw my hand in the sense that I acted on the reason for doing so which the sensation provided. How else then might the pain cause me to act? We assume that there must be some other way, but on reflection this assumption begins to look gratuitous. Indeed, in examples of this kind we may well find that the withdrawal is under way a split-second before the pain is experienced; the stimulus, broadly construed, gives rise to both sensation and recoil, the sensation itself does not cause anything. We have, then, the following important dichotomy: either the pain provides a reason for action or the only cause is physiological. I do not intend these as exclusive, but only that there is not another possibility; accordingly not, in the animal case, the possibility which was advanced as still unaccounted for.

The possibility of giving an adequate causal account of certain of a man's responses in purely physical and physiological terms might be thought to compete with our everyday beliefs, but such beliefs require only the possibility of explanations in terms of reasons, as far as I can determine, or failing this just *some* causal account, which may well prove to be physiological. It is only certain philosophical positions that suffer. Notably, we have that approach to the other minds problem from which the objection proceeded, the approach which would require us to *postulate* mental phenomena, to introduce them as part of an explanatory hypothesis to be appealed to in accounting for observed behaviour, but there is another position which is likewise threatened, namely, that variety of physicalism which takes as its starting-point a characterization of the mental in terms of whatever it is among the states of the person that brings about certain kinds of behaviour, the hope being that we shall eventually be able to identify this with some physiological cause.

The first of these views founders in the face of the adequacy of a purely physiological account of the relevant responses, since if such an account really is adequate there is nothing left for the hypothesis of pains as causes to contribute—as could easily have been foreseen:

if it is only as hypothetical constructs that sensations can be introduced there is always the risk that an alternative hypothesis will
prove superior, and, as in the present case, that the point will be
reached when we shall have no need of any hypothesis at all.
Since it is just such an account that the physicalist wishes to see
carried through successfully, he need not be troubled by this
conclusion—although he ought to be concerned on more general
grounds if he has no independent means of introducing reference
to sensations. Furthermore, if we are right in refusing to allow the
relevant causal role to sensations, then the neutral characterization
of mental states which he wishes to fill in with physiological
detail misses its target. However, it is only the crudest form of
physicalism that is vulnerable in this way.

Our discusion of animal sensation is not at an end, but for the
moment we shall leave the topic and shift our attention to the
peculiarly human form of awareness which appears so far removed
from any animal capacity. Let us go back to the contrast between
the man whose mind is and the man whose mind is not on his
surroundings. In both cases, I claimed, if it really is a matter of his
using his eyes to find his way around, then we are entitled to speak
of *seeing*, and by the same token, of *awareness*: the fact that the
man's thoughts are elsewhere does not prevent him from showing
his awareness of an obstacle in his path by walking around it;
perhaps we can say that he was not *fully* aware of it, but not that he
was not aware of it at all. What, then, is lacking in such a case?
In what does this 'higher' awareness consist?

One answer which comes readily to mind is that *self-awareness*
is involved: I am aware not just of what I perceive but of myself as
perceiving it; I may even have the impression of standing apart
from myself, observing myself engaged in my current experiences.
As already indicated, self-awareness may well enter into the kind
of experience which we are trying to characterize, but it does not
seem to be sufficiently prominent in the less reflective examples of
fully conscious perception in which we are constantly engaged. Is
it then a matter of an awareness which involves thought? Certainly,
without a capacity for thought such awareness would appear to
be impossible, and it seems that it is only because it lacks this
capacity that an animal is prevented from enjoying this state. But
what thoughts? It is surely possible for us not merely to be engaged

in thought—like the preoccupied man—but even to have our thoughts occasioned by what we see and yet not have the awareness in question.

Both of these answers are near the mark, but they do not define the essential difference between the two forms of awareness. The difference is, I believe, simply between being aware of the object seen and being aware of seeing it—to take just the example of sight—which in this context comes to: being aware *that* one sees it. If this is accepted, it is slightly misleading to represent the difference as between two kinds of awareness of one and the same thing, since what the subject is aware of in the one case is different from what he is aware of in the other, though it is true that the man who is aware of seeing *y* is at the same time aware of *y*. Both forms of awareness can be understood in terms of knowledge: awareness of the object is knowledge of its presence and awareness of seeing *y* is knowledge thereof, or knowledge that one sees *y*. Thus, to the extent that we can elicit some response from the man about what he saw, to that extent he demonstrates his 'second-level' awareness, however vague, of having seen, and shows that he did not *merely* see, that his awareness was not confined to the objects presented to his senses.

To think of the difference in terms of self-awareness is not incorrect, but it suggests an emphasis where none need be present: the lower-level awareness is merely awareness of the object, something of which an animal is perfectly capable, whereas at the higher level we have awareness of our seeing, which is a matter of awareness that *we* see; the subject thus finds a way into the characterization of the awareness, but this need not mean that appreciation of *oneself* as seeing need be to the fore. The characterization given also explains the connection of second-level awareness with language, and hence with thought. After all, how could awareness *that one saw y*, as opposed to simple awareness of *y*, show itself in a creature lacking language? The animal's awareness of *y* can reveal itself in many ways, but if we deny it the use of language it would seem that anything which we might propose as showing that it was aware of seeing *y* would simply reduce to an instance of awareness of *y* itself. But, of course, this consideration does not make language, or thought, anything more than a necessary condition for second-level awareness.

When, as philosophers, we think of seeing, we naturally take an instance of second-level awareness and not merely awareness of the object seen. Understandably, we then have difficulties imagining how it is that animals can see, and we might even come to doubt that they can really be said to perceive at all. Even with human beings it is easy to exaggerate the extent to which one's consciousness is involved in perception. It may be that my exposure to a scene has resulted in certain physiological changes within me, and it may be that on a subsequent occasion my experience will be different as a result of my having seen what I now see—when confronted again with the same scene I have an impression of familiarity, for instance. This, however, is not to be located among my experiences of the moment, but it may be that my observed responses are all that occur of relevance to the question of whether or not I have seen; that I, like everyone else, am forced to rely on the evidence of my behaviour in order to decide the matter and there is nothing which I can contribute by virtue of being the one who saw. It is of course only natural that we should generally be prepared to date our seeing only from the first moment that we are aware that we see; by hypothesis, any form of awareness which preceded this moment would not be something of which we knew—or, at least, not something of which we knew without investigation—but this does not mean that there was not a form of awareness prior to this moment which was sufficient for perception. (Compare the natural belief that we are, when awake, always thinking about something or other, never with our minds a total blank. If our minds were a blank then this would not be something of which we could ever know by dint of being aware of this circumstance at the time.)

I remarked above that the introduction of self-awareness into an analysis of second-level awareness suggests a misplaced emphasis, but, as we shall soon see, it may involve worse than that. The contrast between being aware of the cat and being aware of seeing the cat can be described as a matter of an awareness of two 'different things'. This is acceptable if the intention is to oppose the view that we have here two different forms of awareness of the same thing, but the difference between the respective 'things' is so great that it should not be allowed to pass unrecorded. What I am aware of when I see the cat is a species of physical object, something of which I become aware through its being presented to my sense of sight; when I am aware of seeing the cat it is not as if the cat's place is taken by a new object, my seeing of the cat, only now to fall within the gaze of an inner sense. I am aware *that* I see; no more than this is involved in my being aware of my seeing, and here there is no object of awareness, even, it could be argued, in a grammatical sense.

The last point is neither clear nor non-controversial when clarified, but I shall not explore it further since I am only offering it as an analogy for a more important consideration. We invite confusion if we think of the two forms of awareness as awareness of different 'objects'; similarly, I claim, we go wrong if we think of second-level awareness as involving something like first-level awareness of a self. I may have first-level awareness of a person, in that I may see, hear and touch someone, and I may equally have such awareness of myself. This is the awareness I have when I am aware of myself walking, eating or singing; in such cases I am aware of my body and what it is doing; it is an awareness dependent on perception and one which others may have. (There are cases here where our knowledge is perhaps not based on observation, but so long as there are cases in which it is, that is all I require.) On the other hand, when we are aware of (ourselves as) seeing, hearing, or thinking about something, this reference to a body will surely vanish; certainly, to be thus aware does not require us to be aware of our body.

First-level awareness relates to a body, a person, in a straightforward way, but when we move to second-level awareness we are tempted to base this on the model of the first level: there is no physical body to be the object of awareness here, so we introduce an *immaterial* self as what we encounter in self-awareness. However, this step is unwarranted. I can watch or observe myself much as I might watch or observe another, and all this requires is that I identify a body. Nor does self-awareness end there, but it enters into such experiences as being aware of oneself seeing and thinking; this is to be aware that I see or that I am thinking, and such awareness does not require that I identify a body. But, of course, the absence of any such identification does not mean the identification of a non-physical subject. There is no call to elevate the negative condition, 'non-identification of a body', to the positive condition, 'identification of a non-body'. (For a similar argument see chapter 3 of Sydney Shoemaker's *Self-Knowledge and Self-Identity* (1963).) On the other hand, it would also be fallacious to infer from this that no non-physical subject existed, for all that has been established, along with the invalidity of the inference, is the inappropriateness of terms such as 'identity' and 'observe' with reference to the subject involved in self-awareness. Consider the more familiar parallel in the context of sensation. One who asserts that he is in pain does not base his avowal on observation of his behaviour or any physiological states of his body. Nor, on the other hand, is he obliged to observe non-behavioural or non-physiological phenomena. But all we are entitled to infer here is that 'observe' has no part to play in this context, not that nothing non-physical or non-behavioural is involved in being in pain.

A minimal specification of the knowledge acquired in seeing is as knowledge of the presence of the thing seen, but for both men and animals the range of information extracted by use of the eyes will frequently be far in excess of this minimum: by directing my gaze to the person before me I learn that she is blonde, pretty, of medium height, looks foreign, is seated, and so forth. Much of this knowledge is manifested in what I say rather than in what I do, and sometimes it goes no further than the thoughts which I have and which I keep to myself. I have mentioned the tendency to make an immediate association of seeing with second-level awareness in such a way as to cast doubt on the very possibility of animal perception, and it is likewise natural to conceive of the knowledge acquired in perception as a matter of thoughts prompted by what is seen. And likewise uncalled for, if it is to be a matter of the acquisition constitutive of perception on a given occasion, and if thinking is to be understood in terms of 'occurrent' thought, as when we say something to ourselves in a more or less articulate fashion. Here we risk committing an error comparable to that involved in locating seeing somewhere in the animal's responses; just as there is nothing in the animal's behaviour which can be thus identified, so the situation is no better if we take the responses to be the thoughts which the object elicits rather than the bodily movements brought about. Generally, such thoughts will occur against the background of an accomplished perception, and it will be only by accident that the moment of seeing and the moment of thinking coincide.

However, thinking and seeing can be drawn closer together if we adopt a more liberal test for the occurrence of a thought at a particular time: it is not necessary that I should have as much as said inwardly the words which I subsequently utter in reporting my thought, but it is sufficient that I be disposed to utter these words for it to be the case that I did have that thought, or that I should agree with a statement in those terms as a formulation of what I thought. So you ask, 'did you think there was a cat in front of you when you turned on the light?', and I say sincerely 'yes'; that may be what I thought the moment the light went on, the first moment that I saw, even if I did not make the thought explicit to myself. However, it is important to remember that whatever significance the thought has in this context it has only through expressing the knowledge required for perception; we may have the knowledge without the thought, and the thought as stated need not exhaust the knowledge.

There is a perceptual term worth mentioning here which has close ties with both 'thought' and 'seeing', namely, the more specific 'notice'. A person may have seen the cutlery which he is using to eat with—the ease with which he locates his knife and fork and the skill with which he manipulates them may testify to that—but the awareness which he has of the cutlery may not be sufficiently sharp or well defined for it to be the case that he has noticed it; no feature of the cutlery has struck him, prompted any reflection from him or otherwise intruded upon the sequence of his thoughts, but he has learned of its presence and what it is, and that is all. The more specific character of 'notice' shows itself in our unwillingness to say that we noticed something, even though we are prepared to say that we must have seen it. I ask you whether you noticed the doorknob or the doormat as you arrived; you may confidently reply that you did not, but at the same time be reluctant to affirm that you saw neither; on the contrary, you may well agree that you can hardly not have seen them. Similarly, I may see every word on a page, but notice only one or two of them, words which for some reason catch my attention, and I can even see something quite plainly without noticing its colour.

Incidentally, it should not be inferred from these remarks that 'notice' has no application to animals: we hope to escape the lion's gaze, but unfortunately he does notice us and immediately comes heading our way. We could say of an animal that it had seen but not noticed something if the sight led to action only on a later occasion: no sign of seeing when face to face with the object, but subsequent recognitional behaviour. Compare this with the phenomenon of subliminal perception, where nothing is noticed at the time but the man's subsequent behaviour shows that he did see something; the words flashed momentarily on the screen register visually with us, but not in such a way that we can speak of noticing them. Here, we may also note, there is no second-level awareness: I see but without knowing that I see. However, although they are generally co-extensive, noticing and being aware that one sees can part company, as is evident from, among others, the example of the lion.

Although I may not formulate any thoughts explicitly to myself on seeing an object, I shall be able to say various things about it, and it is in terms of this extended ability, not simply the ability to act, that we are to think of the knowledge acquired. Of course, an ability to *say* is not just an ability to mouth certain words which happen to be correct, it is an ability to say *authoritatively*, a matter of being in a position to say how things are; where, indeed, it is in part one's words which determine how things are. And when, we may ask, can an ability to say enjoy this status? With sensation it is no more than a matter of being the one affected and having a command of the relevant language, but with perception more is involved; it is analogous—though no more than analogous—to our original question concerning the responses which are to give proof of sight, where with animals we were to trace a causal connection between the object perceived and the possession of the ability. We might suppose that in this instance the matter is complicated by the possibility of rash responses, judgements occasioned by the presence of the object in conditions of illumination, but where the object was not in full view or where in some other way too many possibilities were left open for the man's conjecture to count as knowledge. However, this is to lose sight of the knowledge which is central, if our concern is merely with the broader question whether or not x has seen y. It does not matter what the man takes what he sees to be, or whether or not he judges hastily; his judgements are of interest in so far as his awareness of the object shows through any misconceptions as to its nature which his words betray. The possibility which does arise, and which will exercise us later, is that the man should be insincere; this, rather than rashness, sets an obstacle in the way of finding out what he knows, and hence what he has seen. On the other hand, a man's particular judgements may be of special interest as regards the question whether he is aware that he sees something, and I shall now take up again the question how this awareness is to be recognized.

Must we grant the possibility of second-level awareness as soon as we allow that a creature is capable of linguistic responses? In the extreme case, the answer to this is surely negative. We might train a parrot to say 'red' whenever confronted by something red, but I do not think we should wish to attach any more significance to this isolated ability than we should to the occurrence of some physiological reaction which was brought about when and only when something red was presented to the bird. Certainly, there is not enough in this performance for us to be able to say that the parrot knows that it sees something. If, on the other hand, an adult is in a position to say of something 'this is red', then we can say without further ado that he can see something red, and if we can say that, then he surely does or at least can know that he sees something red. Why are such simple steps to be denied the parrot?

It should be mentioned here that there is more than one point at which we might draw a line between the various degrees of consciousness, actual and possible. For instance, we might make a division according to which the child with only a rudimentary grasp of language was grouped along with the linguistically sophisticated adult, each being contrasted with the animal. In characterizing higher-level awareness in the way chosen I have been drawing attention to a more extreme contrast, but without denying the existence of intermediate cases, and by way of approaching the question just raised I wish to consider one such case, that of a child at an early stage of his linguistic development.

A child has occasion to identify and describe things as they fall within his experience, but this is an ability which can exist without his having a conception of things falling outside his experience, things judged to be so-and-so by others. As far as the child is concerned, a thing's being red is just a matter of its being red for him, of his taking it to be so—and conversely; similarly, he makes no distinction between something's tasting sweet and its tasting sweet to him; the only world is his world, and that is all the world. I do not mean that there is a possibility which we acknowledge but which the child rejects. Neither alternative is one which he can as yet even contemplate, let alone decide upon. What, essentially, I wish to suggest is this: a distinction between *there being a φ* and *his perceiving a φ* requires a recognition of the possibility of other subjects of experience, and with this recognition can come the possibility of using 'I see . . .'—or the version with his own name— to mark a contrast which is not marked by 'there is . . .'; even though what licenses the child to assert the latter may be such as to justify his assertion of the former, if the child lacks a grasp of the concepts involved in 'I see . . .' he cannot be said to have that knowledge which second-level awareness requires.

The child's concept of himself might develop in terms of two contrasts, that between himself and the inanimate world, and that between himself and other people. It is the implications of the latter that interest us. Thus, his understanding of the concept of himself as a subject of perception may be seen to develop in his use not only of 'I' or his name as subject but in his recognition of other subjects—'does Daddy see?', and so forth. However, when he does come to exercise this concept in such a context as 'I see the cat', this does not require him to make an identification which he failed to make when he was still at the stage of merely describing the object which he saw. From a stage in which, without making any reference to himself as an observer, he merely lists the contents of a room which he surveys, he can make a transition to the stage where he speaks of himself as seeing these things, without making use of an ability to identify himself on these occasions.

It is, then, not just with language that the awareness which I have singled out as peculiar to human beings is attained; or, more accurately, possession of language is not logically sufficient below a certain level. It could be that in practice the requisite competence was in evidence at the very beginning of a child's mastery of language, and that the stages described here bore no resemblance to actual development. All I wish to maintain is the logical possibility that a child or an animal should be capable of giving verbal expression to the knowledge which it has of what it sees without having any appreciation of itself as a subject of perception, so without the knowledge that it sees.

It is of considerable interest to develop the preceding argument further with regard to questions concerning the nature of persons and personal identity, but for our purposes we have come far enough in that direction, our aim having been to extend the discussion of human perception and to prepare the way for a more detailed examination of human sensation which might be set beside the account of animal sensation presented. This latter account has been, broadly speaking, behaviouristic, but it is more usefully considered in the more general terms mentioned in passing. There is something to know, so something of which we might be ignorant, only if there is something which some being, whether man or beast, might know. From this, supposing that animal knowledge of the relevant kind can be ruled out, a behaviourist account follows, if it is indicated as the only possibility which confines animal sensation to the realm of what is humanly knowable. Admittedly, the general thesis is perhaps as much an assumption of the argument as a conclusion which can be extracted from it, but it seems reasonable to hold that the arguments put forward, taken with the difficulty we have in making sense of any alternative, give strong support to this central tenet of anti-realism.

7

SENSATION AND KNOWLEDGE

VERIFICATIONIST theories of meaning maintain that we cannot give an intelligible account of the meaning of psychological predicates unless it is possible to find out whether their ascription to others is correct in a given case, or at least in favourable cases, and in this chapter I shall try to elucidate the forms of definition of certain of the relevant predicates with a view to ascertaining how their ascriptions connect with verifiable conditions. The preceding chapters have taken this subject a certain way, and with regard to animals it seems that the anti-realist has met with some success, but we have barely broached the question in relation to human beings, and in particular the traditionally central topic of human sensation has yet to be explored. And here, it must be said, the problems look formidable for the anti-realist. Thus, when I report a pain my words cannot come into conflict with the findings of others. The knowledge which they have of my behaviour and the state of my body may make them doubt my truthfulness, but they cannot be in a position to contradict me, for however comprehensive the data they have, it is never more than evidence. As the possibilities of proof and disproof diminish, so the problem of meaning becomes more acute: the absence of publicly ascertainable conditions which might decide the matter as far as others are concerned seems to mean the absence of conditions in terms of which 'pain' may be defined to the satisfaction of the anti-realist. If we decide to rest content with this situation we are likely to find ourselves vulnerable to some form of 'private language' argument, while any move away from this uncomfortable position seems likely, if followed through consistently, to bring us to a form of behaviourism—a prospect which is hardly more inviting.

The most popular middle way between these alternatives is one which at first sight enables us to avoid any reduction of sensations

to observable phenomena without going to the extreme of divorc-
ing sensations entirely from their outward manifestations. I have
in mind here the suggestion that pains, itches, tickles, and so forth,
are to be defined by reference to the circumstances in which they
typically occur, but are not to be identified with such circumstances—where 'circumstances' covers behaviour, physical states,
causal conditions, and any other relevant observable features of the
situation. For instance, itches and tickles are produced in certain
specific ways and give rise to certain specific forms of behaviour,
and we need consider no more than these surroundings in seeking
the conditions which are to be formulated in our definitions. Note
that we throw away all the advantages of this approach—perhaps
even contradicting ourselves—if we hold that the sensation is to
be defined as the *accompaniment* of certain behaviour and so forth,
but not in such a way that sameness of circumstances makes for
sameness of sensations. To say that, as judged by the circumstances of their occurrence, the sensations which are troubling us
are to be described as 'itches', but perhaps in reality our individual sensations are altogether different from each other, is to
suppose that we have some further means of comparing sensations. Of course, agreement at the general level of 'itch' leaves
room for disagreement in other respects, but at each level our
understanding of sameness and difference—as far as it exists—is,
on this account, to be spelled out in terms of such public criteria;
we do not have a further understanding which, because it is not
subject to such tests, results in conjectures which must remain
eternally speculative. I say 'as far as it exists', since I do not in
fact believe that we have much use for a terminology and associated criteria in terms of which we might compare sensations in any
detail. The point is rather that, if we do envisage a comparison in
which finer distinctions might be brought into play, then, on the
more plausible interpretation of the account, it requires to be
fitted into this framework of public criteria if it is to make sense in
the familiar way.

However, even without this unnecessary distortion the approach
meets with difficulties. Most obviously, there is the circumstance
that psychological predicates have a tendency to recur in the
definitions of the prescribed form. These I take to be represented
by such sentence-frames as 'an x is what you feel when . . .', or
'an x is the sensation which . . .', but if we say, for instance, that a

tickle is a sensation which makes you want to laugh, we have in 'want' an occurrence of the very sort of term which we are trying to define, and it is not clear how we are to break this circle. Further, there is the problem of giving an illuminating re-phrasal of the general schemata such as 'what you feel when . . .' on which the particular definitions rely so heavily, and until this has been dealt with there is a broad existence question which is left unanswered. *If* I feel a sensation when you run a feather over my skin, and if as a result of this I want to laugh, then there *may* be no denying that what I felt was a tickle. Similarly, a more general characterization may enable us to complete the definition of a *feeling* as 'what you experience when . . .', but at some point we shall surely stop, left with the general notion of an experience or a state of consciousness, and with no alternative but a definition in behavioural terms if we are to stay within the framework of the definitions recommended, or at least a definition in terms of observable conditions of some sort.

In the form which I have given it, the approach just presented ascribes no particular role to the language associated with the experiencing of a sensation. A man's utterances may be reckoned amongst his behaviour, and this the account can allow, but there has been no suggestion that they contribute anything which distinguishes them from the rest of what he does. And this neglect of language may seem only right. After all, if a man's avowal is not superfluous, i.e., does not simply duplicate knowledge which the observable circumstances may furnish, then it would seem impossible to carry through the programme of definition to the end, and if it is superfluous then we are unable to avoid a behaviourist reduction. Either way, the reference to language appears to offer no real advance.

Of the two alternatives, the second—that a man's behaviour should render his avowal of experience superfluous—appears the less plausible: not all our pains disturb us to the point that it shows in any way, or have causes of which we have any knowledge, but even the total absence of any such clues is of no account when held against a man's honest word as to what he feels. On the other hand, the remaining possibility has its own share of difficulties. If we have *just* the man's avowal, quite divorced from attendant circumstances, then it seems we are without any guide as to how it should be understood; there is no accompanying reality which determines any interpretation for us. It is no good introducing a reference to the man's experience in this regard, since we rely on his word for any knowledge which we might have of this; there is no independent way of getting to know what he feels, and so of checking the truth of his report.

But there is another possibility. We run into difficulties if, concentrating on the man's utterance as an assertion, as something which may be true or false, we see the problem as one of confirming what is asserted. Perhaps, then, it is a mistake to look to anything, behaviour or whatever, as bearing out what the man asserts, but we should instead consider his words as in some sense *constitutive* of the state whose existence we are trying to verify: the words give proof of the state, not by giving an accurate report upon it, but because the state in question can be characterized as a propensity to utter certain words. We need not deny that what the man says can be capable of truth or falsity, but we are to think of his words as, in the first instance, adding to any other data which behaviour and so forth might provide, not as a comment on the latter, but as an item which, possibly in conjunction with these, defines a more complex state by being a part of it. That, roughly indicated, would appear to be the direction which the argument must take if we are not to come to grief on one or other of the two more obvious alternatives.

Our general question is one of how language is to be fitted into an account of sensations and mental phenomena properly so-called. At first sight, it seems obvious enough why language is so important; how, after all, could we know what a man was thinking or feeling if he lacked the words to tell us? If we conceive of the role of language in this way we may even suppose that animals too could have thoughts, say, only be unable, through lacking words, to tell us of them. However, on the account which I propose to follow up, this is not how language is to be regarded. It is not that, but for language, there would be no means of knowing what another was thinking or feeling, or that he was feeling or thinking; rather, without language there would be nothing for us *to* know, apart from what we could learn of by observation.

The theme which has now been introduced will be developed with respect to perception, sensation and thought, and the case with which I begin is that of taste, a sense which has so far been ignored. You give me something to taste and I judge it sweet; not meaning to imply anything about how others will find it, but just stating how it tastes to me. It is perhaps conceivable that I should be able to advance reasons of some sort for my description of the taste in these terms, but there appears to be no room for saying that I base my judgement on signs or evidence of the thing's tasting sweet to me, as before tasting it I might be presented with signs or evidence, based on its appearance, that it *would* taste sweet. Further, if something tastes sweet to me then I know that it tastes sweet to me; its tasting sweet is not something which might be manifested in some other way so that I could, by observing my behaviour, or by some other equally indirect method, come to the same conclusion. There is a possible contrast here with tasting unpleasant. While unconscious I might conceivably pull all sorts of faces on being fed some evil-tasting medicine, and you could perhaps use this display to give sense to the suggestion that it tasted unpleasant to me, even though I was not aware that I was tasting anything. No such association with behaviour appears to arise with sweetness, but anything we might think of here, apart from verbal behaviour, is likely to have to do with sweet things being liked or disliked, and not essentially with their character as sweet. Thus, we can say of an animal that it can taste sweet things, that it likes or dislikes sweet things, even that it can discriminate sweet-tasting things from others, but to speak in these ways does not seem to be to go so far as to say that certain things taste sweet to it.

Whether we like or dislike sweet things is accidental to their being sweet, as far as our understanding of 'sweet' is concerned. Some people do and some do not, and a given person may change in this respect. Nor does there appear to be any other behavioural disposition which is associated with sweetness sufficiently closely for it to enter into a definition, as, it might be alleged, a tendency to avoidance-behaviour is associated with 'pain', for instance, or a propensity to scratch is associated with an itch. Indeed, there is no trait or family of traits exhibited by all sweet-tasting substances which our understanding of 'sweet' enables us to cite; we expect there will be something which they have in common, but there need not be, even viewed scientifically, and if there is it certainly has no bearing on the meaning of the word.

I have suggested that it is impossible that something should taste sweet to someone without his knowing it, but it might be wondered whether this really is so. After all, I can recognize a variety of tastes prior to having names for them; surely it cannot be said of me that I do not experience these tastes until I learn the words for them? Certainly, it is not to be denied that you taste something in such cases; the question is: *how* does it taste to you? If you can indirectly identify it as sweet—'that taste which sugar has'—then perhaps that is as good as having said explicitly that it was sweet, but if your description is only at the level of, say, 'familiar', 'strange', 'sickly' or 'pleasant', I still believe it would be incorrect to say that it tasted sweet to you; to say that it did is surely to say that that is how you were inclined to judge it, and the supposition is that you have no such inclination. It would be like saying that it tastes like sugar to you, when you are quite unable to make the comparison. In either case you will be able to make a number of observations about the taste, but these observations may well not amount to an identification of the right feature, a making of the right comparison with other cases, whether implicit, as with 'sweet', or explicit, as with 'like sugar'.

If the argument to date is correct, the only feature analytically connected with something's tasting sweet is a disposition to say that it tastes sweet, and if this is so then we find ourselves defining the word in terms of itself, in terms of a disposition to use that very word—either that, or there is nothing at all associated with the use of the word by reference to which it may be interpreted. We might seek to dispel any impression of incoherence here by the observation that it is not as if we were offering a definition of *tasting sweet* which called for an understanding of 'sweet' as it occurred in the definiens, where it occurs just as an uninterpreted vocable, but doubts are likely to persist. If it is true that the only essential mark of y's tasting sweet to x is provided by x's preparedness to say that it does, then the same could be said to hold for other taste terms as well—for 'bitter' and 'sour', say. (There is some justification for saying that a certain 'face' goes with these tastes, and this would mark a difference with 'sweet', but there are many other examples available if these prove unsuitable—e.g., the taste of butter and the taste of peanuts.) But now, since there is nothing to be found in the respective situations which correlates in any essential way with a man's utterance of 'y tastes sweet to me' and 'y tastes bitter to me', it is difficult to see how we might account for the difference in meaning between the two; all we appear to have is a difference in the words *qua* sounds, and we could hardly extract the difference in meaning from this, let alone determine what each meant. It is not that we cannot allow the possibility of a proposition which is true when and only when a person is prepared to assert it; it is just that in the present context it is difficult to envisage the possibility of there being *two* such propositions.

But this may all seem a fuss about nothing. After all, we do associate more than *x*'s words with the situation in which it is true to say that something tastes sweet to him; it is clearly necessary that he should taste the substance in question, and his judgement does not guarantee that he has done so. There is this connection, it is true, but it is one which holds equally for judgements of sweetness and judgements of bitterness, so it is of no help if the problem is one of distinguishing such judgements. So let us try the following. I suggested that the only feature analytically connected with something's tasting sweet is a disposition to say that it tastes sweet, but this must be construed as meaning more than just a disposition to describe the thing in terms of 'sweet' or some synonymous expression; 'saying that *y* tastes sweet' must be so understood that, for instance, the assertion '*y* has the taste of sugar' satisfies this description. An indirect specification of the taste must be allowed, and this enables us to link 'sweet' to certain kinds of substance, 'bitter' to others, and in this way the distinctive identity of each term is preserved and accounted for.

But now we may question the significance of this connection. It is true that each of 'sweet' and 'bitter' is correlated with its own specific class of substances, but the disposition to use one of these words takes priority to the extent that it is only by reference to the disposition that membership in the class is determined; there is no independent way of identifying the relevant substances. More importantly, the intelligible use of 'sweet' does not require any standard class of sweet-tasting things. It could be there was nothing which enjoyed the role which sugar has in this regard, nothing which always or even generally tasted sweet, but that would be of no consequence provided that by and large people would agree in their judgement of things as sweet at a given time.

So where does this leave us? We started with the observation that something cannot taste sweet to someone without his knowing it. From this it follows that a disposition to describe something as sweet is necessary if it is to be true that that thing tastes sweet to the person, and since such a disposition appears to be all that is required, it seems we are left without suitable non-linguistic conditions in terms of which we might understand 'sweet'. If we cannot specify a difference in the circumstances associated with the use of 'sweet' and 'bitter' respectively, it would seem we cannot distinguish these words on anything but the trivial difference of their sounds. But what more is called for? The words have their distinct identity because we, the speakers of the language, refuse the one on those occasions when we are disposed to use the other. It is true that the occasions on which we are disposed to describe something as 'sweet' may be known to us only as occasions when we are thus disposed, but there is no possibility, let alone necessity, that we should be able to give reasons for a judgement in every case, or that we should be able to specify evidence on which our judgement is based, so no necessity that we should be able to give a more informative characterization of these occasions.

To take another illustration of this point: on the evidence of a tickling sensation which I have I say there is an insect crawling on my back, but there is nothing that I similarly regard as a sign of or evidence for the sensation itself, and if asked how I know that I am having the sensation I cannot answer. It will not do to say 'from the experience', if, as is natural, it is held that the experience comes only with the knowledge that one is having the sensation; knowledge which is a necessary condition for the very existence of an experience cannot be subsequent to that experience, but what we are called upon to determine—and of which we are likely to be ignorant—are causal antecedents of the knowledge which are below the level of thought and experience. Again, if asked to explain why I say that one whistle sounds louder or higher in pitch than another, I can only say 'it just does, that's all'; I can give no reason for this judgement, in the sense of a ground on which I base it, but the best I can do is to speculate about how my learning and physiology may have contributed to the formation of this judgement, how I come to be able to say what I say.

And so too with sweetness. We reach the point where there are only causal conditions to be sought between y and our disposition to judge y sweet; further investigation at this point may well yield information about other features common to substances which we at present group together only as giving rise to this disposition, but the coherence of our talk about tastes can survive a failure to find anything common at this level. The connection pertaining to the meaning and truth of the individual's (unqualified) judgements is not with anything else in his behaviour or in independently observable features of the object tasted, but what is crucial is the making of the same comparisons, the agreement in judgements between him and others. Since this means agreement in our responses to the same things, it is not a question of the language's occurring in total isolation from non-linguistic conditions. The intelligibility of 'sweet' requires such agreement, but once the usage has been established we can readily allow an individual's judgement on a given occasion to diverge from the judgement of others, so that without implying a change in the meaning of 'sweet' we can say that that is how y tastes to him, if to no one else.

The question whether x sees y and the question whether y tastes sweet to x are at opposite extremes: sight connects with knowledge which is readily manifested in behaviour, and this circumstance enables us to make sense of seeing without knowing that one sees, whereas the knowledge expressed in a judgement of sweetness is not associated with any characteristic behaviour, so that when the ability to make such a judgement is absent we do not know what to make of the suggestion that something tastes sweet to a creature. This is not to say that we are entitled to rule out altogether the possibility of giving some sort of sense to the suggestion that, say, sugar tastes sweet to a cat. We might find behaviour of a distinctive kind associated with tasting sweet things, behaviour which could be deemed to manifest knowledge of their sweetness. It must also be noted that the contrast intended is not between sight and taste, but between sight and tasting sweet; it could equally have been a contrast *within* sight, since we could have considered 'looks red' in place of 'tastes sweet'. Here again we should have had the same argument: a man may know how something looks to him in that it looks an unusual colour, say, but even if it is a red object that looks thus it does not follow that it looks red to him; and, once more, it is the agreement in judgements, not some connection between the word and either behaviour or other features of red objects, that is behind the intelligibility of 'red'.

We can see but not know that we see, but if something tastes sweet to us then its tasting sweet to us is something of which we must be aware. The concept of *pain* is both difficult and interesting because of the conflicting tendencies we have to locate it now towards one of these extremes, now towards the other. This conflict is reflected, I suspect, in our uncertainty as to how animals should be regarded: on the one hand, they display the appropriate pain-reactions in response to injuries which undoubtedly cause pain to us, and it seems that we can at least say that they dislike and avoid things and situations which produce such injuries; on the other hand, it may be held—giving a sharper formulation to an earlier point—that words such as 'pain' and 'sensation' go only with second-level knowledge; so given that an animal lacks the knowledge that it is in pain, perhaps it is only in an extended sense that it can be said to be in pain at all.

What makes for the difference with sweetness is the greater plausibility of making a definitional connection between being in pain and having a disposition to act in a certain way, a connection which allows talk about animals being in pain to get a grip, whereas there is not, as things stand, any animal behaviour which makes it appropriate to speak of certain things as tasting sweet to them. On the other hand, the connection with behaviour is perhaps not so tight that we cannot allow an alternative which places being in pain closer to something's tasting sweet to a person. If we think of pains primarily as sensations which are brought about in certain specific ways, or at least regard conditions relating to the production of the sensation as in some cases sufficient for the identification of it as a pain, then we can separate pain from dislike and a propensity to behave in a certain way. Pains are on this account only accidentally disliked, even if this is the commonest reaction. With this separation comes the difficulty, if not impossibility, of making sense of the notion of being in pain without knowing it, and the justification of a refusal to allow that animals can be in pain. If, on the other hand, the connection with dislike is emphasized to the point that a pain which is not disliked is just not a pain, we shall have a conception of pain which allows of application to animals far more readily. It will not be the case that if one is in pain one thereby knows that one is in pain, but being in pain will be a state which can be manifested behaviourally, and which can occur without the subject's knowledge.

In fact there is, as we shall now see, some difficulty in establishing a definitional connection between being in pain and being disposed to act in certain ways. Consider first the question of how we might characterize the notion of an *itch*. There appears to be a straightforward enough connection between having an itch and having a desire or a propensity to scratch; what kind of an itch would it be that did not make one want to scratch? However, could it not be that we have to learn that scratching an itch leads to its alleviation, or to a modification of the sensation which we find more tolerable? On this account a man could conceivably experience an itch, find it disturbing, but not have any desire to scratch it. Similarly, if pains could always be stopped or diminished simply by pressing the body at the point where the pain was felt, it would be natural to think of the inclination to respond in this way as definitive of pain, when in reality it would seem to constitute a rather accidental accompaniment of being in pain.

A pain is a sensation which one wants to stop, to be without— on one plausible interpretation of the notion—but such a want can exist in the absence of an ability to do anything to alleviate it or bring it to an end. Accordingly, it would be a mistake to introduce into a definition of 'pain' reference to a propensity to act in a way requiring some degree of intelligence. On the other hand, if we consider the involuntary reactions which we might take to be in some way integral to feeling pain, e.g., recoiling and screaming, we find that, as regards the character of the sensation, these too seem inessential. Not only need they not occur, but one might conceivably find oneself recoiling, even screaming, yet these be reactions induced by a powerful but non-painful stimulus. What then of the notion of a sensation which one dislikes, or a sensation which one wants to stop? I implied that we might reject the characterization of a sensation in terms of a desire to do certain things where the doing of these things called for knowledge of a means to an end, since it would seem that the relevant sensations could occur in the absence of any such knowledge and any such desire. However, we have already encountered the notion of a want which makes no such demands: a pain could be a sensation which one wanted to stop or wanted stopped, where this is so understood that cessation of the creature's distress on cessation of the sensation is sufficient to establish that this is what it wanted. On this interpretation the difficulty which arises with animals is the difficulty of giving sense to the notion of having a feeling or a sensation; once the propriety of this is established it would appear that no further problem is presented by the specific differentia *painful*. And, since it is difficult to see how one might make a distinction between cessation of the creature's sensation and cessation of its distress, we might propose to interpret being in pain in terms of being in a distressed state, together with certain conditions relating to the way in which that state was brought about.

That the notion of a distressed state requires supplementation by some further condition is clear enough, and more generally we can say that not every sensation that is unpleasant, that one dislikes or wants to stop, is painful. How, then, considering primarily the human case, is the necessary differentia to be defined? One possibility which must be faced is that we should find ourselves totally unable to give any informative account of what makes for the difference, if this is understood in terms of marks of sensations which we go by in judging them painful, and not merely unpleasant or disliked. Perhaps we can give no reason for our different judgements, but only proffer the useless information that one has the property of being painful and the other lacks this property. In such a case the factors which determine our response will be factors of which we know nothing, and this in turn suggests the possibility of a dissociation of judgements of pain from any essential public criteria. When I say that I am in pain I do not do so on the basis of any injury which I note and which may lead you to conjecture that I am in pain; I am trained to say that something hurts in certain circumstances, we may agree, but these circumstances are not such that I must recognize that they hold in order to say I am in pain, but they may obtain only a neural level— perhaps underlying any act of recognition, but not being *what* I recognize. This will explain why I can report a pain even when there is no apparent cause of the pain, no injury to the flesh; since no appeal is made to observable criteria when I complain of a pain in those cases where injury is evident, there is nothing puzzling in the possibility of reporting a pain when such criteria are altogether lacking.

One reaction to this is to object that the possibility of teaching the word 'pain' requires some correspondence of verbal responses with behaviour or other circumstances at a level higher than the micro-level of neural states, and a reaction in turn to this is to claim that we must accept the phenomena as they are, however difficult they make the teaching situation appear: perhaps all we have essentially is people's linguistic behaviour, without any further connection which need in general be evident. The first response risks involvement with the familiar irrelevancies concerning teaching, but it does appear to be more plausible than the uncritical rejoinder. To see where the truth lies let us return to a point which emerged in the discussion of sweetness.

We found that the understanding which we have of judgements of taste required agreement in such judgements; it was not necessary that there be a particular class of sweet-tasting things, constant paradigms of sweetness, but so long as people's judgements at a given time were more or less in agreement no problem arose. The alternative to this did not necessarily mean total unintelligibility; if different people divided things according to taste each in their own individual way it might still be possible to detect enough of a pattern in an individual's responses to be able to say that certain things tasted the same to him, but given the lack of agreement overall we could not identify our 'sweet' and 'bitter' among the words of these people. Again, the agreement underlying the use of colour words is agreement in response to a common object of perception, and something similar holds for pain: burns, cuts and blows are almost universally described as painful. Once again it is not necessary that it should be such phenomena that give rise to pain reports, nor that any phenomena should typically have such an effect, and it is even conceivable that there should be enormous differences from person to person, so that fire was no more generally avoided than water, say, though if we contemplate this possibility we must look for our constancies in another direction, linking the words with a more or less uniform disposition to act in a certain way, for instance.

In the present context we are not concerned with the more general notion of a sensation which one dislikes or finds unpleasant, but we are to consider how a distinction might be introduced within this broader genus to circumscribe the notion of pain more precisely. Behaviour is likely to be the same in either case, whether the sensation is painful or merely unpleasant, like an electric shock or a feeling of nausea; the interesting possibility is whether we could allow the absence of any correlation between linguistic responses and other known features of the situation, and the difficulty with this hypothesis is that it appears to divorce avowals of pain from any accompaning reality in terms of which they might be understood by an observer. Once more, however, we are simply looking in the wrong direction if we try to define the required regularities in terms of an association between people's avowals of pain and the presence of further observable features of the situations in which they are uttered. There is a regularity, a connection between a given man's utterances and something other than his utterances, but it is a connection with the utterances of others; provided there is a constancy of response, provided we do concur in calling the same things painful, there is a foundation for the distinction between what is and what is not correctly described thus, even though we may not have the remotest idea what it is that accounts for a differential treatment of the various situations.

We started off with a crude picture according to which sensations are to be defined in terms of accompanying behaviour and/or observable conditions generally. Unfortunately, it may be that the only feature which is common to the situations in which the sensation occurs is, as far as anything we know is concerned, the sensation itself, so it seems we shall be hard-pressed to produce the desired correlation in such a case. However, the argument which has been developing suggests that it is a mistake to insist upon a correspondence of the kind envisaged; the individual's word is to have 'observable' connections beyond itself, but these are of a rather indirect kind: it is a question of his linguistic responses agreeing, by and large, with those of others, not of an agreement with further features of the situation, on a par with, for instance, a man's gloomy words and the downcast expression on his face, or a man's complaint of the cold and his presence in an icy pond. Of course, the agreement in question is agreement *in the same situation*, so there is at this point an extra-linguistic connection. Furthermore, there can be a non-contingent tie-up between the having of a certain sensation and the propensity to act or react in a certain way. However, the *same situation* is identified by means of words, as too is any relevant behaviour, so the regularities are all in the last analysis a matter of a connection between words and words.

I shall return to this sweeping and seemingly extraordinary claim at a later stage, and I shall also fill in a gap in the argument by considering more thoroughly the case of sensation in the absence of relevant observable conditions. Now I wish to turn to an unexamined assumption which might be held to vitiate the argument to date, namely, that we can meaningfully speak of a person as *knowing* that he is having a certain sensation. Allowing for the sake of argument that we may speak of a creature, even a man, as being in pain without knowing that it or he is in pain, there is still an incongruity in the assertion 'I know that I am in pain'. The source of this incongruity is not difficult to identify: if we have to do with an assertion, not just a sequence of sounds, then 'I know' tells us nothing we could not infer from the rest of the statement; that the subject knows he is in pain is evident from this remainder. But, of course, this explanation depends on the meaningfulness of saying that the person knows that he is in pain, so if this is being questioned along with the first-person utterance, a further argument is called for. First, however, it would seem that even the first-person utterance can have a point, as when one utters in exasperation, 'Of course I know I am in pain—that is hardly something that could escape me', and the possibility of its having such a point is surely derivative from its making sense merely as an assertion which can be true or false. At all events, when one says 'I know that I am in pain', emphasizing perhaps 'I', 'know' or 'pain', there is an obvious enough general contrast, namely that with ignorance, which gives point to the assertion.

This contrast might be made explicit in two ways. First, we could be implying that if one is in pain then one *ipso facto* knows one is in pain, in which case the remark can be taken as a reminder that being in pain is not a condition of which the subject can be ignorant—i.e., the point is a point concerning the 'grammar' of 'pain', a grammar which can be contrasted with that of words like 'tired' or 'lazy'. Second, if it is in fact the case that one can be in pain but not know it, as perhaps with a child, then there is a more obvious point to the assertion that someone knows that he is in pain on a given occasion, the contrast being with other conceivable occasions of someone's being in pain, rather than with occasions of being tired, for instance. Such ignorance is in fact excluded, we are saying, though not ruled out as inconceivable. In such a case the first-person utterance continues to suffer from redundancy, but there is no hint of this with the other forms.

It would be a mistake to rule out either formulation on the grounds that we cannot speak of *knowing* where the possibility of doubt is excluded as senseless. That is to suppose that doubt makes for the only contrast, as if *not knowing* and *doubting* were co-extensive, and the preceding remarks indicate that this is not so: on either of the accounts of being in pain there is the contrast with simple ignorance. Wittgenstein recognizes the legitimate use of *knowing that one is in pain* to make a point about the grammar of pain, but it appears that in his eyes this recognition is not enough to give sense to the use of the notion by the sceptic who argues 'only I can know whether I am really in pain; another person can only surmise it' (*Philosophical Investigations*, para. 246). Wittgenstein seeks to destroy the basis of the sceptic's argument by refusing him this contrast. He counters: 'it can't be said of me at all (except perhaps as a joke) that I *know* I am in pain'. If he had cited the first-person utterance the oddity would be apparent, though not destructive of the sceptic's contrast, but it is hard to see how the version presented—'it can't be said *of me . . .*'— could be rejected. It may often happen that I am the only one who knows that I am in pain; this is not to say that others could not know, but it is to say that I alone in fact do. Perhaps we could rule out as senseless the suggestion that I should doubt that I am in pain, but there is a clear enough contrast between me and others on this occasion in the contrast between my knowledge and their ignorance. (Here para. 409 of the *Philosophical Investigations* is more to the point.)

When discussing earlier the second-level knowledge involved in seeing I spoke of this as an ability to *say* that one sees. This parsing seems particularly apt when the knowledge is not the result of investigation or of finding out from others, though, as mentioned, the 'say' must carry a particular force for the ability to have the implications required of it. When I say that a man may be said to know that he is in pain I mean no more than that he may be able to say that he is in pain, in the sense of *say authoritatively*— which means here that what he says is, if sincere, true. It is not the authority of one who is in the best position to *find out*—a common suggestion of 'knows' which may be behind the reluctance to allow it in this context. If it is accepted that one cannot be in pain without knowing that one is in pain, then we rule out the possibility of finding out by observation or investigation that we are in pain, as another might by noting our screams and injuries; nor is such knowledge to be based on the analogy of that which others may have, as if I came to say that I was in pain as the result of an *inner* observation or investigation. My authority is not that of one who is in the best position to tell that I am in pain, in the sense that I might tell *from* anything that I am in pain, but it is a question of telling as in telling others.

A man may be unable to speak, yet capable of thinking, and that suffices for him to have the knowledge that he is in pain. The central notion, however, is that of being able to say, and it is ultimately in terms of the spoken word that the relevant notion of thought is to be understood; without language in some form there could be no thought in any interesting sense. I shall now give more specific attention to the topic of thought, not merely to indicate the connection between thought and language, but with an eye to the more general questions concerning awareness with which thought, as the paradigm of the mental, so readily connects.

Suppose we try to conceive of thought as standing at the end of a scale which begins with words spoken out loud and proceeds through the intermediate stages of whispering followed by mere movements of the lips. The spoken word is something which both the speaker and his audience can hear, and so too with the whisperings; even the lip movements can be observed by the man whose lips they are if he looks in a mirror. Now much of our mental activity we think of as interiorized speech, and this we might construe as a continuation of the progression which began with the spoken word, became a whisper and then no more than movements of the lips, the man's words finally taking one step further away from the public world, passing to a realm where he is the only witness—though it might also be held that with increased powers of detection we too could pick up the man's thoughts; as if the difficulty were just that they were below the level of audibility. According to this account, then, a man's awareness of his thoughts is to be understood as a privileged extension of a situation in which there is no significant difference between his relation and that of others to a common object of experience. However, I believe the picture here is distorted: the man has first-level awareness of the words which he speaks out loud, but a quite different awareness of his thoughts.

Consider these clauses in turn. It might be suggested that my relation to my words is not on a par with the relation which others bear to them, in that it is not by observation that I know what I am saying. Now it is true that our positions are not the same in all respects, obviously, but this is not the way in which a relevant difference is to be introduced, and we can appreciate this by linking the question with the general issue of how we are to characterize intentional actions. Knowledge of what we are doing when we act intentionally is often taken to be a central case of knowledge which is not based on observation; or, it is more cautiously said, if it is *only* because I am able to observe what I am doing that I know what I am doing, then my action is not intentional. However, this is an unnecessarily strict condition. I may be writing a word intentionally; what I know without observation is what I intend to do, but I need to watch what I am doing to tell whether I am succeeding, whether I am doing what I set out to do. Trying to do something or acting intentionally is here a matter of acting in the belief that my actions will have, or stand some chance of having, a certain outcome, and what I know without observation is what that belief is. Now, as regards one's knowledge of what one is saying, the question what one means or intends to say is certainly not one which is answered by 'observing' what one says, but what one *actually* says must be determined by using one's ears: there is a feedback from the spoken word which enables me to detect a discrepancy between what I intend and what I actually say.

The difference, then, between my relation to my spoken words and the relation of another is not to be expressed by saying that I do not, but he does, 'observe' what I say, so we can accept the account given of the first stage of the progression from speech to thought. However, when we reach thought we do not reach sub-vocal words which, it so happens, another cannot hear. There is not something which unfolds before me—my thoughts—which I can 'monitor' in the way that I can my speech, which I can attend to or not, as I please. If I am having such-and-such a thought, then I *ipso facto* know that I am having that thought, and my thoughts do not go on in the absence of my knowledge of them.

However, the significance of this point might be queried. It is

surely intelligible to suggest that a man may want or desire something unconsciously; why should not a similar possibility make
sense for thoughts? I have no fundamental objection to an extension of 'thought' in that direction; the question of interest is, as
ever, just what this would involve. Well, what is involved in the
notion of an unconscious want or desire? It might be suggested
that to want something unconsciously is simply to act as if one
wanted that thing, at the same time disowning, in all sincerity, any
such want. Such a suggestion is acceptable, so long as it is understood to embody the requirement that the behaviour be persisted
in only to the extent that it leads to satisfaction of the supposed
want. Certainly, whatever the details, it is to the man's behaviour
that we turn to interpret the notion of *wanting* when there is no
question of a conscious want; and, further, it is not a matter of the
behaviour being no more than evidence for the want; given that he
acts that way, there can be no doubt about what he wants. There
is no question of 'postulating an unconscious' to provide a framework for such findings; we may hypothesize underlying physiological conditions, but it is not in terms of these that we give sense
to the notion. Similarly, we may be able to give sense to the notion
of thought without awareness that one is thinking. As far as ordinary usage is concerned, this would seem to disqualify such thought
from being *mental*, and the alternative is not a different, possibly
only conjectural compartment of the mind, but either behaviour
or certain neurophysiological activity, more likely the latter: thus,
if someone wishes to say that I must have been thinking about a
certain problem when I was unaware of doing so, this is most
naturally taken as ill-defined assertion about my cerebral processes,
understanding 'cerebral' in its literal sense. Whether we invoke
physiology or behaviour here is, as far as we are concerned, a
matter of comparative detail. The important consideration is
that, in order to make out a case for the possibility of thoughts of
which the subject is unaware, we are obliged to interpret such
thoughts in a way which makes it possible for others to know of
them.

   To return to the main point, I mentioned earlier the curious
tendency to think of an unconscious thought as like its conscious
version but for the fact that the subject is unaware of the thought
in the former case—as if this were just an incidental difference.
Thoughts, and other mental phenomena, are thus modelled on

physical objects, which can exist both while we are observing them and when we cease to do so. However, the transition from speech to thought represents a transition to a different kind of awareness: a thought is not an object of an inner version of first-level awareness, but the awareness is awareness that I am thinking about so-and-so, or that I think such-and-such. (Recall the discussion of self-awareness.) Finally, to repeat an earlier point, the awareness or knowledge of which I am speaking is not to be thought of as necessarily anything more than dispositional. If I am engrossed in thought, just as when I am engrossed in watching a film, I may give no thought at all to my state; my knowledge that I am thinking about a certain problem or that I now see the hero on the screen may be elicited at any point during these activities, but such knowledge is not continuously present by virtue of my constant dwelling upon it.

I have spoken so far as if thought was to be conceived of as interiorized speech, but this is not the only form it can take. Think of what goes on when you have a tune running through your head, or, if this does not strictly qualify as 'thinking', consider what takes place when, asked to imagine how you would rearrange a number of differently shaped pieces of wood to form a triangle, you try out different combinations in your mind in an effort to picture the right one. Such an activity qualifies as a species of thinking, but can we say that language is involved? Yes and no. We cannot, in the sense that we cannot allow that the thinking which occurs is in any way a version of speech; I do not think to myself in words when I imagine the different shapes in various positions—though this activity may be *accompanied* by verbal thought. On the other hand, such thought seems, *par excellence*, to involve second-level awareness: I cannot picture or imagine something without knowing that I am; and it does not seem possible to make sense of knowledge of this kind with respect to a being which lacks any form of language. Consequently, while certain mental activities, such as various forms of imagining, need not themselves involve language, that does not mean that they could be enjoyed by a being which had no language.

This enables us to correct an earlier overstatement. When we think of thought in terms of speech there are two ways in which we may do so. First, there is the central conception of thought as in-teriorized speech, where it is *our* speech that is being interiorized.

By this I mean that, instead of saying out loud what we want to say, we say it to ourselves. When such thoughts are spoken it is often a matter of saying what we think in the sense of what our opinion is. However, as well as thought based on our own speech there is thought which has as its starting-point the experience of hearing others speak, where we are not expressing anything ourselves, but are passive listeners. Now we could have thoughts which derived from this kind of situation; it would be like hearing voices, and perhaps we should be rather surprised at what we 'thought', though I am inclined to speak rather of 'inner voices', just as we speak of images rather than of thoughts when the analogy is with a picture; certainly, it would hardly be a matter of *my* thoughts. None the less, this is nearer the model rejected, and we could extend this conception further to provide for the possibility of a common object of thought-experience: you and I having the same thoughts, not in the sense of being of the same opinions, say, but experiencing the same inner voices, where, on a given occasion, there was but one voice to be experienced.

This discussion of thought has been extremely sketchy, to say the least, but I think that enough has been said to show that thought and the mental generally can be brought into line with sensation as far as the connection with knowledge is concerned, and hence that we have vindicated something like the intermediate position proposed at the beginning of the chapter. Only something *like* this position, perhaps, since the original suggestion that language be construed as actually constitutive of the specifically human states of consciousness seems to be an overstatement, but the more careful formulation in terms of propensities to say does seem to be acceptable. Thus, the reference to language comes in via the consideration that, if behaviour and other observable conditions do not suffice to establish a certain state of consciousness, then it is because it is necessary to such a state that the subject know that he is in that state, and this is a form of knowledge which we have been able to interpret only with respect to creatures having a language. A capacity for speech is accordingly required, but there need be no actual exercise of this capacity on a given occasion when a person is in a certain mental state. On the other hand, not just *some* command of language is sufficient here. For instance, more is required than is provided by mere ejaculations

such as 'ouch!'. The language of pain is more than simply a substitute for cries: stay with cries and you will not move to a level
where we can say that there is something to be known because
there is something which the person or creature knows.

To conclude this chapter I should like to add a few words on
the distinction between the notion of sensation as applied to an
animal and the notion as applied to a language-user. I do not
wish to say: Smith can have a pain, and in the same sense Smith's
cat can have a pain; only, Smith can tell me of his pain, the cat
cannot. According to our analysis, the cat can have a pain of
which we do not know and which is not to be manifested in its
behaviour, only if at the same time it is able to say that it is in pain,
i.e., if it can make known its pain through its verbal behaviour.
This is what I had in mind in the last chapter when I claimed that
the problem with animals arose because we both denied them
language and allowed that they could have sensations in conditions
in which possession of language was presupposed. Since the cat's
inability to tell us that it is in pain is matched by the absence of
any pains of which we might know *only* if it could tell us, it
would seem that the only problem is one of decision; not: how
can we find out? but: when is it appropriate to use 'pain' of
animals?

But now it is perhaps beginning to look as if there were such a
difference between the human and the animal case that a decision
to speak of pain in the latter would be quite unfounded. This is
not so, I believe, and to present a more balanced picture I should
like to consider the transition from the one state to the other, a
transition which does not take place with animals, but which can
be illustrated by the development of a child. Consider the example
of a small child who knows, can tell, where a sound is coming
from, but has not yet learned to say as much. So, that he does
know is shown to us by his behaviour; by, for instance, his crawling
towards the sound to investigate. Eventually, the child learns to
say where a sound is coming from, as well as continuing with his
locational activities. This *learning to say* is a matter of learning to
say in the situation as previously defined: where before there was
only a behavioural manifestation of such knowledge, there is now
a verbal expression. What the child can now express, what it
becomes aware of in a further way, is not the behaviour which we
observe and which we regarded as giving proof of such 'practical'

knowledge, and it would be patently absurd to understand 'knowing where the sound is coming from' in terms of 'knowing how it is behaving'.

In other instances, however, it is perhaps easier to make just that mistake, to look to behaviour to provide a reference for the words added to the behaviour. For example, characteristically human seeing would appear to involve awareness of seeing, and for this to be a genuine possibility it would seem that there must be logically sufficient conditions for seeing construed more broadly, conditions which fall short of being adequate to the specifically human case: how could seeing involve second-level awareness if this awareness is itself to be defined as awareness of seeing? Accordingly, we might say that we not only see in the way that animals do, but that we can in addition be aware of the seeing which is common to us and them. However, this approach makes out a man's awareness of seeing y to be awareness of his practical knowledge of the presence of y, and while this does not quite reduce it to first-level awareness of his own behaviour, there is surely something wrong in understanding this second-level awareness in terms of the subject's awareness that he has such knowledge. It was a mistake to say that the person who knows where the sound is coming from knows that he has practical knowledge of the whereabouts of the sound, or is aware of the behaviour of his which shows such knowledge, and if that implication fails it would seem that the present instance fares no better. The words attach to the new situation not by virtue of, on the other hand, a non-behavioural reference having been provided, as though they had been introduced to cope with the development of a new mental state, but it is simply the very disposition to use such words that defines the extended state

Let us run through the argument again, taking this time the example of pain, and assuming that we are prepared to speak of a small child as feeling pain. So, before he has mastered any language, the child hurts himself, and he eventually learns to say that he is hurt or that something is hurting him. This *learning to say* is a matter of learning to say in the situation as previously defined, where we spoke of the child as 'hurt' on the strength of his distressed state, occasioned by cuts, scratches, burns, and so forth; where before there was only a behavioural manifestation of the state, there is now a verbal expression. What the child can now express, what it becomes aware of, is not the propensity to cry, and so on, the behaviour which we observed and which we regarded as entitling us to speak of pain, but it would be wrong to understand 'knowing that it is in pain' in terms of 'knowing how it is disposed to behave'. On the other hand, the words are not introduced to meet a need presented by the emergence of a new state; there is a new state, or an extension of the former one, but it is the very disposition to use such words which is to be added to the former state to give rise to the new, and which constitutes the development which the child has undergone.

This way of indicating what the difference in the two states consists in brings out the continuity which makes it plausible to speak of the child as feeling pain before it acquired the use of language. However, whether or not we agree to speak in this way is perhaps of no great importance. If we do not, then of course the child's experience of pain will be held to begin only as its higher consciousness develops, the consciousness which comes only with language—though some notion of distress is surely applicable throughout. If we do agree, on the other hand, we are not to take such agreement as committing us to saying that the sensations which the child had before it could speak were sensations which, because it could not then tell us about them, we could never know of, but only conjecture. If the child could think then it could appreciate that it was in pain and refrain from disclosing this awareness to us; then, as a fact known to the child, there would be something for us to know, but rule out knowledge in this quarter and anything still to be learned is to be learned by observation and investigation. It is true that if the child, prior to its acquisition of language, is in a distressed state, then this distress need not be expressed or manifested. We can make sense of perception in the absence of behavioural signs, and we can likewise allow that a child or animal—through being paralysed, perhaps—is in a distressed state, even though it does not show it at the moment; that is a question concerning how it would have reacted if its natural responses had not been inhibited, and in theory we can have any amount of evidence pointing one way or the other on such a question. The important difference lies in the respective problems of recognizing as such the expression of the state in the two cases. When the proof of the distress is given in purely behavioural terms there is no significant difficulty in this regard, but when it is a matter of accepting the subject's word we have to ascertain that what is said is true to what is known, and this is the source of a major difficulty, in theory as well as in practice.

8

OBJECTS OF SENSE

THE topic of objects of sense and, in particular, objects of vision, has been held over from chapter 4, where it arose in connection with the problem of identifying an organ as an *eye*, and it has been held over until this point because of the further possibilities which the subsequent discussion of awareness has introduced. When we left the topic I had been arguing that vision could be established if it could be shown that a creature's responses to an object were mediated by an eye, provided that whether or not an organ was an eye was, fundamentally, a matter to be decided by reference to features of the object perceived and not by reference to the general appearance of the organ. If, by using its ostensible eyes, the animal is able to show its awareness of illuminated objects placed before it, then we are close to narrowing down the awareness as *visual*. We can say only 'close to', since this condition does not rule out other possibilities: adding the qualification 'illuminated' does not ensure that the organ in question is not one of hearing, for instance; I can hear an illuminated object, even though this owes nothing to its being illuminated. Accordingly we must insist that the illumination, whether reflected light or light emitted by the object perceived, be necessary to the creature's perception if the organ is to be an eye and the sense to be sight. However, we did not go beyond this to the further claim that what we actually and invariably see is light, but it has yet to be determined whether light, or indeed anything else, can enter into an account of vision in this way, as a 'proper' object of the sense.

The term 'proper' calls for a word of clarification. On the one hand, an object may be proper to a particular sense in that it can be detected *only* by that sense; I can smell a smell but I cannot see or hear it, whereas I can both see and hear a dog; 'smell' signifies a proper object of the sense of smell, but 'dog' does not signify such an object of any sense. On the other hand, there is a usage according to which the term 'sound' provides a proper object of hearing in the sense that whenever one hears one hears a sound, whatever else one may at the same time be truly said to hear. Similarly, if you smell anything you smell a smell, and, it would seem, you inevitably taste a taste. However, it has often been observed that there appears to be no term related to 'see' in the same way; no term 'x', that is, such that if you see anything at all you see (an) x. (I should point out that I shall use the term 'object' sometimes to signify a grammatical item, sometimes to signify a non-linguistic item, the appropriate interpretation being clear, I hope, from the context.)

We shall set off presently in search of a proper object of vision in this latter sense, but first let us stop to look more closely at the suggestion that 'taste' is a proper object of the sense of taste. We speak not only of tasting stuffs and liquids but also of tasting the taste of something, and it might appear that a simple grammatical transformation is all that is involved in the move from 'taste x' to 'taste the taste of x'. If this is so, then since no knowledge of extra-linguistic fact is necessary in order to justify the move, we are assured that a proper object of taste can always be invoked, even if it does not receive explicit mention. However, I believe that this is incorrect and that there are assumptions underlying the use of 'taste the taste of x' which are not necessarily present with the simple 'taste x'. By using its tongue a dog can discriminate variously tasting substances; the animal undoubtedly has a sense of taste. Yet can he be said to taste a taste? The inference seems at first sight irresistible, but our earlier discussion of *tasting sweet* should make us suspicious. Is it not possible that all we are entitled to say is that the animal tastes the various things with which its tongue comes into contact? We can say that much, surely, but it would appear that tastes themselves are not to be numbered among such things; the taste of the meat is not something which I or the dog can put a tongue to, and a natural hypothesis at this stage is that when we have the internal accusative, 'taste the taste of x', we have to do with a more sophisticated form of awareness: when 'the taste of x' is object of the verb the tasting is not a matter of manipulating the organ, but tasting the taste is just a matter of having or experiencing the taste, and this seems to be a matter of knowing *how* the substance tastes. In this case, the apparent proper object turns out to be nothing of the sort: animals do not taste tastes, since they cannot acquire the requisite knowledge.

If this argument can be sustained it might seem that *any* object of a given sense can be shown not to be proper: since the senses which we have are to be found in animals, and animal awareness is just awareness of physical objects, or at least of physical phenomena generally, it would be a mistake to think of these various internal accusatives as specifying proper objects; indeed, a mistake to conceive of them as even *possible* objects of first-level awareness. However, I think that this generalization would be in error. Animals can hear sounds, and sounds are proper objects of hearing. Furthermore, if you hear a shirt tearing then you hear the sound of a shirt tearing; with sound the expanded version is always warranted, both for men and for animals. Why should there be this difference? An answer to this question will eventually emerge, but I propose to leave these preliminaries at this point and turn to the problems posed by sight.

We have steadfastly spoken of visual perception in terms of knowledge of the presence of *objects*, material things, and we have paid no attention to shadows, lights, shapes, sizes, differences, heights, and of course colours, which we readily enough speak of seeing. Colours will be particularly missed by the sense-datum theorist, for whom colour patches enjoy a central position in his account of perception, and I shall begin by considering in some detail the behaviour of 'colour' in conjunction with the verb 'see'. The word 'colour' is one among a group of 'quality' words—others are 'shape', 'size', 'height', and, for these purposes, 'number' and 'difference'—which function in an unexpected manner when governed by a perceptual verb. Consider the sentences:

(i) I've never seen the colour of her eyes before,
(ii) I've never seen that colour before.

A superficial comparison would suggest that the first differed from the second only in the specificity of its description, 'the colour of her eyes', but if we have regard to the normal sense of each it becomes evident that this phrase is not on a par with 'that colour'. It is conceivable that in asserting (i) we should wish to claim that there is a certain colour—turquoise, let us say—which we have never seen before, a colour which is to be found in the person's eyes. (i) might, that is, come to something like 'I've never seen that colour—the colour her eyes have—before', featuring 'the colour of her eyes' in a role comparable to that of 'that colour'—

i.e., both being alternative expressions for securing reference to or identifying a particular colour. But it is far more natural for (i) so to be read that it invites comparison with

(iii) I've never before seen what colour her eyes are.

It is not a question of there being some particular shade or hue which I have never before encountered, in the sense that (i) would be false if her eyes were of a colour which I *had* seen before.

If it is thought improbable that a noun phrase should behave in this way we may point to other contexts in which a similar meaning is intended; for instance, when 'the colour of x' follows the verbs 'know', 'find out' or 'remember'. A claim to know the colour of a person's eyes is not likely to be a claim to be acquainted with a certain colour, but it would generally amount to stating that one knew what colour they were. Furthermore, this pattern of interpretation is extendable to other quality words: to know the height of the Eiffel Tower is to know what its height is (or how high it is); to ascertain the number of people present is to ascertain what the number is (or how many people are present); and to see the shape of something is to see what shape it is (or how it is shaped).

The same phenomenon is evident when 'the colour of x' is conjoined with phrases of quite a different type. Suppose I say I am amazed at the colour of a person's eyes. Then, even if this colour is the same as the colour of her hat, it would not necessarily follow that I was amazed at the colour of her hat. In each instance the qualifying phrases 'of her eyes' and 'of her hat' play an essential role, a role which is not confined to the mere identification of the colour; what amazes me is that the person's eyes should be the colour they are, or at least should be ϕ, for a certain ϕ, though perhaps there is nothing amazing about the colour except as the colour of her eyes. Similarly, if I am disappointed, fooled, or annoyed by the colour of x, then it is x's being the way it is colourwise that disappoints, fools or annoys me. There is in such cases a predicational tie between 'x' and some (implicit) colour term which is essential to the sense of the statement and which we of course lose if we eliminate 'x'.

There are, then, uses of phrases of the form 'the colour of x' in which the description 'x' is not such that it serves its purpose provided only that it assists us in identifying the colour in question, but in which reference to x is an essential part of the assertion.

Other expressions which secure reference to x can of course be used, but it is vital that we do not lose sight of the predication with x as subject. To see the colour of x is, roughly, to see that x is ϕ, for appropriate ϕ. This formula is preferable to the less general: 'to see the colour of x is to see what colour x is'. There are certainly contexts in which the speaker's intention in asking 'did you see the colour of her eyes?' could be adequately conveyed by the form of words, 'did you see what colour her eyes were?', but it is also the case that the person could so intend his question that not only answers which were answers to this suggested variant were acceptable, but also other answers which would not qualify as 'saying what colour her eyes were'—e.g., 'I have no idea what colour they were, but I did note that it was unusual'—and the formula suggested covers this case as well.

Note too that it is no part of this analysis to say that the context 'to see the colour of x' is 'referentially opaque'; i.e., that this is a context in which truth-value is dependent on the precise way in which reference is secured. There is a case for saying that such a statement as 'he knew that the man on the bicycle had been hit by a car' is referentially opaque, in that we cannot be sure that truth is preserved if we replace the phrase 'the man on the bicycle' by 'his father', even though it is in fact true that the man on the bicycle is his father. However, to say that a context is referentially opaque is not to deny that a certain noun phrase has a reference, but to assert that *how* the reference is achieved is relevant to the truth-value of the statement, and I wish to leave open the possibility that the phrase 'the colour of x' performs no referential function at all, but is resolved into a grammatical unit having quite a different status, sometimes an interrogative clause, sometimes a phrase functioning predicatively.

If 'the colour of x' always functioned in this way there would be some doubt about even the trivial-sounding view that colours are *possible* objects of vision, let alone proper objects. The situation is akin to that in which we have to do with so-called 'propositional' objects of the verb 'see', as in the context 'I saw that he was coming'. Here too superficial grammar is misleading: the clause appears to function as object—after all, it does follow a verb which is generally transitive—but in view of the failure of a passive transformation to 'that he was coming was seen by me' we might well regard this appearance as deceptive. The possibility of such a transformation is surely necessary to the parsing of 'see' as transitive with the following clause as object, and if it fails, then, despite the general transitivity of 'see', we must look elsewhere for a model on which to base an understanding of the construction. (For more on the possibilities here see my 'Transitivity and Indirect Speech', *Proceedings of the Aristotelian Society*, 1967–8.)

The curious use of 'colour' to which we have drawn attention is not the only one, However, it is far from clear that the use which does provide an object in a less problematic way is satisfactory for the purpose for which it is here required. Consider once more the sentence:

(ii) I've never seen that colour before.

There would appear to be no possibility of a paraphrase which would show 'that colour' to do the work of a clause, or to be anything other than the simple noun phrase which we take it to be. Nor is such a construal necessary, for the moves which we are inclined to make, taking it at its face value, are not moves which lead to paradox. We could not argue: 'The colour of her eyes is turquoise; he has never seen the colour of her eyes; ergo, he has never seen the colour turquoise.' We could not, that is, if 'see the colour of her eyes' is equivalent here to 'see what colour her eyes are'. One possible account of the fallacy would be to say that in functioning as a clause the phrase 'the colour of x' does not serve to designate some colour, and hence cannot be replaced by an alternative designation of the same colour. Compare: 'He doesn't know what is written on this page; his name is written on this page; ergo, he doesn't know his name.' The 'what' in the first premise of this invalid argument is not a relative 'what', expandible as 'that which', but an interrogative pronoun: what the man does not know is the answer to the question 'what is written on this page?'.

Whatever the precise reason for its fallaciousness, it is clear that the argument is unacceptable. However, if someone points to the wallpaper and says 'I've never seen that colour before', you can say 'he had never seen that colour before', pointing now to your car—supposing it to be of the same colour as the wallpaper. Here moves which broke down with (i) are now legitimate. Again, contrast 'I saw the colour of her hair for the first time yesterday' with 'I saw this colour for the first time yesterday'. It is unlikely that 'the colour of her hair' is intended as one among a number of possible identifications of a particular colour, but there is no doubt that 'this colour' is aimed at drawing attention just to the colour; that it should be the colour of some particular x is of no account. A more straightforward use of 'colour', from a grammatical stand-point, is then possible. In this use, on the other hand, 'that colour' is associated with a criterion of identity which makes it unsuited to taking over the role enjoyed by physical object terms—which signify the standard, though not proper, objects of vision. And, as we shall see, if we adjust it to this new role we simply have to introduce a new term to perform the function of which it has now been deprived.

The distinction between these uses of phrases containing the word 'colour' has been worked out in terms of a distinction between the case where the predicational tie is important and the case where the qualification 'of x' serves merely to identify the colour. In considering the examples which lead to this distinction it is natural to hark back to the distinction between colour as a 'particular' and colour as a 'universal', and it might be thought that the analysis which I have sketched is a formal reflection of such a distinction at an 'ontological' level. Thus, the example of the colour which the man had never seen was an example of a colour which was at the same time the colour of the wallpaper and the colour of a car. This, we might say, is colour as a universal, a property sharable by more than one particular. But when I said that I had never seen the col-our of her eyes before, what I meant was the *particular* colour, the colour which her eyes have but which cannot literally be shared by other things, no matter how closely their colour should resemble it.

However, this way of speaking is not what I wish to give ex-pression to at any level. Such an attempt to draw the distinction fails because of its reliance upon a move which rests on an under-standing of 'particular' appropriate only when this occurs with expressions of another type, e.g., 'particular car'. Prefacing 'colour' by 'particular' does not give a logical guarantee that the colour cannot be shared by more than one thing; indeed, it does not give *any* guarantee of exclusivity. No one else can have this particular toe, I can say, pointing to one of my toes, only one just like it—the same size, shape, and so forth. But no such distinction has yet been drawn for colours, viz., a distinction between being exactly alike and being the same, such that the first is possible where the second is not. In fact, in so far as 'particular' has application here it is to the case where we are tempted to regard the reference of the description as the *universal* colour. In (ii), that is, we could insert 'particular' to give 'I've never seen that particular colour before', whereas in (i) a similar insertion does not result in a sentence which we can interpret so readily; or, at least, the most natural interpretation has the effect of bringing it in line with (ii).

When, in the style of (i), 'see' is used to govern 'colour' or other quality words such as 'height' or size', it does not generally have quite the sense it has when we speak of seeing a shell or a lake or any other straightforward object of vision. Sometimes it has the force of 'tell by looking', sometimes it is less specific: to see the size of something may be to see or tell how big it is, but only to the extent of seeing or telling that it is *so* big; to tell how big it is suggests much more detailed knowledge. We should not want, without some reinterpretation, to say that an animal saw the height or size of something—though not because of any defect or limitation which we might impute to its sense of sight—and it is not obvious how we are to interpret the suggestion that animals see the colours of things, if this means attributing to them anything like the ability to tell by looking what colour an object is, or anything about it in respect of its colour. For their case we shall, it seems, have to abandon the phrase 'see the colour of *x*' where this involves a predicational tie, or else assign it a rather different interpretation from the one it typically receives in application to human beings.

If we simply speak of an animal as seeing colours, and not as seeing the colours of things, i.e., we take (ii) rather than (i) as our model, we shall not have to cope with this difficulty. However, it is remarkable how little scope there is for speaking thus even once the unwanted interpretation is put aside. If Fido chases after a bright red ball then it is simply the ball, or perhaps (at the same time) the movement of the ball, that we have good grounds for believing Fido has seen. Of course, if Fido sees the ball and the ball is red, then Fido sees the red ball; that much is guaranteed by the extensionality of these contexts. But the correctness of this redescription has no tendency to show that Fido sees the colour of the ball, and indeed it is obvious that there is no necessity that he should do so. Not only may Fido be colour-blind and yet see, but he will, we may suppose, chase after objects of any colour, and will

chase after this ball even when conditions of illumination are poor
and its colour is not detectable. It is possible that dogs should have
greater sensitivity to colour in a bad light than do we, but it is not
necessary to make any such supposition in order to explain Fido's
continuing ability to locate the ball by using his eyes. It is true that
if it is not to be lost to sight the ball must stand out from its surroundings by being of a lighter or a darker shade. However, it is
possible for a person to make out an object without having any
awareness of it *as* lighter or darker than its surroundings, and *a
fortiori* the same holds for an animal.

To establish colour vision with respect to some particular hue
we must establish not only that the animal is able to see things of
that hue, but also that it displays some differential response to it.
So, we might train Fido to react in a certain way to a certain colour,
and we could be sure it was the colour that was instrumental in
producing the reaction if we found that it occurred whatever the
size, shape, or other characteristics of objects having that colour;
and, moreover, if only things of that colour brought about that
reaction. Even so, I find it much more natural to keep to terminology which does not suggest anything more than a behavioural
response in such cases, to say that it can discriminate between
differently coloured things rather than that it can *see* colours, and
I think that this preference connects with features of the phrase
'see colours' to which we have already alluded: in seeing colours
something other than a behavioural response is typically involved.

Be that as it may, even when it is established that an animal has
colour vision it still does not follow that some description in terms
of 'colour' is appropriate to what the animal sees in any significant
number of cases, unless the description is licensed merely by
considerations of extensionality: the house is brown and the dog
sees the house, so he sees something brown. Part of the reason why
we feel that colour must enter more significantly and more generally
into vision is presumably the fact that to us colours are such
obvious features of physical objects, features which, we imagine, we
surely perceive *first* among visually detectable characteristics of
the scene confronting us on any given occasion. However, it
requires only a little reflection to realize that this picture is in no
way generally valid, even for human beings. At a late hour we may
be able to make out objects without too much trouble, but have no
idea as to their respective colours. Conversely, there may be so much

light or glare around that, while we can discern shapes, colour is impossible to detect. Again an object may move too fast for us to determine its colour even though there may be no doubt that we saw it, and even when an object is motionless and illuminated it is quite possible to be aware of its presence without being at all aware of its colour. Finally, the following point is worth mentioning. The function of the eye appears to be primarily the detection of movement. At all events, the oldest part of the eye is the periphery of the retina, and the cells here respond to movement and not to colour. As evidence of this you may make a movement of your hand, holding some brightly coloured object which can only be seen out of the corner of your eye. The movement will register, but the colour of the object will not be discernible.

It may well have been felt that in certain of the contexts which concern us it is slightly more usual to speak of *noticing* rather than seeing—'did you notice the shape of his head, the colour of his teeth, the size of his feet?'—and this accords with the readiness of 'notice' to join up with a clause, to connect with thought and judgement. However, as already remarked, the connection is not so tight that we cannot speak of animals as noticing; it is just that a plausible interpretation is not so obvious with respect to them. A related notion which may also seem at first to have no application to animals is that of something's *looking so-and-so* to an observer. Psychologists and zoologists frequently have occasion to remark that the world must look very different to creatures endowed with a form of eye quite different from our own; we may share such wonder, but there is considerable difficulty with the question just *what* we are puzzled about. This question is similar to the earlier issue about whether something could taste sweet to an animal. Tasting sweet I construed in terms of the subject's having a disposition to judge as sweet, and in similar vein something's looking pink (blurred, bent, etc.) to me appears to be a matter of my being disposed to describe it thus.

This analysis calls for a few words of clarification before we consider how it might be extended to animals. First, it is clear that it is not as it stands a full account, since the disposition must be brought about in the right way, viz., as a result of seeing the object taken to be pink—I might be disposed to judge or describe something as pink as a result of being hypnotized, for instance. Second, we may note that the notion of a *tentative* judgement

enjoys no central place here, contrary to what is commonly supposed. What we are chiefly concerned to explain is the notion of
something's looking ϕ to someone, not the first-person statement-
form, 'x looks ϕ to me', where the speaker actually uses the word
'looks'. It is true that if I say 'that looks pink to me' I may do so
because I am uncertain as to the true colour, but when I say that
something looks pink to another I do not mean in the first instance
that he is disposed to offer the merely tentative judgement 'it looks
pink'. The disposition is to be thought of as covering this possibility, but there is no need for there to be any hesitancy in the
mind of the subject; the disposition is primarily a disposition to
judge x pink, not to assert that that is how it *looks* to him—a point
which is constantly overlooked in discussions of this topic.

Suppose we have established that Fido enjoys colour vision
comparable in range and discrimination to our own. If we look at a
piece of paper bathed in red light, it will look pink to us. Can we
ask 'does the paper look pink to Fido in this light?'. On the one
hand, this sounds absurd: we have a picture of Fido turning over
possible descriptions in his mind and rejecting or opting for
'pink' or some synonym. But, although the situation does not
prompt any colour judgement from Fido, it would seem that we
could reasonably speak in this way if Fido started to respond towards the pink-looking paper in the same way as, we shall suppose,
he had been trained to respond to pink things. Imagine that he had
been taught to pick up pink things, and only pink things, in his
mouth. If he proceeded to do just that once the paper was under
the red light we might well say that it looked pink to him. And, of
course, when I claim that we might well say this I do not mean:
say this by way of a plausible hypothesis. I mean rather that we
can give sense to this form of words by reference to the behaviour
which is like the behaviour which human beings display when it is
true to say that something looks pink to them, or behaviour which
they are at least capable of displaying to give evidence of such a
belief. Note too that there is no necessity that the object should be
one which merely looks pink, but is really white, for instance. The
argument is unchanged if we consider the dog's reactions only to
things which *are* pink.

The discussion so far indicates that, whether or not it provides a
possible object of vision, the term 'colour' certainly does not

provide us with a *proper* object: it is just not the case that whenever we see we see colour, not at least in the ordinary sense or senses of these words. Still, it might be argued, if 'colour' is not altogether the appropriate term for describing what it is that we see whenever we see, this is so for accidental reasons. We can surely envisage a term which is like 'colour' but without its grammatical peculiarities, and which can be used to formulate more accurately the view which, as stated, has proved to be false; there must after all be some common denominator to all our visual experience, call it colour, light, or what you will. I will try to give some support to this impression shortly, but first let me indicate briefly and without drawing out all the relevant consequences an alternative grammar for 'colour'; it is a grammar which defines a word of a very different character, but a grammar which, I suspect, the term is obscurely supposed to have by those who wish it to furnish a proper object.

A consideration of the way in which 'colour' enters into discourse leads us to regard colours as essentially properties or qualities. Not necessarily properties of physical objects, in any straightforward sense of this expression, since we attribute them to flames, the sky, and other things which do not readily fit into this category. But, although there may be no useful term to describe the multitude of things to which colour may be ascribed, we can say that a colour never occurs except as the colour of something. A patch of colour, we may note, is a coloured patch, where the identity of the patch is something over and above the identity of the colour: the colour of the patch may change, but that means that the patch, the same patch, has changed its colour. The patch is not purely an expanse of colour; it is not only red, it is also hard or soft, wet or dry, and so forth. This, certainly, is the situation with which we are familiar; colour is not self-subsistent, but one way or another it is always referred to something of which it is a property. (I continue to phrase this view in a misleading 'material' mode of speech, for the sake of formulating a common view, not for the sake of clarity.)

Suppose now we encountered patches of colour which had no properties save those logically implied by being extended in two dimensions, along with properties which, like brightness, could be ascribed to the colour as now; no thickness, weight, stickiness, or any of the other properties which require a material substrate. If we used 'this colour' to refer to such items, somewhat in the same way as we now use 'this pigment', or better, 'this patch', the logic of the phrase would alter considerably. Let us, to avoid confusion, write the word so used with a 'k' in place of the 'c'. Just as we now distinguish patches according to their different spatial locations, so we could oppose this kolour to that kolour on the same grounds; 'I have seen that kolour before' would not necessarily be true if, as we should now say, I had merely seen something of that colour; 'I have seen one just like it', would be the most we could say. Similarly, the wish to have a certain kolour on one's wall would be capable of fulfilment only if it were somehow possible to move these kolours from place to place. What is worthy of note here is that there would still be just as much of a need for a term to do the work that 'colour' at present does, for we should surely wish to say that two of these kolours were or were not the same in colour. What we have done is introduce an item which resembles an impoverished kind of physical object more than it resembles a colour, as the term is now understood, and if these kolours were proper objects they would be so only by accident—only because they had become the sole occupants of the visual world. And even then, we may observe, colours would not be proper objects of vision, since you could conceivably see a kolour without seeing its colour.

In this connection we may mention the misconceived dispute as to whether colours are mental or physical. Perhaps the most obvious resolution of this dispute would run as follows: there is no clear sense in which it is true to say that colours are *mental*; as with the description of pains as 'mental', only a sensitivity dulled by exposure to philosophical jargon would refuse to balk at this description of colours. On the other hand, the epithet 'physical' seems to apply only in a transferred sense: colours are physical in the sense that they are properties of physical things, things made of matter; they are not, obviously, physical in the way that a pigment or thin veneer are physical. We might question whether colours always occur as colours of physical things in any relevant sense, but this aside, the defect in this solution is that it does not do justice to the 'adjectival' status of 'colour'. The propositions 'colours are mental' and 'colours are physical' all too readily suggest 'colours are mental entities' or 'colours are physical things', or other construals which assign to 'colour' a logic which is more appropriate to 'kolour'. 'Colours are mental (physical)' compares more with 'sizes are mental (physical)' or 'heights are mental (physical)' than with 'pains are mental (physical)'. Such statements about sizes and

heights are obvious nonsense, and, while less obvious, it is the same
nonsense in the statements about colours.

What is required by those who look to 'colour' as giving a proper
object of vision is, I suggest, a term which functions more like
'kolour', but without designating just one among the various things
which we may speak of seeing, and I propose now to examine the
term 'light' to see if this does not provide a more promising candidate. Light compares more with kolour in that it is not a property
of objects, or of anything else; indeed, light is one of the things to
which colour can be attributed; i.e., light can be light of a certain
colour. When speaking here of light I mean light which we can say
is cast upon something, not a light in the sense of a lamp, lantern,
torch or flame which is the source of the light cast. These, of
course, can be coloured, but it could be maintained that the light
which emanates from a light source and which illuminates objects,
picks out the colour in them and is reflected or radiated, the light
which has been found to be a wave-form, is not best described as
'coloured'. Red light is light which makes surfaces of objects look
red, or at least reddish or redder; it is not red in the same way as
a piece of paper may be red, but it is deemed red by virtue of the
effect which it has on physical objects, making them look red. We
may describe a ray or beam of light as 'red', but the redness of the
light resolves itself into the redness of the particles of dust, say,
which it illuminates.

If the light were red in the way that a particle is, shining a red
light on to a white surface would be like adding a pigment or a dye
to the surface; the red circle which the light casts is not like a
detachable disc or a coat or paint, however thin or thinly spread. If
we think of light in this way we shall not think of it as a peculiar
kind of coloured stuff on a par with other coloured objects—something which could obstruct our view of the latter—but then we
shall not think of it as what is seen either; light so conceived may be
a universal stimulus in vision, but it is not the proper *object* of
vision which we have been seeking.

That is one way of understanding 'light', but only one way. We
shall be prepared for another possibility when we have considered
the connection between light and properties other than colour and
the contrast between the visual and the auditory worlds, and to
these topics I now turn. It is a familiar fact that variations in a

light source give rise to changes in the appearances of objects illuminated by it, but that throughout such changes certain features may remain to a greater or lesser extent detectable by vision. As the light fades the colours of objects stand out less, but even with very little light, less than is required for colour to be perceptible, the discontinuities in the pattern of light between an object and its background may still enable us to make out the spatial boundaries of an object. Not only can the object be distinguished from its background, but its shape may remain recognizable if we bathe the scene in red light, yellow light, and so forth. The variability in the apparent colours of objects observed in such circumstances has generally been turned to serve some theory of the 'subjectivity' of colours; what it does show is how unimportant the colour which something is or seems to be is to our perception of that thing. It may be that nothing constant can be defined solely in terms of colour, but what matters is the persistence of the relative light and dark of adjacent objects. Reflected light also makes possible the perception of the inclination or slant of the surfaces of objects, the texture of their surfaces, the spatial relationships of objects to one another, the sizes of objects, and so forth, and the detectability of such features is able to survive considerable variation in the intensity and coloration of the light source. Once more it is the relational character of these properties, considering them in terms of light and shade, that enables them to survive such variations. The dents, bumps, scratches and grain on the surface of this desk can still be picked out with ease as the sun goes from the room, the light fades and is eventually replaced by artificial illumination. (The role of invariants in the perception of physical objects and various of their aspects is the recurrent theme of the psychologist J. J. Gibson's work. See especially his *The Perception of the Physical World* (1952) and *The Senses Considered as Perceptual Systems* (1968).)

It is easy enough to grasp how sound can be a proper object of hearing and how at the same time we can hear things other than sounds: we speak of hearing x just when it is a matter of hearing the sound which x makes. The relation of sight to light is clearly of a different order, and to bring out the facts which underlie this difference I shall now consider a world in which light and sound are closer to one another in a certain respect then they are at present. Suppose we had a source of sound which had a role analogous to that of the sun, emitting sound waves which were then reflected by physical objects with various modifications depending on the nature of the surface which they presented to the sound, or on their constitution more generally. Thus, we suppose that differences in reflected sound correspond to differences in the objects reflecting the sound, much as differences in the pattern of reflected light match corresponding differences in objects and make possible the perception of shape, texture and movement. The world is, of course, already somewhat like this, at least to the extent that sound is bounced off and absorbed by different objects in different ways, but it requires a much more thoroughgoing change to bring about a situation of the sort I have in mind, in which differences in sounds could go along with differences in properties of physical objects. One obvious complication would be that the source of sound would threaten to drown out all reflected sounds, so that we should have to suppose either that objects reflected sound in a narrower beam, or else that our hearing was more directional, in that we could hear only those things at which our ears were directly pointed, or in some way focused upon. Two ears placed as at present would lead to a problem, and there are other complications concerning 'white' sound, for instance, but the general picture seems to be coherent.

Descriptions which now apply only within the category of sounds would in this new world attach to objects as well, to things from which sounds were reflected. To describe a book as 'shrill', say, would not be to imply, in this extension of present usage, that it made a shrill noise, in the sense of *originating* such a sound, but that it sounded shrill when exposed to a—or to the—sound source. Similarly, the possible objects of the verb 'hear' would increase enormously, both in kind and in number, if we were to suppose that the quality of the reflected sound varied with the nature of the surfaces from which it was reflected to such an extent that we could speak of hearing the dents in the side of a car or the outline of a hedge.

Note that both in this novel state of affairs and in the world as currently constituted the phrase 'hear the sound of x' lacks the peculiarities which we pointed out in connection with 'see the colour of x'. Sound, which can be both originated by an object and reflected by its surface, has thereby a status comparable to that of light, not of colour, and what corresponds to 'colour' is 'pitch'. In the extended situation, terms such as 'shrill', 'flat' and 'melodious', which apply now only to sounds, are going to apply to physical objects as well, describing objects in auditory terms much as 'red' describes them in visual terms. At present, 'red' can be used with reference to colour, to light or a light, and to the surface of a physical object, but 'C sharp' is used only of a sound, and then not as an adjective. In the world imagined, just as 'red' describes the pen by specifying its colour, so 'C sharp' will, taken adjectivally, describe the pen by giving its pitch.

In such a world philosophical questions would arise similar to those which we have been considering with regard to light and colour. It would no doubt be suggested that what we invariably hear is the pitch of an object, but then it would emerge that to hear the pitch of something is, roughly, to hear *what* the pitch of that thing is, and this is rather a special and sophisticated ability, not something inevitably involved in hearing. In the world as it is you may hear a sound and yet be quite unsure what to say to the question, 'did you hear the pitch of that sound?', and in this other world you could hear objects well enough without hearing their pitch, i.e., without being able to tell by hearing anything about their pitch. Again, since you could not only hear sounds but also tables and features of tables, such as dents, scratches and edges, it could be disputed whether in hearing something you inevitably heard a sound.

What should the answer to this question be? Well, terms in the categories of pitch, timbre and intensity would apply equally to physical objects and to sounds; that would not be a matter of dispute. Nor would it be disputed that sound was essential to hearing objects. Just as it has been found that light is absorbed and reflected variously by various surfaces, and that this accounts for certain differences in visual perception, so a similar discovery would no doubt be made with respect to sound. But, given that certain adjectives would be descriptive both of sounds and of physical objects, would that be enough to allow us to speak of a common object of hearing in both cases, and if so would it be correct to speak of that object as a *sound*? Something neutral with respect to each of the different possible objects of hearing is what is required, and not something which usurps the place of either or of both; not something like the intervening *tertium quid* which traditional theories of sense-data foisted upon us, giving us an object, all right, but an object which threatens to supplant the things which we commonly suppose ourselves to perceive.

In this hypothetical world it does seem that, in a sense, no *more* is involved in hearing a sound than in hearing a physical object—the cover of a book, say—or, equivalently, that no *less* is involved in hearing a book than in hearing a sound. This suggests that in order for the sound not to be in competition with the physical object, but to be something which is heard when the latter is heard, it suffices that in describing what we heard as a *sound*, when it was also true that we heard a physical object, we should in effect proceed by prescinding from the other, non-auditory features of the object. But then this would not give us anything more than we had by dint of our knowledge of the descriptions which apply equally to sounds and to physical objects—nothing further, that is, which would be implied by use of the term 'sound'. In the one case we should attach the descriptions to the subject 'sound', in the other to the subject 'book'; use of the latter would have implications not carried by the former, since a book has further properties detectable by other senses, but the converse does not hold. As it occurs both in this fantasy world and in our own, a sound is something whose nature is definable solely in terms of a limited range of descriptions relating to pitch, timbre and intensity. There is nothing to a sound which we can find out about by further inspection, using another sense; a sound is something having a certain pitch, and so forth, but this 'something' does not relate to anything which can be identified by seeing, touching, smelling or tasting, anything which might be conceived of on the model of a material substrate, a common subject of diverse properties.

If, in the world envisaged, we think of the application of such characterizations as '. . . is C sharp' and '. . . is harsh' as being in the first instance to physical objects, then, when we extend them to apply to sounds, we can think of the term 'sound' as a form of 'dummy' subject introduced when the more customary subjects were lacking. This way of looking at the matter helps make clear just how it is that sounds and objects would not compete with one another as subjects of predication; talk of sounds would introduce nothing which had not already been allowed for in the relevant predications taking physical objects as their subject; nothing additional would be imported, nothing which might oust the material substrate as subject of these predications. Our world is not, of course, like the world so described. However, I do not intend these observations as mere fantasy: the non-linguistic facts are different, but the meaning of 'sound' is the same in both worlds. We often feel that there is something puzzling and rather special about sounds. They are 'entities' of a sort, not qualities or properties of objects, like shapes or colours, but they are unlike the more substantial furniture of the world. They conceal nothing in the way of a material substrate with properties which inspection by another sense may disclose, but whatever there is to a sound can be learned of by using one's ears. The question now arises how we are to answer the man who maintains that sounds and sound-waves are one and the same phenomenon, so that there is, as it were, more to a sound than meets the ear. However, I have taken this topic far enough for present purposes and I wish to return now to the problems posed by light. Sounds will be revisited at a later point.

In our preliminary discussion of light we presented an account according to which light was not strictly visible and not strictly coloured. This is an account which offers an easy transition to the scientist's conception of light, but there surely is *a* sense of 'light' according to which light can be visible and coloured. Furthermore, the investigation of sound which we have just completed strongly suggests that a case could be made out for another workable sense of the term. In the world envisaged we were willing to speak of sounds both with respect to the familiar phenomena of sounds as understood in this world and with respect to what one heard when one could be said to hear a physical object—when it was a matter of reflected sound. The legitimacy of the latter possibility was not thought of as dependent on the discovery that sound-waves were involved, but it rested on the overlap between predications applicable to sounds, as they occur in this world, and predications applicable to physical objects, as in the world contemplated, an overlap which was taken to define a common entity, a *sound*.

Supposing that light allows of a similar treatment, the corresponding predications will be predications relating to brightness, saturation and hue. In the earlier discussion I spoke as if such a predication as '. . . is bright red' could always be referred to a physical object; we might begin by saying that the light was bright red, but on closer inspection we should find, say, fine particles of dust illuminated by the light. Light as an object of sight appeared to be a superfluous notion, and the only notion for which we apparently had a use was that of light as a wave-form, not itself visible, but which through its action on physical objects renders them visible to us. However, we might have put ourselves this question: prior to the discovery of particles of dust which light from a light source illuminated, was there not something visible whose existence would not have been thrown in doubt by the failure to locate a material basis for what was seen? Even when light is patterned so as to suggest a physical object in some detail, it is only a contingent fact that when we extend our hand it meets with resistance at the point where the area of light is located—there are no actual figures on a movie screen, and it is conceivable that we should even find the screen to be missing, without loss to the figures. There is no necessity that another sense should find itself affected. Surely a light in the sky and an illuminated surface have something in common which can survive the discovery of a more radical difference, namely the absence of a material basis in the former case? Indeed, there would appear to be more than a possibility here. It can be granted that, generally speaking, something which we identify as merely light turns out on closer examination to be an illuminated surface, or a physical element in a light source, such as a piece of coloured glass or a filament. There surely are, however, cases in which we see a diffuse light, but which do not involve seeing illuminated particles of matter nor some element in the apparatus or whatever from which the light is radiated or emitted; matter will doubtless be involved, but not necessarily as that to which any colour predications are to be referred.

If we should fail to locate any material basis for the light we see, so that all we can say is there to be seen is light, and not something illuminated as well, we are not to regard the light as on a par with a material thing, as something, identifiable in terms of descriptions from the categories of brightness, saturation and hue, which provides a subject of further possible descriptions from a category pertaining to some other sense, such as 'soft', 'sweet', 'pliable' or 'acrid'. This point is important. Thus, the supposition that there is something common to what we perceive on two different occasions just on the strength of our inability to discern a difference is one of the questionable suppositions of the sense-datum tradition. It is only because 'seeing light' carries no implications which conflict

with 'seeing dust particles', because it is a more general, less informative description rather than a competing description, that
we can use it.

The more interesting consideration here is not so much that
'seeing light' is applicable both when what we see is merely light
and when it is a physical object, but that the use of the term 'light'
in the former case carries no implications as to a material substrate.
I shall set forth one consequence of this shortly, but first we may
note that the other point decides our original question about objects of vision. Light has been shown to be a proper object of
vision in both the senses of this phrase: whenever we see we see
light, and light is something which is perceived *only* by sight.
Accordingly, even though there is an enormous difference in the
way light and sound enter into sight and hearing respectively, on the
question of proper objects, light is to sight as sound is to hearing.
Whenever we see we see light, but there is of course no question of
a reduction of the things which we see to a common denominator
of light, as if allowing light as a proper object precluded it from
being true that cats and dogs were seen.

Light has been characterized as something which it is true that
we see whether or not it also turns out that what we see is at the
same time a physical object, and, as just indicated, this specification gives it a status reminiscent of certain conceptions of *sense-
data* as elements common to both veridical and hallucinatory sense
experience, entities which hover uneasily between the realms of
the mental and the physical. I have not explicitly construed 'light'
as indifferent to *these* two spheres, and since I have been trying not
to depart from the ordinary, everyday notion I am perhaps committed to regarding light as a phenomenon which must be locatable
in public space. But now let us consider what we should say if a
man's brain is stimulated in such a way that he has what, if he
knew no better, he would describe as an ordinary visual experience.
We may not be prepared to say that he *saw* anything in such a
case, but if we are, yet are not prepared to say that what he saw was
light, then of course light will not be a proper object of vision.
However, let us suppose that we extend the use of 'light' to cover
this sort of case as well, so that we may speak of seeing or experiencing a pattern of light when thus stimulated—a sense of 'light'
which requires a separation in fact as well as in meaning of *light*
and *light-waves*. What is the difference between the two cases, that

in which the man's brain is stimulated, and that in which the light
which he sees is 'really there'? How would 'light' have to change in
meaning in order that it might be used in such a context? We
might think that its difference in meaning would be a matter of its
now being used of a different kind of *stuff*: 'light' designates a
differently constituted subject accordingly as it is used of a public
phenomenon, locatable in space and perceptible to many, or as it is
used of a private, mental phenomenon. However, it is clear that
this model for understanding the change is not supported by the
conception of *light* which has been expounded; the relevant extension of meaning does not require us to think of a new kind of
stuff as now also being describable as 'light'; the word did not
previously describe a kind of stuff anyhow. The difference is to
be sought at a different level altogether, at the point where the
concept of *light* connects with that of *location*. This key notion,
and the principles relevant to deciding the question of the identity
of light with light-waves, are a topic for the next chapter.

9

PHYSICALISM AND LOCATION

A NUMBER of the problems which have arisen, particularly in the last chapter, are closely connected with the general problem of the meaning and truth of physicalism, the doctrine which maintains the identity of mental phenomena with physiological states, usually states of the brain, and I propose now to develop the argument in this direction.

As the physicalist's position is commonly presented, it contains two striking oddities. The first of these concerns the range of candidates for identity with the physical: in most cases it is sensations, especially pains, to which he applies his thesis, and yet, as mentioned at the outset, it can hardly be said that pains are typically *mental* phenomena; it is surely states and occurrences which have a closer connection with *thought* that we should take to be paradigms of the mental: thinking about a problem, dreaming, musing, composing a limerick, having a tune on one's mind— these are all mental states, and all at a great remove from pains, itches and tickles, sensations which we are happy to describe as 'bodily' and which we think of as much more directly tied to the physical.

In the second place, given our ordinary, everyday conception of pains as bodily afflictions it is slightly curious to find philosophers arguing for an identity between pains and *brain* processes; their physicalism would not suffer, but would surely be more plausible, if they affirmed the identity of pains with certain bodily states, notably the state of the body at or around the point where the pain is felt. Since we in some sense already believe that pains are such states it seems perverse to try to rid us of this belief and persuade us to identify pains with quite different physical conditions of the organism. After all, half the work is already done for the physicalist if we as much as abide by what we accept as non-philosophers, and since it makes no difference to his overall theory precisely what physical states are identified with pains, he might as well save himself needless argument and choose the most promising among the various possibilities.

Such a move has, furthermore, one very clear advantage over the identification of pains with states of the brain. One of the chief difficulties which physicalism encounters is that of the apparent incompatibility between the predicates which apply to the physical and those which apply to the mental, a difficulty which is particularly acute as regards locational predicates, predicates specifying where something is or is happening. A person's brain state may be in some sense circumscribed by his skull, but that is not where my pain is to be located when I suffer from indigestion. Sensations, on the other hand, *are* locatable in various parts of the body, so there is some chance of avoiding one aspect of the general objection if we opt for an identity between pain and the physiological disturbance which is to be found in the area of the body affected.

The emendation proposed looks entirely reasonable. However, it effects only a superficial *rapprochement* between the two terms of the identity, and it does nothing to resolve the question of meaning involved. I said that sensations are like physiological states or occurrences in being locatable in the body, but it is not clear that the sense of locational predicates is the same in each case. Suppose I report a pain in my leg. Can it be said to be there in the same sense as the accompanying physiological condition can be said to be in my leg? A first objection might bear on the notion of a condition or state as being *in* rather than *of* one's leg, and it might be suggested that we can speak of the whereabouts of a state at best only in a derivative sense; only, that is, to the extent that we can speak of the whereabouts of that which is in the state. Still, we can at least say that the leg is in a certain state at a certain point and this would seem to be good enough, so I shall not press the objection. Similarly, there is no serious objection here if we speak not of states but of occurrences, events, episodes or processes. What is more important by far is the difference in the implications of saying that my pain is at a certain point in my leg and the implications of saying that my leg is in a certain physiological state at that point: these differences are so great, it is questionable whether agreement in words is a matter of any significance.

A dramatic illustration of the difficulty is provided by the phantom limb phenomenon. We are puzzled to learn that a man who has had his leg amputated may report feeling pains in a region which his leg previously occupied, but where there is now nothing but empty space. What are we to say in such a case? Does the man only imagine the pain? Is the pain to be located at the end of his stump? In his brain? External to his body? Or nowhere at all? We become confused here because we ignore the difference between the location of a pain and the location of a body or a state of a body, and we suppose that where the latter are ruled out, so too is the former. There certainly cannot be the appropriate physiological disturbance some six inches external to the sufferer's body, but our understanding of pain location in no way presupposes such a possibility. The man's claim that his pain is where his leg used to be does not have to face tests relating to the presence or absence of physical conditions to be found at that point; such an assertion has no logical implications whatsoever with respect to what you will find if you inspect the area.

The putative identity between sensation and physical state is not like an identity in which we have to do with two items which are indisputably from the same category. If it is conjectured that two bodies or two physiological states are the same, then any discrepancy which we may find in their respective spatial locations or boundaries rules out an identity; at best the one is identical with some part of the other. But is the sense in which the pain is in my leg and the sense in which my leg is in a certain physiological state at that point sufficiently close for it to be possible that verbal agreement—both the pain and the physical disturbance are in the same part of my leg—should confirm the identity, or verbal disagreement refute it? If there is no way for you to correct my statement about the whereabouts of my pain by reference to anything which you may detect, is the sense which my statement bears such as to even *conflict* with that in which the physiological state can be said to be located in a particular area?

The possibility of a difference in sense of this kind seems to be generally overlooked, the question of identity being treated in terms of agreement or disagreement at a superficial verbal level. However, it is not, we may note, a difference which has anything to do with the mental, broadly construed, but a parallel argument shows that the physicalist will encounter essentially the same difficulty when dealing with a behaviourist account. Thus, consider a context where something like a behaviourist account of the whereabouts of a pain has some plausibility, that of an animal in pain. In so far as we have any occasion to locate an animal's pain we do so on the basis of what we can observe, not what the animal tells us, and what we observe is a point at which an injury has been inflicted, an area of its body which the animal may lick, try to protect and otherwise give favoured treatment. If there is agreement in these various conditions and reactions then we shall have no problem: that is where the pain is. However, there can be the one without the other—for instance, the attention to a particular limb but without there being any sign of injury at that point—and it might even be that the animal favoured a certain part of its body without there being any physiological disturbance in that area; not merely an absence of gross injury, but nothing relevant to be found even on delving beneath the skin. This would present a parallel to those cases where nerves somehow get crossed in the human body and a man locates his pain at a point in his body quite other than that at which the damage occurred which gave rise to the pain. What he says need not be regarded as incorrigible, at least in the sense that even he cannot revise what he says, but neither in this nor in the normal case does his statement of where his pain is allow of contradiction by the physiologist. A similar crossing of nerves could lead the animal to favour a region of its body other than that at which the injury was incurred, and in that case too it would be reasonable to persist in giving priority to the non-physiological rather than to the physiological considerations. After all, if we do have a concept of the location of pain which we apply to animals it will surely be explicable in behavioural terms, or at least in terms relating to readily observable phenomena, rather than to physiological data which have been established subsequent to a time at which the usage of the concept had become fixed.

I have implied that we must turn to animals to find an appropriate context for a notion of pain location based on behaviour, but it might be suggested that this is, fundamentally, what we have with human beings. Let me explain. It is true that when I say I have a pain in my foot I do not do so on the basis of observation of my behaviour; such observation is unnecessary as regards the existence of the pain and it would also seem to be unnecessary as regards the whereabouts of the pain. However, the fact that I do not make use of behavioural evidence does not mean that I make use of non-behavioural evidence, for when I say where my pain is I do not rely on any evidence at all; *a fortiori*, I do not have recourse to evidence which might come into conflict with what an observation of behaviour might reveal. Of course, what I *say* may conflict with what a man concludes from observing me, and the question now is: whose word takes priority? If my statement about where the pain is is incorrigible then my last word is the last word, but it is conceivable that I should have to defer to what is to be learned by observation. Thus, it is quite possible to have one's fingers crossed in such a way that you locate a sensation in one of them, only to realize on disentangling them that it was in another. Again, the amputee is surely wrong if he says that his pain is in his *leg*, as he well might before learning of its loss. Could it be that the location of pain is to be understood primarily in terms of where you are disposed to *point* to? You may misidentify the part of your body where the pain was, but in any case the characterization offered frequently seems to take second place to what is identified by your saying 'it's there' and pointing to some part of your body; or, at least, pointing to some place: the amputee's leg has gone, but there is still the place where it was, a place to which he can point.

There are further complications here to do with the distinction between where you point to and where you take yourself to be pointing, but I mention this only as a possibility which, if it can be defended, would to some extent vindicate a behaviourist account of the location of pain. Certainly, to restate my main point, there is nothing unique about the opposition between physicalism and a non-behaviourist view of the mental, but the physicalist may run into the same objections from the man whom you would suppose to be more congenial to him, namely the behaviourist.

If the notion of location does differ significantly in its application to sensations and its application to states of a body detectable by observation and use of instruments, we shall have deprived the physicalist of the support which, it was suggested, he might have derived from an identification of pains with physiological states occurring where the pain is felt, rather than with states of the brain. By the same token, on the other hand, such apparent counter-examples as that of the pain in a phantom limb are not to be taken as refuting him. Thus, one strain of physicalist might have started by saying that he was merely putting forward a contingent identity relating sensation and bodily state; not meaning that you could logically infer the whereabouts of a pain from a knowledge of the whereabouts of the corresponding state, but only that so long as the two were found in the same place, to that extent his assertion of their identity would be confirmed. If, however, they were found to be in different places, then he would be shown to be mistaken. For a philosopher who adopts this approach the pain in the phantom limb presents a crucial test case: to keep his thesis in the running he will have to deny the reality of such pains or else argue that a person's pain need not be where he points and says that it is—and neither of these alternatives would appear to be defensible.

What I have been suggesting, by contrast, is that when it is found that pain and state are in the same place, the sense in which it is true of each that it is in my leg, say, is sufficiently different in either case for it to be extremely doubtful whether we have in this agreement any support for the identity. The phantom limb phenomenon brings out in a striking fashion the possibility of disagreement at a verbal level, but even if such a discrepancy never in fact arose the same problem concerning the sense of 'where it is' in each case would arise. Our understanding of assertions of the place of a pain owes nothing to knowledge or suppositions regarding what, physiologically, may be detected at that place, and this independence is not altered in the slightest even if there is never any divergence. On the other hand, as I have intimated, it might be argued that finding that sensation and physiological state are in different places does not necessarily tell against the truth of the identity: the very difference in sense of locational predicates as applied to each means the removal of obstacles to their identification.

That is perhaps a possibility, but we are going to have to demand more in the way of positive agreements between unequivocal terms if we are to have any support beyond the mere removal of certain obstacles, and yet we find that the objection presented continues to arise with descriptions other than those to do with location. We might, for instance, describe a pain as 'sharp', 'stabbing', 'throbbing', 'dull', 'burning', 'acute' or 'mild'; all these terms have application to phenomena other than sensations, but none of them, so it happens, can be predicated of physiological states, processes or whatever. More importantly, even if we should find that these terms could be thus applied we should have to ensure that they then had the same sense as they do when used of sensations, and this would present a considerable problem. To take another example, it is sometimes said that when we report a sensation we do not report a brain process (or other physiological state); to this the physicalist retorts that if, as he maintains, sensations just are such processes, then, even though we may not know what we are doing, we are in fact reporting a brain process when we report a sensation. However, both the objection and its familiar reply are equally beside the point. It is not primarily a matter of whether or not '*x* reports *y*' is an intentional context, but what is at stake is whether the sense of 'reports' is the same in '*x* reports a sensation' as it is in '*x* reports a brain process', and whatever we eventually decide on the question of identity, the difference between the two must, I should say, continue to be recognized: reporting on the state of my brain, which is something I might conceivably do if I were wired up to an electro-encephalogram or if I were a skilled surgeon equipped with apparatus which enabled me to see what was happening inside my head, is not an activity which somehow suddenly becomes fused with reporting the pain which I feel once the identity is in some sense established. There are, it is true, descriptions which apply unequivocally to both sensations and physiological states—e.g., 'lasting two minutes'— but the two classes of description remain non-aligned on so many points, it is far from clear what the identity could mean if its truth is consistent with this multitude of divergences. Nor are these difficulties removed if we revert to the thesis in the restricted form, where sensations are held to be identical with brain processes, but, as we have seen, the same kind of point can be made there with equal effectiveness.

Much of the difficulty which the physicalist meets with derives from his assumption that his position requires an equation between *having a pain* and *being in such-and-such a physiological state* such that not simply is it true that to be in pain is to be in a certain physiological state, but, furthermore, that the pain and the state are in some sense one. We might be prepared to agree that being in pain is a matter of being in a certain physiological state, since it may be that people feel pain when and only when certain specific physical conditions can be identified in their bodies, but the argument to date reveals difficulties in making sense of the further step of equating the two. Could it be, then, that agreement is possible at the more general level and that the differences and difficulties only arise on the assumption that we have in 'pain' and 'physiological state S' comparable terms, terms which can be extracted from these fuller contexts and treated as on a par with one another in virtue of the less specific identity? There seems to be no reason for supposing that acceptance of the broader identity commits us to singling out some aspect of the physiological state of one who is in pain as actually *being* his pain. Similarly, for a pain to be sharp is for the state S to have some particular property ϕ; a property yet to be discovered, not a property which our understanding of the word 'sharp' would offer us the slightest assistance in recognizing.

We shall return again to this more plausible identity, but there is still much to be said about the notion of location, and I should like to press on with this topic, first with respect to pain and then with respect to sounds. There is a familiar sense in which two people can be said to have the same sensation. For instance, if you have experienced the pain one feels on stubbing one's toe then there is at least one pain which we have both experienced. And, we may note, we can say that we have both had that pain, or the same pain, even if at the same time we can speak of differences in our pains: perhaps your pain was more intense than mine, or lasted longer. On the other hand, there is also a sense of 'same pain' in which it is true to say that you and I do not have the same pain when we stub our toes. This difference is implicit when we consider the question whether or not our *respective* pains are the same; here it is a question of comparing two pains, and this twoness persists even though we may conclude that our pains are indistinguishable in kind, intensity or duration.

To show that this twoness is not logically inevitable we may invoke the familiar example of the two people with their flesh so united that they share a common hand; this might be as the result of an operation or it might occur naturally, as with Siamese twins. If the shared flesh is cut or burned and both report pains in it, then it would be reasonable to say that both felt the same pain. It is perhaps not a question of one person experiencing *another's* pain, since it would hardly belong to the one rather than the other; neither would enjoy any proprietary status with respect to the sensation. Note too that we need not insist that the two people's reports on the pain tally in every detail, but the kind of circumstances which allow us to introduce talk of one and the same pain being felt by more than one person would also appear to permit the possibility that it should feel slightly more disagreeable, say, to one person than to the other. Complete agreement in this regard is not essential to the identity of the sort in question. To generalize this possibility, imagine that a number of people could be joined together for a time and could locate sensations in their common flesh. As things now stand we make no distinction between how a pain seems to someone and how it really is, and a man's word has a special position on the question of the character of his sensation. In the situation envisaged, however, just such a distinction would become viable; a man who could barely feel the pain which others found most distracting might be deemed to be less sensitive than the others to the pain which was, as we might put it, there to be felt; it did not seem particularly painful to him, but in reality it was quite severe.

Let us now ask how this identity of pains is to be characterized generally, in what circumstances we might reasonably speak of one pain being felt by more than one person. It would not seem to be sufficient that the pain be felt in shared flesh, since the pains could be at different points in this flesh, one felt by one person, the other by the other. If now we require that the two pains have the same location in the flesh we have the different objection that common flesh does not in any case appear to be necessary: it is quite conceivable that when asked to point to the place where he felt a pain a man should knowingly point to a region not occupied by his body. When discussing the phantom limb phenomenon, I suggested that a person would be mistaken in rejecting the amputee's location of his pain on the grounds that inspection of that area disclosed nothing at all in the way of physical signs of pain; the man's word takes precedence over any such findings. This suggests an extension of the possibility provided by the Siamese twins: if I can locate a pain I feel somewhere outside my body and you locate the pain which you feel at the same point, then perhaps we can say that we both feel the same pain, even though we have no flesh in common. So we might suggest that pains be counted according to a spatio-temporal criterion, a difference in either spatial or temporal location being sufficient for a difference in pains, and a difference in at least one of these necessary. If this formulation is adequate then we can see how it is possible that one and the same pain should feel different to different people: its being one and the same is not determined by agreement in their reports as to its character, but disagreement here is consistent with its sameness as judged by spatio-temporal considerations.

In fact, I have no wish to press for this formula. If we did come to speak of shared pains I do not believe that identity of spatial location would become a strictly necessary condition. A more important amendment, though one which is easily made, relates to the following possibility. It might happen that two people point to exactly the same region of space when asked to indicate where they feel pain, but this is not sufficient for sameness of pain if the pain which each feels moves around with him—if the locations of the pains coincided while their bodies were in a certain position relative to one another, but it just needed one of them to move for this agreement to be lost. More than such momentary coincidence is obviously required, and I suggest the following as a more general account. Let us suppose that the pain was strongest, most acute, when you were in a certain position, and that you would speak of it as growing weaker, less acute, as you moved away from the apparent pain source. If we fixed the location of the pain in terms of the place where it was most intense, and if the reports of different people all converged upon such-and-such a point as the source, centre, or origin of the pain, then that surely just is a world in which pains are 'public', where one and the same pain can be felt by a number of different people. This is not, of course, to claim that all the pains of the sorts which we now experience might be thus re-located: a headache cannot be felt outside one's head, nor a stomach-ache outside one's stomach. The suggestion is simply that it is conceivable that there should be pains which are shared and at a distance from one's body, and these are the circumstances in which this possibility would be realized.

A pain which grows in intensity as we move along one line and weakens as we move in an opposite direction, and which thus seems to emanate from a certain point in space: that is much the way a sound is in our world. This is the parallel I am interested in drawing, and to complete the fantasy I wish now to apply in reverse the same argument to sounds. In the world as it is there is no difficulty, either logical or empirical, in having two people hear the same sound, in either of the two senses which this commonly covers: someone gives a whistle, we both hear it, we both hear the same sound; on another occasion someone whistles, I hear it, you do not, but you hear someone else give exactly the same whistle, so in another sense we both hear the same sound. In the first case, where there is only one sound to be heard, we have a use of 'same sound' which compares with the use of 'same pain' in 'no two people can feel the same pain', when this is used to make a contingently true statement. The corresponding statement about sounds is, of course, false at present, and what we are to do is consider the changes which would have to take place for it to be true, for sounds to become 'private', in one possible sense of this term. Traditionally, the problem has been conceived the other way around: what philosophers found difficult to contemplate was the possibility that sounds might be public. However, to acknowledge this is just to acknowledge the existence of conditions in which we can intelligibly speak of two people hearing the same sound, and appreciation of this familiar fact requires no exercise of fantasy.

More accurately, we are to consider the possibility that sounds should cease to be located as at present. Their failure to be located in public space is very naturally taken as showing their privacy, and it is interesting to develop the topic in this connection. However, it can be questioned whether privacy of sounds need follow so readily on this possibility, and I have no wish to rely on the claim that it inevitably does. First, let us consider the case where sounds become private through being located in the body, like pains. Such a possibility is not to be thought of as being comparable with a person's stomach-rumbles, for instance. This is a sound within a man's body, true enough, but he does not bear the requisite unique relation to it, even if he can hear it more clearly than others. It is the sort of noise that others can with luck hear, and which they locate in the same way as they locate any other sound; it just happens to be within a person's body, and for our purposes there is no significance in this fact. We want to rule out the circumstances which underlie the location of a sound in the same place by more than one person, and this means ruling out the familiar phenomenon of noting a difference in the volume and direction of sound as we move about; to the extent that we have this systematic scale of increases and decreases relative to the position of a person's body and the sound source, we have the location of the sound at a point external to the individual's body, and the way in which, in general, the locations which individuals offer single

out a common point as the source of the sound provides the background for speaking of one and the same sound as audible to many.
So we may suppose such circumstances not to hold, but that hearing a sound is more like the exceptional auditory experiences which
we have when we have a ringing sound, say, in the head or ear,
and which no one else can detect.

Unfortunately, if such 'internal' sounds are to be our model for
hearing generally, there will be considerable doubt about our
justification for speaking here in terms of 'hearing sounds'. When
I hear a sound in my foot, say, there will presumably be nothing
quite like directing a pair of ears to a sound source, and in the
absence of anything like our present organ of hearing being
affected by the familiar causes, I am inclined to think that we have
no right to extend our sound-terminology to such a case. Instead,
let us pass to the following modification: we suppose that we have an
ear as now, even two, and that it responds to such things as doors
slamming and dogs barking, but that there is not the same pattern
of varying intensity of sound which leads us to locate a sound at a
particular point of space. If everything is as now except for the
question of location, I think it is reasonable to continue to speak of
hearing sounds, and we can preserve this much without introducing
the more problematic complication that sounds are to be located in
various parts of the body; they become private—if they do—not
by virtue of being located in the individual's body, but by not being
located anywhere.

We are, then, supposing three things: first, that variations in the
strength of a sound which enable one or more persons to converge
on its source are absent; second, that there is no inclination, or not
necessarily any inclination to locate a sound within one's ear or
head or any other part of the body, but that the ear is necessary for
the experience of sound; and, third, the same sorts of physical
phenomena—doors slamming, and so forth—give rise to the production of sound. It is tempting to think of this situation as like
that in which a sound 'surrounds' us, where it comes just as much
from one direction as from another, but it is doubtful whether this
description would have a meaningful contrast for us in the world
being considered, since, if we had no use for speaking of a sound as
coming from a given point, we could only vacuously say that a
sound seemed to come as much from here as from there. Note too
that when we are surrounded by a sound we can still locate that

sound in space, though being in the middle of it we do not at the time have any awareness of the variations at the 'edges'—louder this side than that—which enable us to ascertain that it is centred on a limited region of space, it being necessary for us to move about in order to find the boundaries of the region which circumscribes the sound. As with thoughts, so sounds are not anywhere, we might say in this world; or as with thoughts we might speak of sounds as being 'in our heads', or perhaps 'in our ears', but in either case the sense of 'in' would not be the same as that in which a sound can at present occur in a person's head or ear.

Before indicating the main point of this discussion of sounds I should like to consider what happens if we try to make the parallel moves with sight. There are a number of reasons why sounds fit my fantasy more readily than does any object of sight. Thus, in the world as it is there are many occasions when we are not aware of a sound as at any particular distance from us or as coming from any specific place. It may be that it is only upon moving our heads, so making for a difference in the sound reaching one ear and the sound reaching the other, that we become aware of a sound as at a distance from us and as coming from the left rather than the right, above or below us. As we remain motionless the sound seems to have a peculiar proximity or intimacy and we have no sense of its being external to us—though no sense of its being inside us either. With objects of vision, by contrast, there is no comparable experience, and it is correspondingly more difficult to imagine the lack of location with them. More difficult, but not impossible; thus, imagine that the scene remained the same as you moved your eyes and head about and as you moved generally in relation to the things around you; imagine too that we could not cut off the view before us by closing our eyes, and that more generally there was no question of interposing something between our eyes and what we saw in such a way that we came to see the object interposed and could make out only the non-occluded part of the background. With the abolition of the phenomenon of occlusion and the disappearance of all the other perspectival variations which come with movements of the body and the organ of sight and which serve as clues for depth, we should be left, not with the experience of gazing at a flat picture— since that suggests confrontation with something at a distance from us—but with the experience of 'seeing' something which stood in no spatial relation to us. There is no question, we shall suppose, even of running our eyes up and down a stable scene, but we cannot move our eyes about, attending now to one, now to another part of the 'scene', while more vaguely keeping the whole of the scene 'in view'. This last condition introduces complications, and is not strictly necessary, but in any event I think we can soon come to an idea of what it would be like to have no conception of the object of sight as at a distance from us; not as, instead, situated within our body, but simply not locatable anywhere. And with this would come the lack of any impression of what we 'saw' as something independent of us, something to which we could return to re-examine, but which had continued to exist whilst our attention was elsewhere.

The hypothesis that to be in pain is to be in a certain physiological state is not free from difficulties concerning meaning and verification, but it fares better than the simple identification criticized. Similarly, it is the more general thesis, if any, that has application to perception: to hear a sound will, on this account, be a matter of being in a (suitably caused) physiological state, although the sound heard is not such a state, indeed is not to be identified with *anything* physical. The physicalist might be reluctant to extend his thesis to perception generally; at least he may suppose he has a particular problem here, since sounds and so forth are not to be located at the same place as any bodily state with which they might be identified. Still, it is what is more generally physical rather than what is specifically physiological that constitutes his preferred class of existents, so he will no doubt opt for an identification of sounds with their physical correlates, namely sound-waves, and in this way consider his general thesis saved. It is my hope that the fantasies developed with respect to sounds show up the arbitrariness of this identification as well, and I shall take up this topic after reinforcing the earlier argument against his treatment of pains.

We can entertain the possibility of pains locatable in public space and which any number of people can experience. The physiological and physical changes necessary for this to occur would be complex but the situation is conceivable: the externalization of pains is something which can be imposed upon the present situation without negating it entirely. Now, if this complication were to obtain we should have even less reason to identify pains with their associated physiological processes than at present: there would not even be the superficial agreement in location which we now have. Of course, to speak of such a possibility is not to speak of the actual world, but it seems to me that just as a possibility it reinforces the impression of arbitrariness which emerged from our consideration of (naïve) physicalism: pains can be as they are and yet in one set of circumstances be located in our bodies, in another set of circumstances not be thus located (except accidentally). It would not be a very interesting form of physicalism which could survive the former state of affairs but have to concede defeat if the other possibility began to be realized. Or we might put it this way: suppose we allow the physicalist the identity of pains with physiological states in the world as it currently, or ideally, is; is such a state of affairs in some way more intelligible than a world in which, because of the difference in location, this identity cannot be effected? Surely not.

Of course, as I have mentioned, the physicalist will rest content if pains can be identified with *some* physical state, and I have not ruled out all such identifications in my fantasy about externalized pains; might not the identity be with certain properties of the surfaces of objects—as with Wittgenstein's pain leaves? Once more, however, we might wonder what the identity could come to if it were thus indifferent, if in one world pains could be identified with physiological states, in another with physical states of the surfaces of objects. It is not that it would be quite impossible to fix a sense for 'same pain' in such a way that it could survive the differences in the physical phenomena with which individual pains were equated; it is just that the point and the sense of the identity are so far obscure. And, in any case, it requires only a slight modification in our fantasy to ensure that pains occur nowhere at all, as in our fiction concerning sounds, and this is a possibility which this version of physicalism cannot tolerate.

It is becoming obvious enough how the claim that sounds could continue to be sounds without having spatial location can be turned against the physicalist, but before spelling out the objection let me mention a consideration which seems initially to be more favourable to his case. It is tempting to understand the location of sounds along the following lines. As you approach a sound source the sound seems to grow in volume, and as you move away from the source it seems to diminish. On one way of looking at the matter—

the usual way—the sound remains constant, but seems to us to vary in volume because of our differing relation to it. However, could we not give an alternative description of these facts? Let us suppose that in some sense the sound can be conceived of as a state of the person who hears it, and that this state intensifies— i.e., the sound grows louder—as he nears a certain point, to wit, its source, weaker as he recedes from this point. We might put our question this way: is there any difference between the hypothesis of an *internal* sound that varies in strength as we vary our distance from its source, and the hypothesis of an *external* sound that seems to vary according to our distance from the source, but in fact remains constant? (As a matter of fact, we quite happily speak of the sound as getting fainter as we move away, and not as merely *seeming* to.) If we did accept such a translation between internal and external we might naturally think of the public sound as in some sense a 'projection' of the internal sound which we experienced; or we might feel that, although there could be no denying that sounds were external, when we saw what that came to—in accordance with the equivalence suggested—the notion of their being at a distance from us did involve something unexpected enough to be describable as 'illusory'.

I have thought this account appealing enough to be worthy of mention, but it is in fact badly confused. The alternative description which would be justified relates to the question of the *volume* of the sound, not to its whereabouts: you can say that a sound actually is getting weaker or only seems to be getting weaker, when the difference is brought about by your movements away from what is producing the sound and does not reflect a difference in the sound at source. As I say, we already have these two ways of speaking and neither has to be chosen in preference to the other. However, the possibility of saying that the sound *is* and not merely *seems* to be faint at this point does not give us any right to speak of it as 'internal'. There is nothing private about the sound, but one and the same sound is faint for everyone at this point—or merely seems to be so: neither locution carries any implications about privacy. We did briefly consider the possibility that sounds might be internalized, in the sense of located within the individual's body and audible to him alone, but we found this difficult to interpret satisfactorily. In any case, it is just not the case that the sounds that one hears are in any sense locatable in one's head, ears, or other parts of the body; we understand the location of sounds in terms of what we ascertain by using our ears, not by inspecting the ears or brain of a person; *a fortiori*, there is no question of our *projecting* sounds from an inner to an outer world.

The possibility which we did substantiate was that which allowed that sounds should be private and without any location whatsoever, but it surely cannot be maintained that when normally I hear a sound it really does not occur anywhere but that I project it on to a certain region of public space. If I do locate the sound as coming from a certain room, say, and this is recognized as correct by ordinary standards, what sense can be made of the suggestion that, at the same time, the sound does not really occur anywhere? And yet it does seem that, in order to give sense to the words which are to translate our familar propositions, it is necessary to deny the truth of the latter; not simply say what they come to— something which we cannot determine in advance and which might well cause us surprise—but actually declare them one and all false.

What is true, and may be behind this misconception, is that hearing can be a matter of the ear and brain being in a certain (suitably caused) physiological state, irrespective of whether or not the sound we hear is at a distance from us. The fact that more than one person can experience the very same sound and that the sound is at a distance from us presents no obstacle whatsoever to the broader version of physicalism. If the preceding arguments are correct, a sound's location is a comparatively minor feature of the sound, something which we can imagine to vary in a variety of ways, and it is, I suspect, only if we persist in ascribing to location the role which it has with physical objects—and generally try to understand sounds on the basis of a material model—that we shall find sounds perplexing and the broader physicalism unacceptable.

Let us return to the thesis that sounds are identical with soundwaves. The arguments which we initially invoked against the identification of pains with physiological states can be appealed to in this instance, and we can also use our fantasy about the location of sounds to show the arbitrariness of a form of physicalism whose truth may depend on agreement, possibly merely verbal, in locational predicates applied to both sounds and sound-waves. There is no necessity that sounds be located as at present, but it is conceivable that they should occur without any location at all, even though,

as now, sound-waves were necessary to their production. Similarly'
the identification of light with light-waves can be seen to be both
arbitrary and unnecessary.

To expand on this conclusion I wish to take further the comparison between feeling pains and hearing sounds, or, more
generally, between 'mere' sensation and perception. There would
appear to be a clear and important difference between feeling a
pain, itch, or other bodily sensation, and feeling a nail, a stone, or
some other physical object. The pain which I feel in my leg is not
something which was there awaiting discovery, something which I
might have felt for in vain but which on this occasion I did successfully detect. This way of marking a contrast between the two uses of
'feel' is familiar enough, but the nature of the contrast is perhaps
not altogether clear. It cannot be simply that between feeling which
may or may not locate something and feeling which cannot know
failure, feeling which cannot exist without its object. It is true that
there is no organ of pain which can be used in an exploratory
fashion, so that I might cast around within me as I might sniff with
my nose or scan the scene with my eyes in search of some feature
which I might detect, or which, on the other hand, might escape me.
But this is not the appropriate contrast, since in the case of feeling
with respect to physical objects it is not feeling *tout court* that
signifies the correlated exploratory activity, but feeling *for*. I may
feel for the nail and meet with success or failure, but if I have felt
the nail I have already met with success. It is not a matter of two
different uses of 'feels', such that the verb can go objectless when its
possible objects are physical but cannot be without an object when
it relates to sensations; it is just that we cannot speak of 'feeling
for' in connection with pains and sensations generally.

It is not entirely irrelevant that there are organs of sense, which
can be exercised effectively or not, but not an organ for the
'detection' of pain, but more important is the consideration that
we can speak of trying to smell, of sniffing without actually smelling
or of using others of our sense organs in vain, because we can make
sense of the suggestion that the object, in this instance a smell, can
exist independently of us. The distinguishing feature of the senses
is, in this connection, that there can be something there to be
sensed whether or not a given individual, or indeed anyone, is there
to sense it. Whether or not we can control, direct, or otherwise
manipulate a relevant organ is secondary. I can bring myself into a

position in which I can feel the warmth of the sun; this is in some ways like, in some ways unlike sniffing, or straining one's ears, but what all three cases have in common, and what differentiates them from feeling pain, is that in their case the object of sense has an independent existence in a way which the individual's sensations do not. Thus, I sniff and catch a whiff of perfume; I might have failed to detect anything, but there could still have been that smell of which others might have become aware. However, if I do not feel a pain, then there is no pain there to be felt. Of course, changes in both directions are possible, according to the earlier argument: if sight became as I suggested there would be no call to distinguish between the sense's being exercised and its object existing. Conversely, pains could have the independent status of sounds.

In the world as it is, however, this difference exists: sounds and smells are there to be sensed by all, the pain I feel exists only in so far as I feel it. Now, since a pain does not extend beyond the individual's awareness of it, but has an existence which is measured by that awareness, we might suppose that there is indeed some chance of equating *feeling pain* with *being in state S*, where S is the relevant physiological state. My perceiving x, on the other hand, is a matter of my going into a certain physiological state, on the comparable hypothesis for perception, but the history of the object sensed is not co-extensive, unless by accident, with my awareness of it; sounds, smells, patterns of light, these may all continue to exist whether I am there to perceive them or not. This being so, even the broader physicalism might be thought to harbour a certain tension, a tension between perception as involving a transitory state of the perceiver, and the constant, independent object of sense which continues in being irrespective of what happens to the observer. But this is not so. The fact that the physiological states of the various observers are individuated by being of their respective bodies does not result in any inconsistency when we say that they sense the same thing, and that this is a matter of each being in a certain, suitably caused, physiological state.

That is one point. To the objection that the physiological account is inadequate to the fact that sounds can exist unheard it would be a mistake to reply that sounds simply do not exist unless there is some sentient being whose ears are being appropriately stimulated, and hence that the existence of the sound is co-extensive with that of the corresponding physiological state. The more plausible physicalist account does not depend for its truth on the possibility of establishing a match at this point in this way, but the truth-conditions for the existence of sounds are quite different from those for the existence of physiological states. There can be a sound in the total absence of any physiological activity, but this is allowed for by the consideration—assuming the correctness of the more cogent version of physicalism—that the categorical assertion of the existence of the unheard sound is matched, ultimately, by a hypothetical proposition about the physiological and physical conditions. This is of course a claim which is much disputed, and it would take us too far afield to follow up the dispute at this point. Let me simply mention that it would be wrong to reject such an account on the grounds that it makes the existence of sounds no more than hypothetical. To say this is like saying that on this analysis unheard sounds do not really exist at all, when we have just asserted what it is for them to exist, what, on the physicalist hypothesis, their existence comes to. A cushion is springy if it will revert to its original form after having been sat upon. That, let us suppose, is both a necessary and a sufficient condition for its being springy; but for its being *actually* springy, not for its being hypothetically springy. For that we should require a conditional with *two* antecedent clauses.

It is conceivable that the physiological state associated with x's being in pain should be quite different from that associated with y's being in pain. This may not be so if the specification of the state is given at a high level of generality, but once physiological detail is introduced and we descend to the neural level the possibility of a difference arises. This is simply a consequence of the difference in meaning between the psychological and the physiological statements and it does not constitute an objection to physicalism in its more plausible form. To take an analogous example, but with reference to the problem of reconciling physicalism and behaviourism, we understand what it is for an animal to be frightened without having any knowledge of the underlying physiological conditions of the phenomenon; the right reactions in the right circumstances will be all that we shall need to justify our description. If the animal's fright were something which could conceivably be identified among its physiological states, then the possibility of a different identification from creature to creature would arise, and this could lead to a difficulty for the physicalist—though once more it would depend on the level of generality at which the description of the physical state was given. However, even the physicalist who wishes to identify pains with physiological states is unlikely to want to say anything more than that to be frightened is to be in such a state; he will surely not be strongly tempted to take the further step of insisting upon a physiological referent for 'fright', and this being so he will not be troubled by the emergence of a difference in the states of x and y, unless such a difference goes with a difference in actual or potential behaviour relevant to the description of the creature as 'frightened'; and by hypothesis this is taken to be ruled out. Further, and in line with our earlier argument concerning sight in the absence of behaviour, we can allow that detection of a certain physiological state might be taken to show that the animal was frightened in circumstances where its fright was not evidenced by more readily observable signs, since we could have ascertained that this state went along with a propensity to act in such a way as to give proof of fright, a propensity which was inhibited in the particular circumstances. But once more we can allow the possibility of two such states, quite distinct the one from the other, provided that the difference is not effective in bringing about a difference at the level at which the sense of 'being frightened' is determined.

Where a problem of some magnitude does arise is in connection with the notion of ascertaining the physiological conditions associated with a particular psychological state. With an animal the practical problem is enormous, and with a man we have in addition a considerable theoretical difficulty, stemming from the almost invariable requirement that we establish a correlation between on the one hand physiological—and more specifically neurophysiological—conditions, and on the other hand certain knowledge which the subject has. The difficulty is not simply that the man might not tell us that he is in pain, say—as the lazy cat may refrain from any actions which would show that she had seen the ball of wool—but that if he says he is then we shall want some guarantee that he is telling the truth; and here the parallel is with doubts which we might have concerning how the cat's actions were brought about.

The problem posed by physicalism and the problem of other minds come together on this point: whether it is to be used to establish the physicalist's correlation or whether we are just interested in it for its own sake, knowledge of a man's psychological states depends on the possibility of ascertaining what he knows in the face of possible deception and suppression of responses on his part. It is true that the major problem for the physicalist remains that of elucidating the sense of the identity which he wishes to establish, but this problem of verification is an important preliminary for him, and one to which we shall turn our attention in the next chapter.

In conclusion, it is of interest to note the parallel between our discussions of physicalism and animal behaviourism. The physicalist who insists on identity at the level of *pain* and *physiological state S* is like the behaviourist who will not rest content with the logical adequacy of behaviour in grounding the ascription of a given predicate, but demands in addition that there be some item of behaviour which corresponds in a simple fashion to that predicate. In neither case is there anything to be gained by defining the general position in such a way that the specific match is necessary to its truth. This point is now generally recognized, even if not consistently observed, and in particular the version of physicalism which I have held to be more plausible has superseded the cruder version in the writings of most physicalists. However, my aim has not been to suggest new possibilities in support of the physicalist so much as to use the issue as a starting-point for questions relating to the location and privacy of sensations.

10

VERIFICATION AND OTHER MINDS

I N the analysis given of human sensation, and suggested of the mental generally, a central place has been accorded to knowledge. I have interpreted this knowledge as, primarily, no more than an ability to say, and while this needs further qualification—a man who is dumb does not on that account lack the relevant knowledge—there need be no question of the improper uses proscribed by Wittgenstein: the use to make a misconceived contrast in terms of doubt and certainty, or that which suggests a finding out, a learning by investigation. As a preliminary to getting to grips with the problem of verification which is still unresolved, I should like to examine a false model of sensation and perception which relies on taking this latter suggestion seriously.

For me to see something, various publicly checkable conditions must be satisfied—that the thing be there to be seen, for instance—but if we are concerned with anything more than a behavioural responsiveness such conditions will not be sufficient: what is wanted in addition is an assurance that I know that I see. It is not, however, a question of knowledge acquired in any way whatsoever, and to illustrate how the knowledge might be inappropriately acquired we may take the example of certain 'split-brain' experiments. (On these see, e.g., M. S. Gazzaniga and R. W. Sperry, 'Language after Section of the Cerebral Commissures', *Brain*, 1967.) If we sever the great commissure or corpus callosum which connects the two hemispheres of the brain we find that a curious bifurcation of abilities results: the subject may respond appropriately to a request to point to an object which is in the visual field of one of his eyes only, and even be able to draw it, but report that he is unaware of seeing anything at all—though if the object is exposed to the other eye he may encounter no such difficulty. We commonly think of the ability to point at something or draw a copy of it as inseparable from the awareness of seeing that thing, and it comes as a surprise to learn that the latter may be lacking without the movements of one's hand degenerating into 'blind' gropings and fumblings. However, there is clearly a logical distinction between this awareness and these abilities, and the experiments with split-brain subjects present us with an unexpected realization of that possibility.

It is, then, quite conceivable that I should see but learn that I see only indirectly, by relying on the evidence of my behaviour, for instance, or on the word of another. When, in the typical case, I say that I see, then, on the view which we are to consider, I am conveying information based, not on the evidence of my behaviour, but on evidence of another kind: phenomena to which I alone have access, events which unfold before my inner gaze and of which I am the only witness. To some extent this picture has already been contradicted: we must allow that our seeing can itself be an object of knowledge as well as being an acquisition of knowledge, but it does not become the former by being the object of another, internal seeing. However, such a rejoinder is perhaps not very useful, since the notion of an internal seeing would surely be conceded to be metaphorical, so it is not clear precisely what it is that we can take ourselves to have refuted. More important, though far from straightforward, is the following observation. When I add the crucial words that I see, the words which are to give proof of the required knowledge, what I say need not be based on evidence at all, and *a fortiori* not on evidence which is available to me alone, or to others only in so far as I communicate it to them. I *can* assert that I see on the basis of evidence, but surely what distinguishes the normal, the typical case, is that there is no reliance on evidence or criteria of any kind.

There is a temptation to push this reply further, in the direction of the view which makes the verbal response constitutive of the state of which it gives proof. It is, we might say, not so much that there is one item of information which I have but which others lack; rather, there is one thing which has to be said and I am the one to say it. My words represent the knowledge crystallizing, as it were, rather than a report of something already known to me. On this view everything is on the surface, nothing hidden, but it neglects the consideration that the knowledge precedes its expression, not merely in the inevitable way that a disposition will precede its exercise, but in the more damaging sense that the knowledge may be fully articulate to the subject prior to its expression; the knowledge, and hence the associated state, owes nothing to the man's words, but is a determinate reality prior to anything he might say. All we are entitled to claim at this stage would seem to be what we have been maintaining all along: I alone can say that I see, in the sense not that I alone can tell, but in the sense that it is only as coming from me that the words can give proof that *I* see, and if I cannot say this then I do not know that I see.

The view which understands knowledge of the mental in terms of discoveries made by a gaze turned inwards may or may not be coupled with the claim that a person can be wrong about what he finds. If the possibility of error is allowed, we have the difficulty of making sense of the notion of things being other than the subject believes them to be, when the true state of affairs is not such that anyone else stands a chance of being able to ascertain how it is. If, on the other hand, we add to this false view the more traditional conception of the subject as infallible about the findings of inner sense, then the error becomes more complex. Independently of whether we subscribe to the underlying view, there is of course a genuine issue of whether a man is capable of error as regards the relevant judgements, and I should like now to consider this matter in terms of the notion of *incorrigibility*.

A man's avowal is said to be 'incorrigible' if it is not open to correction or revision; provided, we must add, that he both understands and means what he says. It is important to distinguish between the possibility of correction on the part of the person who makes the avowal and the possibility of correction from others. There have been a number of arguments directed against the view that pain reports are incorrigible, but most such attacks proceed by drawing attention to ways in which a person might be led to revise his own report, and not by citing circumstances which others can ascertain and which can put them into a position to deny that a man is in pain despite what he avows. The more important contrast is between the position of the person making the report and the position of everyone else—this after all is the asymmetry which we are trying more generally to characterize—and it seems appropriate to speak of an avowal as being incorrigible provided only that it cannot be corrected by others. So, even though I may show some hesitancy about whether or not to say that I am in pain, and even change my mind on the matter, my assertion that I am in pain is not, on this reading of the term, thereby shown to be corrigible.

Although highly unlikely, it does seem possible that we should go back on our claim to feel a pain, an itch, a tickle or a tingle, or on our avowal that we feel hot or cold or sleepy. Having just said 'that feels hot to me', for instance, I may conceivably have second thoughts and decide that the dish really feels very cold; extremes of temperature occasionally prompt a response which we are led to retract once our system has recovered from the initial shock. Again, if we are expecting a particular sensation, one of heat, say, we may be overhasty in judging that that is indeed what we felt, though we may appreciate our rashness almost at once. The cases in which a revision of judgements is forthcoming are generally such that the judgement is no sooner made than the person takes back what he has said, but it is also possible to persist for a time in saying that what one felt was so-and-so, and only come around to revising this on experiencing another sensation which offers a basis for comparison: I declare the taste in my mouth to be sweet; further reflection leaves me with this assessment, but I change my mind on being given some sugar to sample, something which, I now admit, really is sweet and shows up the unsweetness of the original taste.

These various kinds of revision are all possible, but, we may note, unless we have to do with an instance of misunderstanding, the authority of the individual is not thereby threatened, since the last word rests with him and is not dictated by the findings of others. That this is so can be further shown by considering the following possible objection. Suppose it is agreed that I can revise my judgement about a pain, saying one moment that a sensation I felt is painful and the next that it is not—or was not—exactly painful after all, perhaps even that it is rather pleasant. In some cases it might be reasonable to take this curious reaction as defining a particular kind of sensation, but let us suppose that there is no hesitation about my second judgement, and no inclination on my part to revise it again. Not only might I revise my judgements in this way, but it is possible that an observer should learn to anticipate these revisions or reclassifications. He notes that in certain circumstances I tend to retract my original judgement, speaking of an agreeable sensation after first describing it as unpleasant, and he can accordingly contradict my first judgement with a fair expectation that he will be proved right. So I start off by exclaiming 'ouch! that hurts!', he counters with 'no, it really doesn't hurt at all', and sure enough I come around to saying 'you are quite right, my initial reaction was mistaken'. However, it is important to note that the facts which prove him right are not independent of what I avow, but it is my eventual decision that it was after all not a pain that vindicates his contradiction of my avowal. It might look as if I come around to agreeing to something which he had somehow established and of which I was for a time ignorant. In a sense this is so, but what is unusual about the case and finds no expression in this way of stating it is that my agreement, though a concession that he was right, is at the same time what makes him to have been right in what was, in effect, a prediction. His claim that what I feel is not unpleasant is to be construed as a prediction that that is how I shall come to see it—or at least that that is how I should come to see it if I were to give the matter further thought. The man may be instrumental in getting me to revise my judgement, not by presenting me with evidence which conflicts with what I have said, but by suggesting that I think again. So, although the possibility of such revisions on the part of the speaker may be greeted with some scepticism, the fallibility of memory surely requires us to make room for them, and if they are allowed they present no problem for the supporter of incorrigibility.

If the possibility of incorrigibility is coupled with the account of our knowledge of our mental states based on the model of our knowledge of the physical world, the error in the latter is compounded in a curious way. On the one hand, we are invited to think of the individual's mental states as possibly awaiting discovery and investigation by him, and so as having a reality independent of his knowledge: they are as they are, even though their being as they are is not something which anyone else could determine. On the other hand, when he does pronounce upon their nature he cannot be in error; somehow his judgements are invariably in agreement with the way things are.

If we are to speak of a man's judgement as incorrigible, then we surely cannot think of him as judging upon an already fixed reality which is as it is independently of how he takes it to be, but we must attribute to his words the function of determining how things are.

I said above that provided a man both meant and understood what he said his word might be incorrigible. Putting the first condition to one side—as we may if we suppose it to be a matter of the man's unspoken word—it may seem as if, equipped with understanding, a man could set about ascertaining the facts concerning his thoughts and feelings of the moment, understanding being a necessary, but not a substantive part of what is involved in this internal investigation. However, understanding is not just one among other conditions which put a man in a position to make a true judgement, but, granted understanding, there is only the making of the judgement to come; there is nothing to be established as a preliminary, but the man has only to be disposed to make the judgement for it to be true. Turning to the spoken word, we can allow that what is said expresses knowledge which the man already has, but this knowledge is not to be described in terms which make it out to be anything other than the coming to be of the words or thought corresponding to what he says out loud. Any metaphorical description in terms of an inner sense must be consistent with the fact that this is, essentially, all that is involved. To say that the man is in pain we do not have to establish the existence of a reality beyond his words; but neither does he; no investigation, no discovery is required, but he has just to say what he is naturally disposed to say. We are obliged to reject the attractive but over-simplified view which always looks to the man's avowal as an element which is constitutive of the state in question rather than a report of it, but we retain what is distinctive to this conception to the extent that we think of the thoughts reported as themselves having the role of the words which would constitute the natural response which is definitive of the state.

The fundamental error in the picture which we are rejecting resides, I believe, in its misconception as regards *truth*. Let me try to indicate how this is so. When we say that the subject's word is incorrigible, this suggests that the possibility of a mismatch between what he says or thinks and how things are is somehow eliminated. A mismatch can occur, however, only between judgements, and likewise a match calls for a correspondence between two linguistic items, whereas in the examples in question there just are no other judgements with which a match or a mismatch could be established. We naturally think of truth in terms of the agreement of propositions or judgements with reality, but it is only as itself presented or expressed in judgement form that reality can enter into the comparison. This is not intended as a *reductio* of that account of truth—as if the only comparison could be circular —since, when comparison is possible, it will be between one's own judgement and that of others, not between one's own judgement and reality as one takes it to be oneself. However, in the case where there can be only one's own judgement, that judgement cannot be thought of as conforming with reality as determined by what others might say, but it is left to what one says or thinks in such a case to determine how things are, and the notion of truth here is correspondingly to be understood in terms of the judgement's having this role, rather than in any agreement between words and a reality whose nature is independently determined.

The notion of incorrigibility risks contamination by association with a false conception of a man's knowledge of his mental states, but it is not essentially tied to any such view, and it would certainly seem that in the typical cases we must acknowledge that a man's word is the last word on questions concerning his experiences. The problem of determining the nature and existence of a man's thoughts, feelings, and so on, accordingly becomes the problem of how we can establish the two provisos, sincerity and understanding, which are required for acceptance of the man's word as decisive. These two provisos are rather different in kind. The possibility of insincerity is not a possibility which affects the subject's authority in any way, which shows him not to be immune from error in a certain respect, but it is an obstacle which stands in the way of *our* knowing for sure how things are. With understanding, on the other hand, we have a proviso which threatens the individual's knowledge as well as our own, and I propose now to consider whether it is possible to appreciate when this threat is or is not realized.

It may be that a man's word is not answerable to public criteria as regards its truth, but the significance of this freedom from public control is diminished if any doubts are simply transferred to the proviso of understanding. If, that is, the incorrigibility of a man's (honest) avowal is protected by this clause in such a way that any doubts are to be interpreted as doubts as to its satisfaction, then the damage to the subject's authority is equally serious and the incorrigibility which he can claim for his avowal is that much less significant. In order, then, to show that the subject can make good his claim to a proper understanding of what he says, even though it appears to be at odds with the publicly checkable circumstances, we must consider whether it is possible to test for understanding independently, i.e., without having to let the question turn on his use of words in the disputed contexts.

To say that a person understands what he is saying is to make a claim of the kind which defines the general problem of how we are to verify an ascription of a psychological predicate. Fortunately, however, this is not an instance where the subject to whom the predicate is ascribed enjoys a position which from the present point of view is privileged in any special way. Whether or not a person understands something is not a matter to be conclusively settled by asking him, even supposing him to be truthful; nor is he even necessarily in a better position to judge of the question than others. There are two features of word use which we look for in testing for understanding. On the one hand we consider whether the person makes the right intralinguistic connections with the pro-lematic term, whether he draws the right implications from its use on a given occasion, connects it with the appropriate range of predicates, can give, or at least recognize, a reasonably close para-phrase, and so forth. On the other hand, we also consider whether he connects it with the right non-linguistic situations. As regards the first consideration, a person's use of 'pain' is on a par with his use of any other word; it is the second consideration that makes for the difference from the general run of words, since it is pre-cisely the problem of identifying the right extra-linguistic situations that causes us difficulty. However, this difficulty should not be exaggerated. It is only necessary that the subject should associate 'pain' with the kind of situation which makes an ascription of pain reasonable, as when he, or someone else, screams, writhes, groans, recoils and otherwise shows his displeasure on being struck, cut or burned. The person's behaviour will give no logical guarantee of pain, but provided it is a situation which, from the point of view of what can be observed, is of the right kind, and provided that the man recognizes that what is still lacking, if it is, is the avowal, an avowal which is not based on observation or evidence, then he has shown that he does have the requisite understanding of the phrase 'to be in pain'.

There are so many different ways in which a man can show his understanding of a word, it would seem unlikely that a few disputed contexts should upset the overall pattern which our questioning would reveal. If they should, on the other hand, or if it should be a matter of more than a few discrepancies, the problem is one of deciding how to describe the situation in the light of the opposing considerations, rather than penetrating to a well-defined but elusive truth, and the evidence on which such a decision is to be based is evidence which is, given the subject's co-operation, accessible to all, not just to him. In practice, if we doubt that a person is in pain despite what he says, we are more likely to suspect insincerity on his part rather than a failure in comprehension. He complains of pains but as soon as the company departs his anguished expression vanishes and is replaced by a smile. Or, conversely, he protests that he feels no pain despite the fact that he has just dealt his finger a heavy blow with a hammer. It is conceivable that he does not understand what he is saying, but if he can speak the language at all, that is highly unlikely as well as generally being readily detectable. Note, incidentally, that in considering this proviso we should have in mind the more general condition of truthfulness or meaning what one says, where not meaning what one says does not necessarily carry with it any suggestion of an intention to deceive. A person may be forced to say the words 'I am in pain'. He does not mean what he says, but there is no question of insincerity since he is not in a position to deceive and realizes that he is not. Again, an actor does not necessarily mean what he says, nor a person who is asleep, hypnotized, or under the influence of drugs, but this does not mean that we are to impute insincerity to such people.

There is an important division between these various instances of not meaning what one says. In one set of cases we may say this of a man on the grounds that he is not fully conscious. Consciousness has frequently been taken to be an elusive condition, but in fact its verification is not subject to the difficulty that affects so many psychological ascriptions. We need simply check to determine the range of a person's responses, linguistic and otherwise, and we can infer from his performance that he is conscious, or at least partially conscious, without fear of refutation on the score of pretence or deceit. A person can pretend to be unconscious or not fully conscious, but he cannot pretend to be conscious when he is not; consciousness will show itself whatever the

intentions with which he says what he says and does what he does. In a way, this is more significant than the fact that *specific* states of consciousness can be lied about, since it means that it may be readily determined whether a man 'has a mind', in one sense of this expression. It is the particular states that pose the problem. How, after all, can a person convince us that he is not lying? If we distrust him we may well regard his repeated denials as just so many more lies, and if we do come around to believing him this will be an act of faith, not a bowing to the inevitable.

It is customary to insist that a charge of insincerity makes sense only in a setting where it can be backed by reasons, and an attempt might be made to counter our scepticism with this consideration. Thus, the circumstances and our knowledge of children make it reasonable to suppose that the small boy who has been stung by a bee but says he did not feel anything is trying to be brave, or, more realistically, that the child who screams and says that he has hurt himself when he falls on the carpet is only trying to attract attention. If doubt is to be reasonable in the circumstances, there must, it is true, be some ground for attributing insincerity, but its making sense to suppose that P is not the same as its being reasonable to make that supposition: there can be insincerity when there is no reason to suspect it, where, as far as anything anyone can tell is concerned—anyone apart from the person affected—to allege it would be unreasonable. I could easily say that I had a sore finger or was feeling uncomfortable for reasons which were known to me alone, reasons which even the closest observer of my behaviour would not even begin to suspect. And, of course, it is *proof* that is our quarry; anything short of this, no matter how persuasive, is at an infinite remove from what the anti-realist requires.

There is no problem of checking whether a man means what he says unless and until there is a question of insincerity. Thus, if we suspect a slip of the tongue, a joke, or inattention to what he was saying, we may seek confirmation from the subject, and we shall consider the matter settled provided we feel assured of his honesty in dealing with the question. However, if there is a suspicion of deceit, is there any way in which the matter can be finally decided? In some cases, the answer would seem to be Yes. The man observed at the football match who says he has had to attend his grandmother's funeral could perhaps be deemed to

have had his insincerity exposed beyond any shadow of a doubt, if it were found that he knew she was alive and that he was generally in possession of his faculties. The problem arises with less gross instances of deception, where there is no question of the person's words and actions belying his avowal.

Here we might note the following. The anti-realist does not require that the actual circumstances always render verification possible, that we should have verification on demand, as it were. Just as nature is often loath to give up her secrets, so too with men. If the subject is stubborn there may be no way of making him give any indication of what he thinks, but the question is whether insincerity *can* show itself in the most favourable circumstances, when the subject is actually willing and co-operative. But now, even with this liberal interpretation of what is called for, it is still difficult to see how in the troublesome cases we could have *proof*, anything beyond very good reasons for a belief one way or the other. I say that I have a mild pain. I then try to persuade you that I was lying. But how can you be certain that I am not lying now? I have shown that I cannot be trusted, since I must have been lying on one of the occasions, but the assured fact of my untrustworthiness is not a hopeful basis for arriving at the truth.

The problem of insincerity is likely to present itself to us in the following terms: on the one hand there are the man's words, on the other hand there is what he really thinks. What he really thinks is conceived of in terms of occurrent thoughts which he has already had, and the question becomes one of how we are to ascertain what those thoughts were in order to be able to compare them with his subsequent spoken words. Now it is true that insincerity is a matter of saying one thing and thinking another, but sincerity need not be a matter of thinking one thing and correctly reporting that thought. Or, more accurately, the words you utter may be a report of what you think just in the sense of being a statement of what you think, though not a report of a thought which occurred to you in anything like an articulate fashion prior to that time. As long as we establish that such-and-such is what the man thinks, it matters not whether it be what he thinks in virtue of being a report of an already formulated thought, or whether it be what he is giving form and expression to for the first time. In this non-reportive use, saying what one thinks or meaning what one says has a rather negative import. It is a matter

of having one's mind on what one says, being sensitive to one's words; I as it were 'monitor' my speech and note anything which 'jars', but not in the sense that I have in advance a fully articulated intention with which to compare the phrases I actually come out with; it is more a matter of the words not prompting misgivings, second thoughts, or a wish to retract them

Let me mention an approach which these remarks suggest. We can get a lot nearer to establishing a person's sincerity if we can show that his words are an immediate response to whatever it was that caused the sensation which he avows. I dig something sharp into you and you immediately react with 'that hurt!'. Is there any room for doubt in such a case? We can strengthen the negative position by adding that you do not see me do what I do, so have no chance to prepare your false response. Furthermore, if we could have a decisive check in such a case it could also be applied when there was no such simple connection between stimulus and response. You are unable to manipulate the causes of my internal pains in order to determine whether my response is immediate, but you can manipulate events by asking me the question, 'were you telling the truth?', thus giving rise to a repetition of the kind of situation in which you do have the opportunity to ascertain immediacy and spontaneity of the reply. This would allow us to cope with the generality of cases—though there are problems with memory—but unfortunately the idea on which it is based is not, in my opinion, wholly convincing. It seems to me that one could never have the requisite authority to exclude all doubt, but that, no matter how prompt my response, it could still be made in the knowledge that what I was saying was false. There is too much uncertainty here for the benefit of the doubt not to go to the sceptic.

Perhaps, then, there is a stubborn fact which we just have to face: it is not possible to be in a position to say that a man is sincere or insincere except on the basis of evidence. How devastating would this conclusion be? We may combine this with another query: even if someone should show that insincerity is detectable in these difficult cases, that we can have more than mere evidence for it, must we agree that this is necessary to the status which we ascribe to imputations of insincerity? We can agree with the anti-realist that truth and falsity must in some sense make a knowable difference, but is it equally mandatory that this should be a difference of which *anyone* can come to know? After all, there will certainly be propositions which it is impossible for a given individual to verify—propositions about one's death, for instance. Why should there not be propositions which the individual alone is in a position to recognize as true or false without an evidential basis?

To follow up these questions, let us begin with the anti-realist's requirement that a man's avowal of pain should be capable of independent verification. There is a right and a wrong way of understanding this condition. Thus, when you tell me what is to be found in the drawer I can check on what you say; I am not obliged to take your word for it, but I can carry out my own investigation. In such a case we have to do with an independent check in the form of a *corroborative* check: I put myself in the same position in an effort to see if I come up with the same results as you. The general applicability of this procedure is possibly behind the desire to ascertain that a man or an animal is in pain by somehow experiencing, observing, or identifying the pain. This can be seen to be absurd when bluntly stated, but it may be thought to express an ideal of verification against which other procedures are to be compared; so a physicalist will recognize that a man's pain is not something to be revealed to careful observation, but at least the physiological state can be detected, and this may seem to him to place our understanding of pain on a firmer footing.

However, it is doubtful, to say the least, whether there is any gain in introducing reference to the physiological state in this connection, since the relations of meaning are not such that doubts about the existence of a pain could be settled in any but an indirect way by discovery of the state, and more generally it would seem we must break away from the conception of verification which favours this approach. We think of the problem as one of providing truth-conditions for an avowal, and we think of such conditions as being conditions in which what the man says corresponds to the way things are—Aristotle's saying of what is, that it is—whereas in this context the emphasis should be more on *proof*-conditions, conditions in which the man's utterance is to have probative force, in which what he says can be accepted as determining the way things are. We are to establish that the man is in a position to speak authoritatively—that he is fully conscious and understands what he says—but we are not to seek in addition to identify a state of affairs which he is purporting to describe and against which we can check the accuracy of his report. In those cases where a corroborative check is possible, ascertaining that a man knows that P involves ascertaining first that P, but in the present instance the order is reversed: we do not ascertain P as a preliminary, but we identify the subject as a source of knowledge or information, as far as we are able, and we come to accept P on the basis of his avowal of it.

This account makes explicit a more accurate statement of the problem, but it continues to be a problem: the anti-realist is still faced with the question how the relevant proof-conditions can possibly be determined. If this is just a matter of establishing that the man is able to say, if he chooses, how things are, then it can be established, but if we wish to lay down verifiable conditions which show us to be justified in taking his words at their face value, then we run up against the obstacle presented by the man's possible insincerity. This is a blow to the anti-realist; of that there is no doubt. But perhaps its force can be mitigated; perhaps our main concern should be with conditions which count against the man's sincere word as being authoritative, as not excluding all error and hence as not yielding direct verification. The man's authority certainly is impugned by a failure of understanding on his part or a lack of full consciousness, but these are conditions which, in favourable circumstances, can be known to us. Recall that the possibility which we are granting is that there should be propositions which the individual alone is in a position to recognize as true or false without an evidential basis. The qualification 'without an evidential basis' protects this position from attack at a point where it would otherwise be most vulnerable, since if the individual could have no more than evidence, then the state of affairs in question would be beyond his assured knowledge as well as beyond the knowledge of others. However, the possibility of undiscoverable insincerity does not open the door to a profusion of 'facts' having this problematic status.

Perhaps this, the possibility of an assertion not based on evidence, is what is central, with sincerity—which affects the spoken word, not the man's knowledge—of only secondary importance. This appears to be enough on which to build the direct–indirect contrast, and no stronger principle had to be invoked in destroying the false conception of the individual's knowledge of his mental states just discussed. Such knowledge was made out to be like knowledge of the physical world to the extent that it was supposed that things could be as they were independently of the individual's knowledge of how they were, even though—and this was the crucial difference with the physical world—how things were was not determinable by the judgement of anyone else. No appeal was made to verifiability in rejecting this, but what was claimed was that the relevant facts could not be held to be determinate independently of anything *anyone* might know.

Again, there is the consideration that the anti-realist still appears able to deal with the more far-reaching scepticism that we may entertain with respect to other minds, as I shall now indicate in greater detail. Suppose someone says 'I have a pain in my foot'. If we now say 'either he is telling the truth or he is lying', then we have asserted a disjunction each of whose disjuncts has mentalistic implications. If the man is telling the truth then he is in pain, a certain state of consciousness, and if not he is lying, so thinking one thing and saying another, which is again such a state. A more radical objection is accordingly possible, namely, to question whether we have any right to treat the man's utterances as having an intention behind them; they are not to be just sounds which an organism produces, but they must point beyond themselves, be symbolic of another reality, and how could we be assured that they succeed in that when we never get beyond the words themselves? After all, it would be possible to construct something which looked just like a man and which said 'that hurt!' when struck, but which was nothing more than a robot programmed to respond to the relevant stimuli in that way. It is surely too much to hope that words uttered on a given occasion, however reinforced by behaviour, should give incontrovertible proof that a being is in the mental state that its words would imply, or in any mental state for that matter, since they must establish the being as a subject of conscious states.

Now, it certainly is not logically impossible that an artifact should have thoughts or sensations, since our various concepts of mental states make no reference whatsoever to the physical make-up of the beings to which they may be applied—nor, we might add, do they have any implications about whether or not a creature has been in some sense programmed. Consequently, whether or not we can construct such a being is a question which only time, not logic, can tell. However, it is true that it is only too easy to take for granted certain conditions which are necessary if we are to take seriously the claim that x can be a subject of states of consciousness, and it is an enormous step to regard a being in this way, as something more than a mere object, like a clock or a wireless, something which we cannot find out about merely by taking it to pieces and inspecting it, but a being capable of states of which he may inform us, states for which his own word provides a non-superfluous criterion.

On the other hand, it does not appear especially difficult to furnish the justification for taking this step. What is required is that the being be capable of meaning what it says, of *having a mind* in a sense which is to be explained in terms of sensitivity or attention to the words of itself and of others. This is in turn to a large extent a matter of the possibility of its modifying its utterances to meet with changes in circumstances or discoveries which render them inappropriate. If it is capable of correcting itself in the face of conflicting data and of correcting us when we offer interpretations of what it says, then we shall surely establish that it is capable of meaning what it says, even if on a particular occasion we simply cannot determine whether it is sincere. If, on the other hand, it is inflexible, unable to adjust its utterances to the circumstances, then we shall be obliged to deny both meaning and understanding. Its utterances will be like tapes printed out by a computer: they present us with something which may become knowledge for us, but nothing which the machine can be said to know. Furthermore, for there to be a question of a possible 'knower', rather than merely something for us to know, a *subject* of the knowledge is required, and this is not guaranteed merely by the production of the right words in the right circumstances. As we noted in the discussion of conditions for second-level awareness, for the fully-fledged case the verbal responses must reveal a grasp of the concept of the speaker as a subject. But once more it is possible to recognize when that concept has been attained.

In our opening exposition of the anti-realist's attack on the realist's attitude towards the question of animal sensation we mentioned the objection that there is an assumption as to the reliability of A in the description of it as *evidence* for B, an assumption whose justification calls for an independent verification of B. This point was re-expressed in terms of the anti-realist's demand for the possibility of conclusive verification, verification which makes no assumptions as to the reliability of evidence. Both formulations are plausible for the case of animal sensation, where there is no question of the animal's verifying anything, but with human beings the most we can require is, it would seem, the assertibility of the proposition by the subject, without a basis in evidence. The subject himself does not *verify* the relevant assertions, in any sense which would imply the possibility of his finding out that they have been true all along, but only in the sense that his word may verify the conjectures of others. In a way, the notion of conclusive verification has no application here, since we reach conclusiveness only when it ceases to be possible to speak of verification in the required sense. The emendation in terms of direct assertibility does not, however, answer the earlier objection: what right could we have to hold that A gives us a good reason for supposing that B if we could not at the same time say that, when in the past it was observed that A, it subsequently turned out that B? In the interesting cases this will resolve itself into the question of our right to affirm a man's sincerity or insincerity on the basis of certain allegedly good reasons, and it is apparently only if we have an established correlation that there can be any assessment of reliability, of better or less good reasons, so we must inquire whether such correlations are to be had.

It is commonly believed that when a man lies his pulse rate tends to go up. But how do we or could we find this out? Well, perhaps the subjects of our investigation kindly admit to lying in sufficiently many cases for us to be able to establish the correlation. But, of course, on these latter occasions they could have been lying, and here again we may have only reasons, never proof. As long as we are restricted to an appeal to mere reasons we shall never acquire the knowledge we seek, but only transfer the assumption of reliability from one occasion to the other, leaving us with no more than the knowledge that the man cannot have been telling the truth on all occasions. However, let us suppose that there are cases in which insincerity can be detected: the man is caught out by saying or doing other things which show him to have the knowledge which he denies. If there are such cases, as it would seem there are, and if a man's truthfulness can likewise show itself, then the possibility arises of establishing that some factor, F, e.g., a reading on a lie-detector, is a good index of sincerity, or, conversely, insincerity. Furthermore, the reliability of F may be established not merely with respect to ourselves—perhaps we do not even offer our services as a subject—but with respect to a variety of people who lie in circumstances in which their dishonesty is transparent, or who tell the truth when it is apparent that they know what they say to be so. We then make use of F in situations in which deceit is not otherwise detectable.

Even if it is in principle possible to test for insincerity in the troublesome cases, the practice of regarding certain conditions as indicative of insincerity—a reddening of the face, stammering, averting the gaze—has got going without our having done so. On the other hand, the existence of the practice points to more than the possibility of verification; it would seem we have actually found that certain conditions correlate with insincerity, a correlation which is only contingent, so that verifiability in principle has contributed nothing to our knowledge of these contingent connections. This acknowledges a possible insight in the rejected 'pedagogical' version of anti-realism. That version seemed obliged to consider verifiability in principle as too weak a requirement, since our actual understanding owes nothing to a mere possibility of this sort; if you are to train a person in the use of the language of sensations you must, the theory asserted, have actual verified instances to point to, there must be more than the theoretical possibility of verification. There can be no question of reviving this view, but it is true that the whole apparatus of reasons and evidence which we make use of so readily with respect to psychological ascriptions could not have been established unless, it could be argued, we had verifiability in practice and not merely in principle. If A is evidence for B then the relation between the two will be contingent, and this means that the connection between A and B can be arrived at, if at all, only through experience. So an actually well-established system of correlations argues for verification in practice to some degree, though not to the extent that all members of the class of propositions need be held to be verifiable.

Supposing only that verification is in principle possible in the straightforward cases, we can resurrect the possible use of analogy in the context of other minds. The usual grounds for its rejection here are twofold: an argument based on one instance, that of one's own case, is too weak to serve as a basis for any secure inference about others, and, second, the requirement of verifiability in any event relegates the use of analogy to a secondary status, since the requirement means that there has to be a direct way of establishing the conclusion in question. On the first point, it is clear that there is no question of a single instance bearing the weight of proof for the generality of cases, nor are we required to exploit any knowledge which we have of our own case. The analogy contemplated is between those cases where some factor, *F*, has actually been found to go with insincerity and the problematic cases where no such joint verification seems possible; the number and variety of people used in setting up the basis for the analogy could be as great as you please. On the second point, we reject the suggestion that there must be verifiability of a sufficiently conclusive kind to make the use of analogy dispensable. There need be nothing which would count as conclusive verification as far as anything *we* can know is concerned, but neither can it be said that this is, by contrast, a possibility open to the subject. Direct assertibility by the subject is all that we require to establish the possibility of a state of affairs for which the observable data can be evidence.

Although the version of anti-realism presented at the beginning of this book has had to make an important concession on the question of our knowledge of other minds, that does not mean that we can reinstate as genuine hypotheses all manner of logically consistent conjectures concerning the mental lives of animals. A proposition, *P*, is not to be discounted on the grounds of its unverifiability, that is true, but with animals there is no question of *P*'s status as a genuine hypothesis being secured by the animal's possible knowledge with regard to its truth. Anything to be known is, if the earlier argument is correct, knowable by us. The only point here at which the anti-realist appears to be vulnerable is on the question how one could establish that an animal definitely does *not* have certain knowledge or abilities which we may or may not be inclined to attribute to it. This is really a matter of the problem concerning possible disproof of the existence of unexercised abilities and dispositions in general, not necessarily in connection with the mental, but I shall discuss it in terms of the particular question which we left hanging at the end of chapter 2, the question whether animals might not have thoughts which they do not disclose to us. Is it not at least conceivable that an animal should be able to think, but that we should never know of its thoughts?

We can assert the existence of an unexercised ability on a given occasion if it has been exercised at some time in the past and if its exercise has enabled us to establish certain factors as signs of its occurrence, but by hypothesis we are without any such indications in this instance. One way out is to deny the meaningfulness of saying that a cat, say, might actually think, and to claim that there is not sufficient resemblance between it and a human being for this to make sense even as a possibility. However, I have no wish to take such a step. After all, it could turn out that the cat should suddenly start speaking, telling us of the thoughts which it has had over the years, and if that is logically possible it is conceivable that even now the animal has this ability. But what is important is that the only thing that would count as *proof*, or would have counted as such on the earlier occasions, is the sort of thing that we have elaborated for the human case: if a man who is fully conscious and understands what he is saying tells us that he is thinking about his next meal, then we can safely say that he is capable of thought— not necessarily that he thought what he said he did, since he may be lying, but that in turn yields the same general conclusion. To put it slightly differently, the only thing that would count as a reason for supposing that the animal thought would be something which counted as a reason for supposing that the animal was able on the relevant occasion to show in roughly the way prescribed for human beings that it thought.

We might add to this the following argument. There are many things which we can imagine an animal doing and which would incline us to say that it must have in *some* sense thought in order to have been able to do them. However, is anything added to the explanatory value of such a hypothesis by construing the thought as something more than certain events and states in the animal's brain? I can reason out loud and I can reason to myself, but no special significance accrues to the reasonings in the latter case in virtue of their being mental; my overt reasoning is none the worse *qua* reasoning for its being spoken aloud. Similarly, I suggest, the supposition that x's thinking has been conscious, that he could at any time have told us what he was thinking, does not give that thought a greater explanatory power than does the supposition that the relevant neurophysiological happenings were not associated with consciousness; I might consciously work out a man's name or I might recall it with no prior conscious thought. There would appear to be nothing which could be explained *only* on the hypothesis that it was preceded by conscious thought; consequently, the ascription of conscious thought to a creature which displayed no linguistic ability would seem to be entirely without foundation.

We are now in a position to tie up some of the loose ends in our earlier discussion of purposive animal behaviour. Most such behaviour can be understood in terms of action which is engaged upon because of its consequences, where this means consequences which it actually has, rather than consequences which it is taken or believed to have by the agent. However, even if we do not in fact come across cases which fall outside the scope of this formula, it is certainly conceivable that we should, that we should encounter intelligent goal-directed behaviour showing typically human novelty and originality; imagine, for instance, an animal which could play a good game of chess. In such a case we should be reluctant to deny that the creature was in some sense thinking out its moves, that it in some sense believed that its moves would have certain consequences. Given the creature's presumed lack of language, I do not see any way in which we can speak of it as having thoughts and beliefs in a way that is true of us, but there is nothing to prevent us from introducing a sense of 'thought' which is to be understood in terms of behavioural and physiological conditions, a use of the term which would run parallel to the use of 'unconscious thought' as applied to human beings.

The anti-realist's insistence that mental phenomena cannot be introducible *merely* as hypotheses has been mentioned all along. Since we have now cast doubt on his position, as initially presented, this question can be re-opened, not perhaps with respect to animals, where we have had no cause to qualify his theory, but certainly with respect to human beings. Consider first the reasons for his stand. If mental phenomena can be introduced only as hypotheses then (i) we run the risk of finding ourselves with no grounds for asserting their existence—since we might devise a better hypothesis or find an explanation which dispensed with all hypotheses—and (ii) in the absence of the possibility of conclusive verification we cannot even speak of the words as formulating a genuine hypothesis. The second of these points presents us with a position which we must now consider suspect, if not actually refuted, but (i) still appears to hold good. However, when it is said that a pain, say, may be introduced as part of a hypothesis, it must be understood to be a matter of a causal hypothesis invoked to explain a man's words or behaviour, not just something which we cannot know to be true directly. We need only object to the introduction of pains as hypotheses in the first sense; they may continue to be hypothetical just in the sense that their occurrence (as specifically human states of consciousness) need not be conclusively verifiable.

Two distinct kinds of ground are given for the hypothesis of pain by (1) the specification of conditions which appear highly likely to give rise to pain, as a severe burn, and by (2) the claim that being in pain would give the man a good reason for behaving in the way he is observed to behave. (1) does not present us with the kind of hypothesis which need trouble us; there is no question of postulating the existence of the sensation as part of an explanation, so no question of its being rendered superfluous by an alternative hypothesis or by an account in purely physiological terms. There is of course the question of verification, but this will bring up consideration of the man's word, and so take us on to the second kind of possibility, where we are concerned with establishing the man's reasons for saying what he says. With regard to (2) there is no risk that a competing explanation in physiological terms will rule out the kind of explanation given, since an explanation in terms of physiological causes does not exclude an explanation in terms of reasons.

In the first place, 'reason' and 'cause' are to be compared with such pairs as 'sensation' and 'physiological state'; in neither instance is there any simple correspondence which would allow us to replace the one by the other; indeed, in many contexts, e.g., those of the form, 'his reason was that . . .', the result of substituting 'cause' for 'reason' is not even grammatical, so the question of their identity does not even get off the ground. In the second place, even if a more roundabout equivalence can be established—'having R as a reason caused him to ϕ'—it would seem (a) that this leads only to showing what having R as a reason comes to in terms of the relevant physiological processes, and (b) that there is little likelihood that having a reason can in any case be considered a relevant causal factor: to have R as my reason for acting is often a matter of acting in the belief that such-and-such will follow from my actions; the belief is more in the nature of an accompaniment to the action rather than causally related to it. To sum up, while admitting that we may not be able to prove that someone is in pain, the sense in which his being in pain is, accordingly, no more than a hypothesis is not such that we are open to the kind of objection which we found to vitiate the realist's introduction of pains on the basis of a causal hypothesis.

To sum up more generally, the anti-realist's position has finally come to grief, predictably enough, on the question of determining whether a man means what he says, and hence what it is that he thinks, feels, and so forth. It is, as far as the analysis has gone, because of something peculiar to the mental, broadly speaking, that his position has had to be qualified, and not for some more generally applicable reason; it is not because, for instance, there is an *indefinite* number of possible circumstances which would count against the truth of a psychological ascription, an indefiniteness which might preclude us from ever being in a position to say that *all* such conditions had been eliminated; it is this one condition, sincerity, that is a stumbling-block for the anti-realist. However, in rejecting his theory we have not given new life to the position with which it was initially contrasted. It is true that nothing as strong as verifiability has been invoked in arguing against false accounts of sensation and the mental, but the weaker principles which have emerged are equally opposed to the realist's conception of facts which are possible where any knowledge is impossible, and this presents us with an interesting and to my mind plausible position.

CONCLUSION

WE have come to the end of the argument of this book, but only to the beginning of a number of large issues concerning mind and meaning. In this final chapter I shall not become embroiled in any new topics, but I should like to run briefly over the main arguments which have been presented and enlarge upon some of the conclusions which have emerged.

The nature of the problem of other minds, and its solution, depend on the conceptions of truth and meaning which are held to be threatened by the range of conceivable facts which we are commonly prepared to recognize in this area: facts, possibly not ascertainable by us with any certainty, about how another man, a child or an animal, thinks and feels. The particular anti-realist account of truth and meaning which is here put to the test is likely to strike us as more plausible if we have regard to animals, less plausible if we confront it with specifically human phenomena: if we cannot establish with certainty our ascriptions of mental states to other people, we shall not on that account consider their intelligibility imperilled; on the other hand, it is not so obvious that we are talking sense when, for instance, we attribute thoughts to animals, and even the terminology of sensations may be thought to be stretched in its use of creatures other than men. That is how the problem initially strikes us, and by and large the subsequent argument supports this division: it is because of human beings, not of animals generally, that the anti-realist is forced to revise his position.

The anti-realist programme with respect to animals, which in practice means a liberal form of behaviourism, is followed up by considering the notions of *knowing* and *wanting*, these being chosen with an eye to the problems of perception and sensation. Here the task is relatively straightforward. Provided he renounces any requirement that such notions be matched in a simple way with items of behaviour, and concentrates instead on showing the logical adequacy of the latter for the former, the anti-realist does not meet with formidable obstacles. There is a passing difficulty with forms of behaviour suggestive of phenomena which, like insight, appear to allow only of mentalistic interpretations, but the episodes which suggest the initiation of a mental state can be argued to represent the beginning of a state of *practical* knowledge only; not a state which has at the same time an 'inner' realization, in terms of thoughts which the creature has but which it is obliged, for want of an adequate system of communication, to keep to itself. However, we might feel uneasy at the claim, essential to the anti-realist, that to speak of an animal as *thinking* is totally unfounded if such an assertion can never have the status of anything more than a hypothesis. If we require the possibility of proof before we are prepared to speak even of a hypothesis, then perhaps we shall find ourselves forced to regard the putative thoughts of other human beings as in no better a position. Whatever we may learn of a man by observation, there is seemingly no logical compulsion to accept that he has thoughts, and yet it is surely reasonable to hold that others *may* at least think, and not be just so many mindless automata.

One of the most complex questions with which the behaviourist has to deal is provided by the goal-directed behaviour which is found in great variety and sophistication even among the lower forms of life. We are able to provide an interpretation of *φ-ing for the sake of the consequences of φ-ing* which is applicable to such behaviour when there is no question of saying that the animal is acting in the belief that what it is doing will have a certain outcome, and it appears that no more than minor variations on the formula suggested are called for to furnish us with an appropriate pattern of explanation with respect both to behaviour and to the notion of biological function. That is the general picture. However, there remain instances of goal-directed behaviour, possible if not actual, which also require us to consider what behaviour, if any, is explicable only on the assumption that animals can think.

With these preliminaries behind us we take up the topic of animal perception, more specifically, animal vision. We try to keep within the framework of a broadly stimulus-response account, and in one major respect at least this approach stands a fair chance of success: we are able to say with some confidence that suitably caused behavioural responses can give proof of perception; not just render perception a plausible hypothesis on which to explain the observed behaviour, but give us grounds which are logically adequate for an assertion that the animal sees. However, two points

leave us with something less than full confidence at this stage. In the first place, the nature of the response is important: not every response of the animal will be of a kind to give the proof we seek, so there is still the possibility that the requisite differentia will be of a type which the behaviourist cannot recognize. In the second place, there is the possibility of a delay between seeing and responding, and even of seeing in the absence of any response, and it is not clear how the behaviourist can find room for such cases.

Both these difficulties are met by the interpretation of perception in terms of knowledge: the responses which give proof of knowledge, and at the same time proof of perception, are those which, given the creature's goals, are appropriate to the situation, and the anti-realist can allow the possibility that a creature should have knowledge which is not currently manifested in its behaviour. It is important to note that the knowledge which is central here is knowledge of the presence of the object perceived, and that this is an extensional context: if the dog knows of the presence of x and x is the same as y, then the dog knows of the presence of y. This is not to deny the possibility that an animal should know that such-and-such is before him, in the sense that he can know that it is specifically a cat, say, that is there; it is just that such knowledge is not necessary to the awareness of the cat which he had just by dint of seeing it.

While the notion of knowledge is central in the analysis of perception, it is necessary to avoid over-intellectualizing the form which it takes; yet this is the step which, surprisingly, is risked by the supposition that it is primarily colours that we and animals see. The genus of physical objects, broadly construed, proves to be the appropriate genus in which the commonest objects of sight are to be located; there is no difficulty in establishing the cat's visual awareness of the bird, but to show its awareness of the colour of the bird presents us with a problem of meaning as well as of verification: many of the responses which we might cite as establishing this latter awareness turn out, when considered more carefully, to support only the former, and even if we do encounter behaviour of a suitably differentiated kind, it is more natural to speak of the cat as discriminating between variously coloured things rather than as seeing their colours, since the normal understanding of this phrase brings it close to 'seeing what the colour is',

an ability which is primarily intellectual, most readily understandable with respect to beings capable of classifying colours linguistically. However, we can allow some sense to this and to similar expressions, e.g., 'tasting the taste', expressions which prove to have an unusual grammar and an unexpected lack of application in the contexts where they have been traditionally located, and we can even make sense of the notion of light as a proper object of vision, not merely in the sense that light can be perceived only by sight, but also in the sense that whenever we see we in some way see light.

A condition of introducing light as a proper object of sight is that it should not compete with familiar particular objects: seeing a light or a pattern of light is not to exclude seeing the moon, for instance. Using the term still more broadly, with regard, say, to what a man 'sees' when the appropriate area of his brain is artificially stimulated, we find that the same negative condition is to be enlisted: it is not now a new kind of stuff that we see, but the difference between this and the normal case is to be sought at a different level, certain propositions relating to other experiences now failing to be true rather than additional positive characterizations holding. Thus, there is no necessity that the differences which obtain in the different cases should find their way into a specification of the *object* of vision, but it is reasonable to introduce a term which applies indifferently in the three cases—even if we are departing from normal usage in speaking of *light* in the third case. The differences which make for seeing a physical object, and not merely light, will relate to what can be learned by using the other senses, notably touch, and if it is a matter of seeing light in public space, but with no material substrate, certain conditions relating to location and common experience will be fulfilled which fail if it is a phenomenon peculiar to an individual.

The knowledge involved in perception is a matter of awareness of what is perceived, and as such can be ascribed to creatures generally. At the same time we must recognize another form of awareness which is a prerogative of human beings. It would be quite unreal to speak of human perception in terms solely of the acquisition of practical knowledge, but the knowledge we acquire is, in addition, theoretical or intellectual: we rise above the animals in our ability to *say* what is there, and, further than that,

in the more reflective knowledge of which we are capable. We do not merely see, and so learn of the presence and nature of things about us, but we know that we see, and to that extent have self-knowledge, an awareness which is not directed merely to our environment—although, we note, this reference to self-knowledge has to be interpreted with care.

We can make sense of perception without supposing the perceiver to be capable of this further degree of awareness, but it is not so clear whether the same holds good of sensation. Can a creature be said to be in pain if it does not know that it is in pain? We do, I think, feel that there is a lack of reflective knowledge, a lack of self-consciousness in animals which makes for a difference between the notion of experiencing pain as applied to them and as applied to us. The question is whether the difference is so great that we are not really entitled to speak of them as being in pain at all. Perhaps we are not compelled to accept the appropriateness of speaking in this way, but what is more important is that what we say is, if we do so, perfectly intelligible. Thus, the grounds for saying that awareness that one is in pain is not necessary to being in pain are that the creature's behaviour, suitably caused, is adequate by itself, and this leads us to an analysis of *being in pain* in terms of being in a certain kind of distressed state, a kind which is identifiable by having regard to no more than we can observe.

At this point we must avoid the analogy which would compare the animal in pain with the man who is distracted from his pain. We can say that, in so far as the animal can be said to have a mind, it can have its mind on its pain; or, alternatively, to the extent that the animal cannot be said to have a mind, we are *not* to think of it as like a man with his mind elsewhere. To have a better picture of what sensation and perception come to for animals, imagine yourself as, say, smelling something, but without words to describe the smell. This still leaves you in a position from which an animal is debarred, since you can turn over possible descriptions in your mind and you at least know that you can smell something; so imagine further that your conceptual powers are so limited that even this much is denied you. To take this step is not to refuse to allow that you can still be smelling something, but it is to cease to be able to understand this in terms of the acquisition of knowledge which you know yourself to have and which you might communicate, and it is thereby to move to a plane where sensing is something which can be known of only by observing the creature sensing. But, of course, when this stage is reached it is odd to speak of you as imagining *yourself* smelling something. Since the distinctive features of self-awareness are absent from this account, you might as well be imagining *any* creature smelling.

This account seems cogent enough when perception is at issue, but it is not so convincing when applied to pains and other sensations: so long as the analysis of being in pain is confined to analysis of a certain kind of distressed state we are likely to feel that the pain itself has been left out altogether. This is a natural reaction, but I believe it to be mistaken, the result of an improper insistence that a creature's pain be something which could be disclosed to observation, something which we might detect on a closer examination of the animal. We might detect the nervous activity peculiar to a creature's being in pain, and it could even be that the meaning of 'pain' involved reference to some bodily condition which could be filled in in physiological terms, but there is no such thing as detecting the creature's pain in the way that the objection would appear to require. This does not mean that there is anything inappropriate about our ways of speaking of pains—as if we had no right to use a noun 'pain' if we could not make any such identification; the animal's pains can be spoken of as individual items with their own histories, compared with one another in terms of their degree of seriousness, located in specific parts of the creature's body, and so forth. We have not talked pains out of existence, we have simply been re-applying the argument which was used of wanting and knowing: the animal's behaviour and other observable conditions can provide us with logically adequate grounds for saying that it knows something, even though there is nothing in these conditions to be identified as its *knowing*.

In this discussion of animals we defend something like the claim that sensations are to be defined in terms of the typical circumstances of their occurrence, but the general thesis runs into difficulties when we turn to human beings: the characteristically human states of consciousness are precisely those which appear to be logically independent of surrounding circumstances, where language comes into prominence and the importance of behaviour is at a minimum. So we are left with a double problem, that of making clear the relevance of language, and that of ascertaining just what remains, if anything, for behaviour and other observable conditions to contribute.

But for language we could not know what a man is thinking or feeling, and that, it may be suggested, is how language comes to be so important. If that is its role then there is no denying its importance, but this conception does not go far enough; it may even suggest that animals too could have thoughts, only be unable, through lacking words, to tell us of them, and if language cannot be introduced in such a way as to rule out this as a possibility, then it contributes nothing as far as the anti-realist is concerned. But this is not how language is to be regarded. It is not that, but for language, there would be no means of knowing what another was thinking; rather, without language there would be nothing for us *to* know, apart from what we could learn of by observation.

In order to rule out the connection between language and the mental which the anti-realist repudiates, it is tempting to make language constitutive of the specifically human states of consciousness. However, this direct identification involves an oversimplification. The reference to language arises as a consequence of the circumstance that, if behaviour and observable conditions generally can give no guarantee that a certain state of consciousness exists, this will be because the subject's knowledge that he is in such a state is necessary to its very existence, and knowledge of this kind appears possible only for creatures having a sufficiently well-developed language. A capacity for speech is thus required, but there need be no actual exercise of this capacity on a given occasion for it to be the case that the person's mind is occupied in a certain way.

To take the example of thought, it would be incorrect to hold that all thought involves language in the sense that all thought is linguistic in form—silently spoken words like those which occur when we count to ourselves or run through people's names in our head. Whatever we do can to some extent be 'interiorized', whether or not it involves words; thus, eating, walking, falling, hearing—these all have their imaginative counterparts, but language is brought in because of the requirement that when we think or imagine we must know that we do so. The anti-realist's position appears in the principle that if a man is thinking, say, and this is not something which can be read off his behaviour, then it must be something of which the individual himself knows; there is something to know, or something which we may fail to know, only in so far as there is something which *some* creature knows, and of which he can conceivably inform us; either that or something which we can come to learn of by observing the subject. This is the crucial point, that the only possibilities that we have to allow are all within the framework of possible human knowledge; whether exclusively behaviouristic criteria are adequate for animal pain, whether we might appropriately speak of thoughts when there is only neurophysiological activity—these are minor questions of detail so long as it is recognized that none of the possibilities transcend human knowledge.

The concept of knowledge clearly plays a major part in our account of the mental, and it is in just such a context that its use has been challenged. For our purposes, however, there is no need to exploit the connotations which make it suspect, but in the central cases it seems to be explicable as meaning no more than an ability to say. It is not the propriety of speaking of *knowing* in this context that is the source of a problem, but the difficulty arises in specifying the necessary and sufficient conditions, especially the latter, for this knowledge to exist. A dumb man may be unable to say what he thinks, though knowing what he thinks; it is when all capacity for communicating is totally lacking, rather than when the man is merely inhibited in the exercise of such a capacity, that there is nothing to be known, though at times the line between these two may be difficult to draw.

In shifting attention from behaviour to a man's words we acknowledge the separation of the mental from the behavioural which to common sense is evident enough. However, if, as might well be the case, we are reluctant to lose all contact with behaviour and external circumstances generally, we have the task of assigning these to their proper place, and in attempting this we run the risk of ending up at one or other of two unacceptable extremes. On the one hand, we might proceed in the following way. Let us imagine ourselves in the position of a being from outer space who is trying to make sense of the linguistic behaviour of the people whom he observes. Language does not have meaning by itself, the argument runs, but it is only in conjunction with an accompanying reality that a particular interpretation is determined for a form of words; such an utterance as 'I am in pain' does not come with a sense which we could simply read off in ignorance of the context of its appropriate use. But now, if this approach is carried through consistently, it looks as if it will take us back to some form of behaviourism. Accordingly, we switch to the other extreme: could it not just be a fact to be faced about human beings that they produced certain utterances which by and large hung together with the rest of what they said and did, but which had no systematic connections with anything we might observe? Why should we not regard our fellow men as individually 'knowers', and not only as collectively so?

The error in the first approach resides in its misplaced 'corroborative' conception of verification which leads to undervaluing the individual's contribution to the stock of knowledge: there just is not, in the contexts which concern us, a body of already ascertained facts against which the individual's utterances may be checked, but he plays a part in determining those facts by what he says. To make this point is to side with the second position and regard the individual as privileged on the question of truth, but the question of the meaning of what he says, and so of what it is that he knows, is to be answered in a way that favours the first alternative. The demand for intelligibility forces us to introduce a reference to conditions of utterance; in a particular case there need be no connection whatsoever with publicly ascertainable conditions, but if no such connection can be traced, however indirect, then the properties which the word for the 'experience' has would seem to be no more than properties which it has *qua* sound, and we are unable to construe it as bearing a symbolic relation to anything beyond itself. However, the 'observable' connections which a man's words are required to have turn out to be different from what was naturally envisaged, and it is in the last analysis a question of the general agreement of the individual's judgements with the judgements of others that establishes a consistent pattern of usage and hence a determinate sense.

The way in which human perception and sensation involve a more sophisticated form of awareness in conjunction with a capacity for language was illustrated with respect to taste. Let us run once more over the argument, taking this time the example of smell. I can experience all manner of smells to which I cannot put a name, and I can appreciate that two smells are quite different before having any mastery of the terms in which I might record the difference more specifically. This we must acknowledge. However, although it can be said that I smelled something acrid, or that I smelled a smell like that of lavender—the appropriateness of these descriptions being decided by others—it does not follow that these phrases describe how the smell seemed to me; I may be quite unable to make such comparisons, and in that case there will be no such seemings as far as I am concerned. In such a case, as when we encounter a totally new smell, we are tempted to say that there is something incommunicable about our experiences. If this means that we have no words adequate to describing the smell, then the temptation need not be resisted, so long as we take care not to conceive of the situation as one in which there is something of which I know but of which others are compelled to remain ignorant. True, there is—or may be—something which I can be said to have and others to lack, namely the experience, but this does not make for a difference at the level of knowledge in the relevant respect; what I do know, that I am smelling a smell which is quite new to me, is something which I can communicate, but my inability to say anything further about the smell is not to be construed as possession of incommunicable knowledge concerning it. The difference between being the one who is having the experience and one who is not is an enormous difference, and one which no amount of shared knowledge can obliterate, but unless it leads to the possibility of unsharable knowledge it is not a difference which will serve the sceptic's ends.

The circumstances in which we are most inclined to speak of incommunicability are those in which we are able to locate the smell generically, or at least able to say that we are experiencing a *smell* and that it is different from other smells, but not able to particularize beyond this. All that the subject actually knows is that he is experiencing a smell which is new to him, and this, as I say, he can readily communicate. On the other hand, although we are on a par as regards what is known if he does inform us of this fact, he continues to maintain a special position as a continuing source of knowledge, even though at this stage it is only a matter of potential knowledge: he is always a step ahead of us in that the knowledge originates with him; it is for him to say how the present smell compares with others he may come across, for instance— though only if it is a question of how the comparison strikes *him*, and then it is for him to say only in the sense that it is his saying that makes it to be that way. There is also a potentiality for knowledge in the sense that he may eventually acquire a new description with which to replace his mere assertion of a difference, or of unfamiliarity, a description involving a more positive classification or comparison with other smells on other occasions. But still, if he does learn an appropriate term, 'ϕ', and comes around to describing his smell thus, we are not entitled to say that it smelled ϕ to him all along. You can experience the smell without having the words, and without having the means of offering even an indirect comparison, but at this point there is no knowledge of the precise character of the smell in any sense which allows us to say that you have knowledge of something but are unable to communicate it. There is the experience all along, and there is the potentiality for such knowledge, but nothing beyond these two.

From time to time we are tempted to introduce a reference to physiological conditions into our account of perception and sensation. In the case of animal sensation there is perhaps some chance of allowing such a reference, in very general terms, but in so far as we are concerned to elaborate our ordinary understanding of the relevant notions there seems to be little scope for such an approach in the human case. Furthermore, a form of physicalism which makes no claim that reference to such states is to the point in this connection, but which none the less holds out for an identity between sensations and physiological states, is soon seen to be deficient. There is a familiar usage according to which pains can be described as 'bodily' states, but the relevant notion of a bodily state is not interchangeable with that of a physiological state, where the latter is understood in terms of what can be found in a body by using our senses or suitable instruments of detection. (Similarly, it is not that it does not make sense to say that a thought is *in* your head, it is just that the sense of this is quite different from that of 'a neurophysiological process is taking place in your head'.) It is absurd to say that when I feel a pain I feel a certain physiological state; not for reasons which have anything to do with intentionality; it is just that the two kinds of term are not commensurable in such a way that the alleged identity is readily intelligible, if intelligible at all. This, however, would generally be agreed, and our aim is not to advance this particular debate but to find out more about the concept of location as it applies to pains, sounds, and other sensible phenomena, since the notion crops up time and time again in questions concerning the relation of such phenomena to the physiological and to the physical generally, as well as to questions concerning the privacy of sensations.

The implications of saying that a man has a pain in his leg are totally different from the implications of saying that his leg is in a certain physiological state at the point in question. In the latter case there are implications as to what inspection of the leg at that point will reveal to us, but the failure to find any physiological disturbance or condition generally at the point where a man complains of a pain has no tendency to show that he was mistaken in what he said. However, here and elsewhere it is not uncommon to find totally inappropriate criteria being invoked to settle a question of the existence of sensible phenomena, and it has even been thought that taking the scientific account of perception seriously forces us to revise our commonsense beliefs and deny that, for instance, objects are really coloured. We may be impressed by the scientific findings, but we should remain quite unimpressed by the reasoning which sees in the total failure of certain tests to show something to be coloured a reason for denying the existence of colour, when the tests in question are so inappropriate that it is hardly conceivable that they should have yielded any other result. Similarly, it would be absurd to let the reality of colours wait upon the discovery that they were identifiable with, or at least could be correlated with, certain physically definable properties of the surfaces of objects. It could be found that the relevant constancies were as much on the side of the organ of vision as with the object perceived, but that would be completely irrelevant to the question whether things were coloured.

These comments make it seem as though nothing but error could come from physicalism. This is not so. In the case of sensation and perception, the appeal of the more plausible version of physicalism is considerable. The possibility of saying that my hearing a sound just is a matter of my being in or entering upon a certain physiological state, without being committed to saying that the sound itself is a state of me, whether physical or mental, lies behind the possibility of conceiving of perception as an act or state of the individual but with a public object, and at the same time conceiving of perception as involving an intelligible relation to the object perceived, and not, as it were, a merely spiritual confrontation with it: the object there, we at a distance from it, and no positive connection relating us to it. More significantly, if having a sensation or perceiving something is just a matter of being in a certain physiological state, then it is a mistake to regard the sensation or what we perceive as *caused* by the state. This corrects the faulty inferences occasionally drawn from the scientific accounts of sensation and perception, where these are taken as specifying the physical and physiological conditions which must obtain *prior* to those experiences; we may trace the neural processes as far back as we wish, we shall never arrive at a sensation, so how is the transition made from these events in the physical world to a non-physical phenomenon, and in what space does this occur? According to the physicalist, there will be physiological events which do precede the man's experience, but at some time it will be true to say both that the man is in a certain physiological state and that he is perceiving or feeling something, and at this point the latter will not be caused by the former but will simply *be* the former, considered from the point of view of an observer, not the subject. This is how the distinction is to be drawn: the physiological state is not to be taken as the *object* of the subject's experience; it is not something which presents one side to us, observers equipped with instruments which enable us to detect and characterize the state, and another side to the man whose state it is, but the distinction is that between being in a certain state and the state as a detectable or observable condition.

Many of the misconceptions which naturally arise when we try to theorize about sensations and the mental derive from our adherence to the model of a man's knowledge of his mind based on his knowledge of the physical world. We can show the failure of that model by pointing to the inapplicability of such notions as *investigation, discovery, inner sense,* and so forth, but the basic reason for the breakdown of the model lies in the consideration that there are no facts of the relevant kind which are determined other than by the individual's knowledge, no reality fixed independently of his word as to its nature.

If, however, we think of the man's word as a *report* on how things are, then it would seem that some other factor must have been effective in determining how things are prior to the report; indeed, it would seem that in general a man's word is quite superfluous: things are as they are with regard to his feelings whether he speaks or is silent. To see where the truth lies in this complex situation, it will help to consider the following simplifying fantasy. Imagine a time in the development of mankind when men's thoughts always received direct expression in words, so that there was no possibility of concealment, or at least no more than there was with respect to their words. We might modify this slightly to allow for a notion of *what a man thinks* to be understood in terms of how he *would* speak if questioned, but when a man did give voice to his thoughts this would not represent a disclosure of thoughts which he had already articulated but kept to himself up till then. In this world *pain* could be understood solely in terms of non-linguistic responses and circumstances, but there could also be a concept of consciousness which required verbal responsiveness, and it might be that a man was not said to be in pain unless he was prepared to say that he was. A man could be in pain even though he said nothing, since the natural tendency to respond with the right words could have been inhibited, but in such a case there would be no question of knowledge which he had but was concealing from others. Knowledge for everyone would come about only when the crucial item, the man's avowal, came about, and this would have the significance it had only as coming from him, not because he was the only one in a position to know, but because as *his* response the avowal would be part of a sufficient condition for *his* being in a certain state.

This concept of a conscious state is extended in a certain direction when it is allowed, once the interiorization of speech has become a reality, that a response which gives proof of pain has occurred even if the overt verbal response has been suppressed and only the thought has occurred. And this is how it is with us. It is then *thought* which is the source of the problem, since it is thought that lies behind the possibility of undetectable deceit. However, thought can be at the source of a less respectable problem in that there is also the likelihood that the thoughts will be taken to be reflections on an already secured reality, as it were, rather than themselves responses having the role of the overt responses in the fantasy, and so determining how things are. The true picture is distorted still further if the thoughts are taken to be incorrigible, and while we claimed that incorrigibility can be dissociated from the false conceptions of a man's knowledge of his mental states with which it is commonly linked, our examination of the notion must go deeper if we are to see it in proper perspective.

If a judgement is incorrigible it requires only the saying of it to make it true. It can have no entailments as regards the experiences of others, since that would make for the possibility of falsification in the event that such experiences were not forthcoming. On the other hand, we have ruled out the alternative that it should have privately testable consequences, that it should relate to an already fixed reality, only one that is surveyable solely by the individual. But, then, what kind of a *claim* can an incorrigible judgement make if it does not report even the subject's findings, and how can its sense be given in public terms if it is immune from falsification by the findings of others?

There is some pressure to try to understand every case according to this pattern: either the judgement can be corrected by others, or it reduces to a judgement of the form 'it seems to me that . . .', where this in turn can be understood as a disposition to say, and where the words which complete the sentence constitute a corrigible judgement. These unspecified words can be thought of as defined in terms of publicly observable conditions, the incorrigibility of the whole judgement residing simply in the qualification 'it seems to me that . . .'; despite the corrigible character of the dependent clause, a falsification of the whole judgement is effectively barred, but the knowledge which is expressed is no more than a recognition of the propensity to use the words in question. Formulating the contrast in this way makes it clear that it is not a question of there being public criteria in the first case, private criteria in the second, but it is only in the first case that we have any occasion to speak of criteria at all.

Many instances of incorrigible statements are explicitly of this 'seeming' form, and many others can be plausibly rephrased in such terms. But is there always the possibility of such a construal? Consider the example of a sensation which I describe as 'stinging'. I could be misapplying the word through a lapse of memory, but we can suppose that a contemporaneous bee-sting in another part of my body provides me with a vivid reminder of this quality. Given now that I understand and mean what I say, it surely must be accepted that I am having a stinging sensation. Where does the seeming come in? It is not a matter of the sensation's only seeming to sting; it actually *is* stinging. Is it that it seems to me that I am being stung? Well, by hypothesis, it is like what I feel when I am stung, but in the absence of any inclination on my part to suppose that I am being stung in that particular place, this is surely not the most appropriate form of words for me to use.

What is important, however, is that we naturally invoke a locution, 'it is as if . . .' or 'it is as when . . .', which has a very similar role and which preserves the connection with public criteria. And this is what is central, the appropriateness of the particular form of comparison expressed by certain idioms, such as that of seeming, being of secondary importance. To appreciate this, let us return to an earlier, uncompleted discussion. When investigating the relation of experiences to observable conditions I defended the claim that a background of agreement in judgements was necessary to the intelligible use of descriptions of experiences. However, while such agreement secures the place of the description in the language, it is not a condition which can invariably be invoked on the particular occasion, and we have still to accommodate avowals of present experience which are made, as they often are, in the total absence of conditions in terms of which that kind of experience can be identified as such.

The interesting cases to consider here are not those in which the associated observable conditions which happen to be absent are to be defined in terms of behaviour which is suppressed on the particular occasion. It is unlikely that we should have incorrigibility here, but in any case that is not the kind of obstacle to verification which concerns us. This still leaves us with a variety of associated circumstances, such as those concerned with how the sensation came about, and what is being claimed is that it is the possibility of effecting a comparison between what one feels when the typically associated conditions are and when they are not present, that allows us to make sense of the description in the latter case. As already indicated, we must leave room for the possibility of a man's memory misleading him, but this apart it would appear that the connection between the problematic and the unproblematic cases is to be traced via the subject's preparedness to speak of what he feels as the same in both, and that is all that is required. Take the example of sensations of warmth. Many warm things or warm conditions are known by other of their features, but even if in terms of such features there is no further factor common to warm things of which we are aware, there is at least the agreement in judgements in the variety of conditions. I might, however, experience a sensation of warmth which is not shared by others and of whose causes I am quite ignorant. My description does not require confirmation from others; it is enough that I am prepared to say I feel warm, to liken what I now feel to what I feel in cases where my judgement can come into competition with the judgements of others.

But, it may be objected, there surely must be the possibility of a check on the alleged identity, otherwise there is no distinction between the one sensation's merely seeming to be and its actually being the same as the other. Well, of course, we can recognize just that distinction when there is the possibility of a miscomparison due to faulty memory. However improbable it may strike us as being, such a lapse must always be allowed for, and this means that we cannot consistently hold that the individual's word is sufficient to establish the truth of the identity. On the other hand, once that source of error is eliminated, then, always assuming sincerity, there is no other possibility remaining. The man's saying of two sensations which he feels at the same time that they are the same determines their being the same; we have no further understanding of what their sameness might consist in, so no understanding which can make use of a public check. However—and this is the point of the argument—the man's knowledge of sameness is no more significant than the knowledge which he can lay claim to when what he says amounts to a statement of how things seem to him. It is not a matter of an infallible intuition that closer inspection will fail to disclose any point of divergence between the two things being compared; it is simply the knowledge he has that he is disposed to respond in the same way to either, and that is no more than the sum of the knowledge which he had in the two individual cases.

According to the modification of anti-realism which has emerged, it is impossible to maintain that a proposition could be true even though its truth is something of which no being could come to know. This thesis can be traced back to the demand for the possibility of direct or conclusive verification, but with the notion of verification giving way to that of assertibility; it is held that it must be possible to reach a point at which there is no longer any reliance on evidence, but it is required only that *someone* should be able to be in that position, not everyone. Verification goes with corroboration and is a particular case of the more general notion, since what it amounts to is, roughly speaking, multiple assertibility.

The consequent emphasis on the role of judgements is not altogether familiar, and the claim that something resembling direct or conclusive verification is possible might well be challenged. Let us consider further what is involved in these points. Whether or not something looks red to me is a matter which my judgement decides; whether or not it looks red generally is to be decided by considering men's judgements generally; and whether or not something *is* red is likewise to be decided by reference to a general consensus of judgements concerning its colour. In this last case there are additional conditions to be satisfied. These conditions are not easy to detail, but this does not affect the claim that, ultimately, whether or not x is red is a matter of how people are or would be prepared to describe it. In the case of incorrigible judgements there is a familiar objection to this kind of identity. To revert to the example of pain, the thesis that a man's sincere and properly understood avowal of pain gives a logical guarantee that he is in pain has been rejected on the grounds that it prohibits us from maintaining the status of the avowal and the sensation as 'distinct existences': if the sufficiency is logical we surely have a totally implausible reduction of a man's pain to his uttering of certain words.

This objection continues to be relevant to the account given of being red. We do, it is true, require that the judgements which determine the colour of something occur or be hypothesized to occur in certain circumstances, but these circumstances are in turn to be identified in terms of people's preparedness to concur in their judgements, so there is no avoiding the objection in this way. In short, the association of words with circumstances is ultimately an association of words with words, whether it be a matter of an experience private to an individual, or a proposition susceptible of public verification.

There is, we may agree, something disconcerting about 'for x to be red it is sufficient that (with certain provisos) people be prepared to describe it thus' when it is set alongside, say, 'for x to be red it is sufficient that it absorb all but red light'. The sense in which what people are disposed to say determines the colour of something is quite other than that in which certain physical conditions can determine a colour: there is no question of our words usurping the role of an object's absorptive properties; conversely, to assert the sufficiency of our agreement in judgements is not to run the risk of refutation on the grounds that words fail to provide the requisite physical conditions. When looking to what people are or would be prepared to say we are fastening on a general condition for the *truth* of judgements, not just of redness, but of judgements generally, a condition which defines the anti-realist's basic disagreement with the realist.

The realist is content with specifications of the meaning of sentences in terms of their truth-conditions; for him intertranslatability is the central notion in an understanding of meaning; so, for instance, to explain what it is for x to be ϕ we say what this comes to in other words: it is for x to be ψ. For the anti-realist such an explanation is perfectly acceptable at its proper level, but we should not let the accident of there being a synonymous expression blind us to the more general question of what it is for x to be ϕ, or ψ, or anything else, of what the truth of such predications consists in. At some point the question how words connect with reality must be tackled, although, interestingly, the difference between the realist and the anti-realist is misrepresented if we think of the former only as keeping solely within language, since the connection of words with reality is, if the argument is correct, ultimately a connection of words with words, however differently it is envisaged by the two parties.

To repeat. The anti-realist can agree that truth consists in the agreement of judgements with reality, with how things are, but for him 'how things are' can be understood only in terms of how things are to us, how we are disposed to judge them. We are, moreover, to relinquish the picture of the judgement on one side, reality on the other, as though we were confronted with totally unlike terms waiting to be matched.

Ultimately, the 'distinct existences' argument does no more than repeat in disguised form the assumption challenged by the anti-realist, and it is worth expanding the argument to the point where this shows itself more clearly. It is insisted that, however much one person or many may say, mere words cannot give actual proof of a non-linguistic reality, mental or otherwise. This objection is likely to lie behind the belief that what is characteristically sensory has been omitted from an account of perception in terms of the acquisition of knowledge, and it is also relevant to attempts to identify one's imaginings, say, with one's ostensible reports of one's imaginings. With regard to judgements of colour, the claim is that it must be logically possible that something should fail to be red, however extensive the agreement that that is how the thing is to be described, and in the case of thoughts and sensations it is held that it is always logically possible that a person may not be in the state he reports, even granted that he means and understands what he says. How otherwise can the identification of such totally disparate phenomena be avoided?

So, whatever you may say, it is , as far as I am concerned, always possible that your mind is a blank, that you are quite without feelings or any other experiences. I can, after all, never penetrate beyond your words to any reality which they would seem to report. But how is this alleged possibility to be understood? It is suggested that, despite a man's words, his mind *could be* a total blank, but what possible experience of what person does this 'could be' anticipate? Surely no situation is contemplated in which a suitably placed person might fail to encounter anything which would count as a thought or feeling? It is confidently held that there is a real possibility here, that, although no one could ever know of it, it could be that all thought and feeling were absent; but this apparent specification of a possibility fails to look forward to any conceivable human experience, and so fails to define a possibility which might make for the breakdown of the inference. In short, the objection adds nothing new to the realist's case, but is just a reiteration of his faith in the intelligibility of hypotheses which transcend anything that anyone could ever know of.

But now we still have not got to grips with the problem whether, on the account favoured, truth can ever be recognized, whether there can ever be any such thing as conclusive verification. We can agree that in general the individual's judgement does not suffice to establish how things are, and that it awaits confirmation from the judgements of others. But the judgements of others at a given time may likewise be inadequate, since the original judgement may have had implications relating to other experiences which have not as yet been put to the test. The question is whether we are here generating a sequence of possible judgements which can ever be terminated, whether the point can be reached at which the original issue can be conclusively settled, or whether these judgements in turn are always subject to revision in the light of future experiences.

It is clear that it will be difficult to make sense of the notion of truth if the truth of a proposition does lie beyond anything that could be established after a finite time, and, indeed, examination of particular cases suggests that the conception of an infinity of judgements calling for verification is totally unreal. It is sometimes held that even the simplest of our day-to-day propositions go beyond what we could ever hope to verify, but this is to misrepresent the way in which our language works. There is no definite number of judgements which we require before we can assert with complete certainty that the cat is on the mat, but the point is surely reached when we can take this to have been established beyond all doubt, and any subsequent data which are at odds with these findings will be so only in a non-logical way. If the cat suddenly disappears into thin air there may be a reasonable assumption that our inspection of it had not been thorough enough to disclose the seeds of its destruction within it, but such an unexpected development gives no logical guarantee that this is so, that anything at all untoward would have been revealed to us; nor does it prevent us from saying that we had had to do with a cat until its disappearance. We can devise propositions which embody an unrestricted generality, and these may prove embarrassing to the anti-realist, but it is a mistake to see such a feature in the ordinary run of things we say.

The above argument counters scepticism about the possibility of conclusive verification only to the extent of correcting a misapprehension concerning the logical implications for future experience of our ordinary descriptions. It is not intended to confound the sceptic generally, but there are many other points at which he can raise doubts. In conclusion I should like to give one further example of the central position which agreement in judgements occupies, at the same time completing the earlier discussion of perception. The account of animal perception presented in chapter 5 was described as a *causal* account. We began by noting that perception was established once it was found that the animal's responses were brought about in the right way, and we concluded by requiring that the knowledge which its responses manifested be causally related to the object of perception in order for perception of that object to have occurred. Part of this account can be transferred directly to human perception, in that here too the acquisition of knowledge, though not merely of a practical kind, is involved. However, that part of the analysis which relates to the causal condition is emphatically *not* to be carried over. Given our particular aim, the justification of behaviourism with respect to animal perception, it was appropriate to develop the topic in the way we did, but this was a special case, and not the model on which to base our understanding of human perception.

The limitations of that approach can be seen by considering an objection commonly levelled against causal theories of perception, namely, the objection that one cannot in general establish that x is perceived by establishing that x is the cause of one's knowledge (or, in other accounts, of one's sense-impressions), since to establish x as such a cause would require one to perceive it. Since 'perceive' can cover different senses there is superficially an easy reply to this formulation of the objection: the existence of the object, and hence the possibility of its being a cause, could be established by means of one sense, and this knowledge could be invoked in deciding whether the knowledge associated with another sense was brought about in the right way. However, it is clear that the difficulty is barely postponed, and the argument cannot even be initially appealed to if we take as our example of perception a sense such as hearing, which does not have an object perceptible to any other sense. There surely is something absurd in the idea that we should ascertain that we hear a sound by first ascertaining that it is indeed a sound that is the cause of our knowledge or of our impression of hearing a sound. But could we not in theory confirm such an impression by establishing a causal relation between our auditory experience and associated sound waves? In the absence of any physical reality corresponding to the sound, surely we can pronounce what we hear to be a mental figment, not an item in the real world.

It should by now be abundantly clear that this will not do. The reality of a sound is not to be secured by finding *another* reality allied to it, a reality for want of which the sound will become mental or private. If we all agree that there is a sound, and if our further judgements serve to place that sound in public space, then that is an end of the matter, and any physical conditions which we find to underlie such circumstances have significance only as evidence for a state of affairs which such agreement conclusively establishes. This agreement does not stand in need of anything outside itself, and even if we were to insist that other conditions be found to obtain, this would only extend the class of judgements within which agreement was to be sought; it would not introduce a fundamentally different consideration.

The notion of cause is altogether ignored in this account. That is not to say that it has no part to play, but a reconsideration of the arguments which lead to its introduction suggests that its role is only derivative. Suppose, for example, that a man's brain is artificially stimulated in such a way that he has the experience of hearing a whistle. Suppose too that at the same time a whistle of the kind which he reports is in fact there to be heard. Is it not precisely because the latter is causally unconnected with his experience that we disallow it as the object of his hearing and regard the accuracy of his description as mere coincidence? Well, so far we have not ruled out the possibility that the man is aware of both sounds, so we must ensure that the public whistle is inaudible to him. He will say that he hears the latter, we may suppose, but if his ears are blocked or he continues to make this claim after the sound has ceased we may disregard what he says. Now it is true that we may show the sound to be inaudible to him by showing that it was not possible for the sound waves to have any effect on his ears, but this condition can be invoked only because it has been found to go along with inaudibility as established by common agreement. We find out that circumstances in which a sound cannot be heard are circumstances in which the ear drums are not affected by pressure waves. Conversely, the causal conditions applicable to our actual hearing of a sound are discovered subsequent to our knowledge that we do hear sounds. Given that the existence of a sound has been ascertained, we can appeal to causal considerations in showing that a given individual does or does not hear it, but such considerations do not secure the existential premise.

While the objection to the causal theory as applied to human perception has been sustained, it does not tell against the analysis presented for animals. The main point here is that animals are not the sources of our knowledge of the existence of sounds in the same way as are human beings. I do not wish to say that the existence of a sound is always presupposed when we consider whether an animal hears a sound, that we first identify a sound and then, making use of causal considerations, set about determining whether or not the animal heard it. However, I wish to say that either the behaviour of an animal which leads us to say that it must hear a sound gives us only inductive evidence for the existence of the sound, or else the sense of 'there being a sound' is slightly different from its sense when applied to human experience. The first is the relevant possibility if it is a matter of our being led to conjecture that there is something for us to hear, even if this means no more than something which we might conceivably hear. The second is at stake if there is no prediction intended about our possible experience, but if none the less the way in which sound waves and the ear are involved make it natural to speak here in terms of 'hearing sounds'. In short, we can apply a causal theory of perception to animals because it is only in a secondary way that we appeal to animals in establishing the existence of sensible phenomena, and so of possible causes.

INDEX

ability, 26, 38, 49, 101–3, 107–8, 206, 224–5
to say, 133, 152–3, 206, 219 232, 236
ache, 117–18
achievement, 94–6, 110
action, 31, 34, 42, 228
adaptability, 58
agreement in judgements, 211–12, 246 f.
analogy, 5–8, 16, 110, 121–2, 124, 223–4, 233
anti-realism, Intro. and Ch. 1 passim, 30, 32, 36, 41, 91, 112, 116–17, 119–20, 124, 137, 215–18, 221 f., 229, 235, 245, 247, 249
'partial', 8–9
appropriateness, 46, 85–90, 231
Aristotle, 94, 97, 218
assertibility, 222, 224–5
attention, 121
avowal, 37, 139, 150, 208 f., 218–19, 242, 244, 246
awareness (see also consciousness), 44, 52, 93, 114–17, 120, 127 f., 153, 156, 159, 162, 202, 206–7, 231–3
'first-level', 130, 154, 156, 164
'second-level', 128 f., 156, 159, 221
Ayer, A. J., 15–16

behaviour, passim
behaviourism, 6 f., 17, Ch. 2 passim, 67–8, 77, 107, 137, 186, 203, 205, 231, 237
belief, 70, 104–5, 228, 230
bodily movement, 32–3, 50, 67
state, 8, 184 f., 197, 239
brain process, 184 f.

capacity, 26, 48, 102, 235–6
categorical, 18, 24, 27, 203
causal theory of perception, 106–9, 249–52
cause, 29, 59 f., 72 f., 111, 118, 125–7, 144, 227–8
certainty, 4–5, 8, 16, 206, 229
colour, 73, Ch. 8 passim, 231, 240, 246

conditional, indicative, 19 f., 203
subjunctive, 17 f., 117
consciousness (see also awareness), 37–8, 61–2, 120–1, 134, 139, 214–215, 218–20, 225–7, 234–5, 242
consequences, 43, Ch. 3 passim, 226
corpus callosum, 206
corroboration, 218–19, 237, 245
criterion, 8, 37, 138, 207, 212, 243–4

deceit, 75, 214–15, 222, 242
decidability, 3, 13, 17
Dennett, D. C., 115
design, 62–4
differentiation, see discrimination
discrimination, 84, 92–3, 100, 163, 170
dislike, 141, 146
disposition, 26–7, 41, 47, 156, 159, 207, 224
distinct existences, 246–7
distress, 36–40, 45, 87, 125, 147, 159, 233–4
doubt, 3–4, 9–11, 16, 152, 206
dreaming, 13
Dummett, M. A. E., 2

electric sense, 105–6
'electrocate', 106
electro-encephalogram, 190
end (see also goal), 62
end-state, 39, 52, 59, 62, 66
evidence, Intro. and Ch. 1 passim, 32–3, 36, 115, 137, 141, 144, 187, 207, 210, 214, 217 f., 245, 251
evolution, 66, 88
explanation, 56, 64–5, 67, 125
explanatory hypothesis, 6, 126
extensionality, 103–4, 169–70, 231
externalization of pains, 197 f.
eye, 73, 81, 84, 100–1, 162, 171

feedback, 113
feeling, Ch. 6 passim, 139, 201, 248
foresight, 68
fright, 204
function, 61–6, 86, 230